# *The Future, Declassified*

## MEGATRENDS THAT WILL UNDO THE WORLD UNLESS WE TAKE ACTION

# MATHEW BURROWS

palgrave
macmillan

All statements of fact, opinion, or analysis expressed are those of the author and do not reflect the official position or views of the CIA or any other U.S. Government agency. Nothing in the contents should be construed as asserting or implying U.S. Government authentication of information or Agency endorsement of the author's views. This material has been reviewed by the CIA to prevent the disclosure of classified information.

# Contents

# *Acknowledgments*

I'M BLESSED WITH HAVING SO MANY INSPIRING AND GENEROUS COLLEAGUES AND FRIENDS who have helped and guided me throughout my career. Ambassador Robert Hutchings, who was then chairman, brought me on the National Intelligence Council (NIC) in 2003. I was thrown in at the deep end, having to produce *Global Trends 2020* a year later. Ellen Laipson and David Gordon, two former NIC vice-chairs and authors of *Global Trends 2015*, also showed me the ropes. The other NIC chairmen I've worked with during my ten years at the NIC, Tom Fingar and Chris Kojm, were also very supportive.

The NIC is relatively small but packed with original thinkers who have taught me much about how to think and write about global trends. The list is far too long to name them all, but it was my privilege to work with them for ten wonderful years.

*Global Trends* is unique in that it is more than an intelligence product. It has many backers outside government. And foremost among them is the Atlantic Council's Dr. Banning Garrett, who has been architect, promoter, chronicler, and, above all, friend throughout the past eight years. It was his vision for *Global Trends* as a vehicle for expanding international exchanges that was critical when the NIC started its overseas outreach. Over the years, we've visited upward of 20 countries, meeting with as many outside experts as government ones, which the Atlantic Council facilitated.

I am very grateful to Atlantic Council President and CEO Fred Kempe, who has taken to heart the message about the United States and the world being at a critical inflection point where it's important to shape the future and not just let it play out. His redesign and revival of the Atlantic Council has been driven by an appreciation of the global challenges facing all of us.

There have been literally hundreds of individuals I've encountered who have helped me think about the future. Among the many, I would like to express my appreciation to Jonathan Paris, Philip Stephens, Barry Hughes, James Elles, Alvaro de Vasconcelos, Lars Hedstrom, Darryl Farber, Howard Passell, Moises Naim, Giovanni Grevi, Alexander van de Putte, Sergio Bitar, Richard Cincotta, Paul Saffo, Drew Erdmann, Aiyaz Husain, Dan Twining, Will Inboden, Peter Feaver, Greg Treverton, Chris Layne, Cat Tully, Alun Rhydderch, Bruno Tertrais, Bob Manning, and Alexander Mirtchev.

I will be always grateful to my literary agent, Rafe Sagalyn, who conceived the original idea for the book and sought me out. I could not have had a better editor than Elisabeth Dyssegaard at Palgrave Macmillan, who expertly guided the novice book author to the finish line. Her team, including Donna Cherry, Bill Warhop, Christine Catarino, Lauren Janiec, and Michelle Fitzgerald, have bent over backward to be helpful.

Finally, as everybody knows, the best luck you can have is a loving family, and I have that in spades thanks to my mother, late father, late grandparents, and my brother and his family. This book is dedicated to them.

# Don't Kill the Messenger

WE'VE HAD A BAD DECADE OR TWO IN THE UNITED STATES, IF NOT AROUND THE WORLD, FULL of nasty surprises and shocks. First 9/11, then the wars in Iraq and Afghanistan that did not work out the way we anticipated. In the 1990s we were told there could be no more financial crises, which was reassuring until the Great Recession happened in 2008. The impact of the financial crisis was worse in Europe, all the more as it was imported from America. The Arab Spring—though welcomed at first—was largely a surprise; no one anticipated that the Ben Ali or Mubarak regimes would fold so fast or that authoritarianism could come back so quickly in the case of Egypt. Equally, two big natural disasters—Hurricanes Katrina and Sandy—showed us just how vulnerable we are. And how much we have failed to heed the warnings about extreme weather. Finally, more recently, Russian aggression against Crimea seems to have come out of the blue, rattling our assumptions about Cold War divisions having been overcome.

You could look on this in a couple of ways. It's a bad patch that everybody—countries down to individuals—goes through from time to time. Our luck will return. It always has. America is bound to bounce back. That's how most of us see it or would like to see it.

Another way is to see shocks and surprises as the new normal. There are multiple reasons: globalization, greater interconnectedness, new extreme weather patterns, and dynamic new technologies that are reaching tipping points. There is more than enough evidence from what we feel in our daily lives that change is ever increasing, making the future seem more unpredictable.

This book takes the second tack. I'm a firm believer in America bouncing back, even if the United States and other countries are seeing the old status quo crumble away, but all of us will need more than luck to succeed and excel in this new, faster-paced world. I believe we are in a new era that we are only just beginning to understand. Unlike in the past, the United States doesn't have much margin for error. We do have to be smarter.

In truth the future doesn't have to be bad. But it could be if we don't watch out. We're at one of those junctures in which it could go different ways. But many of us don't seem to care, or maybe believe we can't do anything about it. In my view, that's not so. We have so many ways to ensure it does go in a direction that benefits us all.

This book grew out of ten years working at the US National Intelligence Council (NIC)—a privilege and an honor in the truest sense. My job was an analyst's dream, working the really big topics: Which way is the Middle East headed? Will we live in a nuclear-proliferated world? What are the key threats facing the United States? Are we winning the global war on terrorism?

Indeed, for the ten years I was on the NIC, I was actively engaged in thinking about and authoring many studies about the big challenges facing the United States and the world, but most of that work remains classified. One study the NIC produces every four years for each new US administration is not classified, however, and that one is about the longer-range future. That is the basis of this book. Of the five *Global Trends* editions so far produced by the NIC, I was the principal author of the last three.

The *Global Trends* works are increasingly influential within and outside government circles. I briefed Presidents George W. Bush and Barack Obama on them. They are used in strategic planning by the White House, State Department, Pentagon, and others. Within the intelligence community they are used to think about how to position intelligence operations for the future. Outside, they are widely used by other governments as well as in university courses everywhere. They have been translated into seven languages.

I am not a pessimist, but I'm also not a starry-eyed optimist. I was raised with the notion that God helps those who help themselves, and I believe it applies to nations and civilizations, not just individuals. We can and should plan for our future.

I have grown more and more concerned that we Americans are not planning for the future. Part of that may be ignorance about the sheer magnitude of the developments unfolding. Never has humankind stood at the threshold of so much technological change, for example, where the ground is moving under our feet. As I'll address in this work, human nature is being transformed. The old limitations—whether in mental or physical capabilities—are being lifted. For billions of people in the developing world, it is not a cliché to say that a new and more prosperous era is dawning that was unimaginable even two or three decades ago.

As Americans, we should revel in those changes. The liberal world order we established after 1945 allowed other nations and societies to prosper and rise. Today's more multipolar world is part of the US dream, and we should glory in it.

Unfortunately, we seem to feel increasingly threatened by it. *Multipolar* was not a word in the official government lexicon until recently, and many in the Washington foreign policy establishment are still loath to acknowledge the less US-dominated order. The insertion of the word in the second edition of *Global Trends* I worked on was a hard-fought victory. Some of my colleagues opposed it. In the end, then NIC chairman Tom Fingar supported its inclusion. We should not have had to argue about what was reality. We should have been proud and not threatened by it.

The United States' *relative decline* was another term I used that was highly controversial in the last two editions. Some US critics thought I was under-cutting the United States by using it in an official government document. Ironically, senior Chinese officials puzzled over why it was used in an official document but concluded it showed that the United States was indeed so confident about itself that it could be open about its weaknesses. I don't think relative decline represents a weakness, just a fact that the rest of the world is getting richer. But I think the Chinese are right that we have nothing to be embarrassed about. And the fact that we can be frank about ourselves gives the document an enormous amount of credibility in others' eyes.

It's a shame we spend so much time on the decline issue because the world ahead offers so many opportunities for the United States. It's still the case that much of the world—though not all—wants basic elements of our way of living—the traditional middle-class lifestyle that obviously involves materialism like cars and houses but also the freedoms that Americans have and the ability to plan for their children's future. So much of the rest of the world until relatively recently could not hope for a better future for their children. If it happened, it was either by fluke or by birthright. The growth of the middle class—a big theme you'll see—is tailor-made for America as it engages others in this more multipolar world. Part of the reason I wrote this book is to get that positive and uplifting story out.

For me, while a lot about the trends is worth celebrating, there is justification for worry. You could say there's a lot of treacherous driving ahead as we navigate slippery pavement, dangerous hairpin turns, and a lot of sheer drops along the side of the road. Having our wits about us is key. The problem is that there are so many different kinds of dangerous threats to keep our eyes on. It would be far easier if there were just a couple threats that we knew were definitely out there. A theme in the book is that individuals and small groups have the ability to do harm on a level formerly reserved for states. In government, we've had almost five centuries of experience—at least in the West—of navigating our way in the state-run international order. But this is a new world in which you have to worry about terrorists blowing up iconic buildings in Manhattan or Washington. The British in the heyday of the Empire also had their worries about Afghan jihadism, but it never threatened London. Irish terrorists did explode bombs in the imperial capital, but there was no hijacking of airplanes and ramming them into buildings, causing massive casualties. Sadly for the future, the kind of destruction witnessed on 9/11 is the tip of the iceberg of what terrorists, insurgents, and states can do.

I can't tell you how many times US government officials—particularly when they are frustrated by the nebulousness of terrorist or insurgent threats—have leaned back in their chairs and gazed out wistfully, murmuring that it was so much easier in the Cold War. In the Cold War, we knew who the enemy was (the Soviets and Communism) and what they wanted (world domination). And even when the liberation struggles were waged in Central

America or Africa, at least we thought we knew who the real enemy was behind it all. We're again seeing rising tensions with Russia over its aggression in Ukraine, but I don't believe we're going back to a bipolar world of two superpowers trying to stare down each other. Unfortunately, it's going to be a lot messier if the world is both globalized at one level and also fragmented as multipolarity increases.

We've gone from a black-and-white to a gray world, and at an intellectual level we know this change to be true. However, in our hearts we are still searching for that clean and simple explanation for the new era that is unfolding. We all want to be a latter-day George Kennan, who invented the concept of Soviet containment. It was a clean and concise concept that gave meaning and direction for all our actions in the Cold War.

I wish it were that easy. The best definition I've found of the era that we're in comes from the opening lines of Charles Dickens's *A Tale of Two Cities*—that entrancing and enduring novel about the French Revolution that began in 1789: "It was the best of times, it was the worst of times...it was the spring of hope, it was the winter of despair...." Dickens wrote that at a time of immense change when the outcome was not apparent. We're in a similar period. Besides 1789, I would compare this time to other pivotal historic moments like 1815, 1919, 1945, or 1989, when existing political, social, and economic systems were upended. Either we take charge and direct the needed changes or change will take charge of us. Although profiled once in *Foreign Policy* as "the Fatalist," I am far from it.[1] The whole purpose of this book is to help us shape the future. As an American, I think the stakes are particularly high for the country's standing in the world and for ordinary Americans who want to maintain their quality of life, but the stakes are high for everyone, everywhere. The justifiable inclination after being at war for over a decade is that Americans want to turn to problems at home. And there are urgent challenges that have been ignored for too long. However, without staying engaged and shaping the global environment, there won't be a bright future either. So we must do both, which won't be easy.

**CAN WE PREDICT THE FUTURE?** I get the question all the time. Of course, the answer is no. No one has a crystal ball. But we can know enough about the future that we can plan. There is a difference between prediction and foresight. Prediction is trying to divine the precise future—an impossible task. Foresight is understanding the factors or variables that can or may produce the future. Inevitably, foresight talks about alternative futures—because how we shape those trends can lead to different futures. President Dwight D. Eisenhower's famous saying that "plans are worthless, but planning is everything" is good advice here.[2] Thinking systematically about the future—even if we can't exactly foretell it—helps us prepare for it.

The *Global Trends* works have had a good track record in identifying the key trends shaping the future. Before undertaking the last edition, I commissioned a report from two academics to examine the earlier findings. We got good marks on identifying key trends and scenarios, less so on the rate of change. The rate of change has been much faster than anyone anticipated.

More than any weaknesses in the analysis, the government planning falls short. It's better than before. The White House re-created a strategic advisor's office when Stephen Hadley took over as national security advisor during President George W. Bush's second term, and that office was retained in President Obama's national security staff. It increasingly coordinates interagency strategic reviews and produces the National Security Strategy. However, crisis management still crowds out longer-range strategizing. The Pentagon does best at systematic planning for the future, but US strategy needs more than just a military component. I am not the only one who has plugged for a more strategic approach. So far the US government is not alone in trying to get ahead of the curve. Everybody else is equally swamped. The country that finally develops a way to operate strategically will have a huge advantage over the others.

This is the big challenge facing us—how to reform government so it can keep up with the drumbeat of new events but not be swamped by them. Since 1945 the United States has reformed our national security apparatus as the US global role increased. The changes needed may not require a full-scale overhaul, but we have not begun the discussion. All we do is decry the reactive nature of what government is doing.

What makes this book different from the NIC report? For one thing, I can be franker about what needs to be done. The NIC study is an intelligence community document and can't flag the policy gaps or point the blame at policy failures. This volume can be more forthright about the risks of weak US leadership. More than the NIC report could, this volume updates and zeroes in on the key global issues. I can't escape being an American, but hopefully the perspective here is global and integrates the views of others. The NIC reports triggered a veritable avalanche of interest from across the world, and this volume utilizes those reactions in gauging possible global pathways going forward.

This volume seeks to forge a comprehensive look on the future. Too many books on the future deal just with one or two strands, providing a distorted view. Many play up the bleaker or scarier aspects, which is easy to do. It is important, though, to put all the changes into context, because what we arc looking at is a systems change. Just as the French Revolution and advent of mass manufacturing portrayed by Dickens in his novels ushered in a new era of nationalism, class conflict, and budding democratic politics, we are witnessing profound structural changes that will lead to a wholly different world. Or, as an American Indian proverb puts it, "For new music, a new dance is needed."

This is also a different kind of book. A good chunk is fiction, telling a story about the future through invented characters shaping the new world, sometimes in unintended ways. I did not want this book to be another wonkish policy document pretending to be a trade book. We all need to think about what kind of future we want for ourselves and our families. The book tries to capture what is at stake for the individual, not just governments or international businesses or institutions, which are the usual customers for futures analysis. A big theme in the book is that, more than ever, individuals matter. The losers in many ways are governments and other established institutions. The future won't necessarily be kind to them, for a variety of reasons. But individuals can also lose out if they don't have an understanding of what is happening.

I don't believe the future will be like many science fiction novels, where everything is so unfamiliar and strange. Yes, we are in for some big structural changes. And I do agree with science fiction writer William Gibson: "The future is already here, it's just not very evenly distributed."[3] We often have difficulty understanding the future's significance. The past won't disappear, either; it will continue to exert an influence on how we approach the future. There will be choices we will need to make about the kind of future we want. And it is up to us to choose. Hopefully this book will help us all make the right choices.

BEFORE I CONCLUDE, it might be wise to say a few words about myself. I came to do foresight for US intelligence by a circuitous route. My training was as a historian of the United States and modern Europe. After graduating from Wesleyan University with a degree in history, I studied abroad in Cambridge, England, and Paris and finished a PhD in European history in 1983. I got a job at the Central Intelligence Agency in 1986.

Twenty years ago I don't think I would have thought foresight mattered a lot. I don't think I was alone. At that time most of us thought we could predict the rough contours of the future; there was so little structural change. The fall of the Berlin Wall and the disintegration of the Soviet Union had not happened when I started at the CIA in 1986. We did not worry much about change. The world seemed to be frozen, and at most one anticipated only incremental shifts.

In 2003 I joined the National Intelligence Council. For an intelligence analyst, this was a dream job. The NIC is the premier analytic intelligence institution, drawing from all the intelligence produced throughout the whole intelligence community and providing the president and his senior foreign policy team the most authoritative analysis on key issues facing the United States. It was at this point in my career that the changes underway became more frightening and disconcerting: 9/11 and then seven years later the 2008 financial crisis signaled the start of a new era—a less predictable and more disturbing one.

Beginning in the mid-1990s, the NIC began publishing quadrennially a major work forecasting future trends to coincide with the presidential election cycle. Members of the NIC recognized that there were new forces shaping the world that had not gotten due intelligence attention, such as demographics, globalization, and the changing environment. One of the original motives behind the work was to pull outside expertise into the intelligence community. The publications were titled *Global Trends* and looked out 15 to 20 years.

My involvement with the NIC began in 2003, when then NIC chair Ambassador Bob Hutchings brought me onto the NIC as the director of analysis and production and assigned me the task of writing the next *Global Trends*. As a trained historian, I was fascinated by the possibility of situating the changes underway into a broader context, comparing what we were living through with other historic transitions. What were the drivers and what kind of forecasts could be made? I don't think there is anything more exciting—or taxing—than analyzing all the possible trends shaping the future and thinking about how they might interact with each other to produce potentially different futures.

In the fall of 2013, I retired after 28 years in government service and now work at the Atlantic Council, a Washington think tank, as director of their Strategic Foresight Initiative. This new work is an extension of my NIC efforts, involving new clients in the private sector who want help thinking about the future. This book will hopefully help all of us not only think about the future, but ways to shape it.

# PART I

# Megatrends

WE LIVE IN AN ERA OF PROFOUND CHANGE. THE STATUS QUO IS NOT AN OPTION. FOR MANY of us the megatrends detailed here may represent a threat. We would rather put off the inevitable than deal with it today. The coming changes are not all bad, though; I will argue that most of it is very good. Our future world *could* turn out to be what previous generations everywhere have wished for—the chance to be prosperous and live in peace. Through science, we can enhance our human capacities to design a richer, more environmentally wise and equitable world, if we so choose.

But these megatrends have the capacity to destroy, too. And that destructiveness is heightened if we are not proactive in channeling those negative elements into a less harmful direction. Ironically, we are on the cusp of being more empowered than ever as individuals, but also more dependent on machines. With artificial intelligence, machines will someday have more brainpower than humans. This is no longer a science fiction fantasy, but it need not be a scary prospect, either, if we ensure that the automated systems operate the way we intend.

We've had a foretaste of how our capacities can outdistance our decision-making power with the Edward Snowden revelations on US government surveillance of all our communications. The intelligence community defends itself by saying they were adhering to the law. But the law was designed when such ubiquitous surveillance capacities did not exist.

For the West, some of these megatrends present a special challenge. The next couple of decades will see the end of Western dominance that began roughly in the late fifteenth century with the age of European discoveries. The end of Western dominance need not mean Western decline. We have already seen a global expansion of many traditional Western values even as traditionally non-Western countries are becoming the dominant force in the global economy. The rise of the West in the 1490s through the twentieth century was a traumatic experience for much of the rest of the world. The "rise of the rest" could prove equally conflicting, but it need not be.

The final issue is how much inequity we are prepared to tolerate. At a time of spectacular technological advances, we might see parts of the world being pulled back to a Malthusian or dog-eat-dog age because of a coincidence of factors happening from climate change, rapid population growth, resource scarcities, and bad governance. As we learned from the 9/11 attack, coming as it did from an obscure and impoverished part of the world, deprivation and misery might not be any easier to contain going forward.

## CHAPTER 1

# *The Power of One*

WHAT MAKES THIS COMING ERA DIFFERENT? A LOT OF PEOPLE IN WASHINGTON WOULD SAY China. Some years back when I was preparing earlier versions of *Global Trends*, I would have said the same, maybe with the difference that it's not just China but other countries too that are now being galvanized and becoming regional and global powers. The rise of new actors on the global stage—beginning with China—still contributes to what makes this coming era different. But the biggest change may be the one that is all around us in our daily lives and has to do with our own increasing powers as individuals.

My own bias was that individual empowerment is a good thing. As good as it gets. How could it not be? People—men and women of all races and nationalities—finally being given a chance to live up to their full potentials. Wasn't this the democratic dream? Wasn't this what all the generations before us have been striving for? Why wouldn't we rejoice?

I still think that way, but when I put on my analyst's hat, I can see the complications.

My first clue that others were not so high on individual empowerment was when I went on the road with the *Global Trends* works. The first NIC chairman I worked for had the wisdom to see that we could never forecast future trends by staying in Washington. We needed to get out. From that first edition I worked on in 2004, I met with academics, businessmen, scientists, academics, students, government officials, and others all over the United States and then, increasingly, overseas too. In 2004, we went to five places overseas; for the last edition I authored in 2012 it was 20. On these trips, I often had a preliminary draft to show and would ask for a critique. On this issue of individual empowerment, I got an earful.

First, to a man and woman everyone instantly agreed that the power of the individual was increasing, government officials particularly. They could feel it. It was not just a trend on paper. It was happening and people could see it. That's where the agreement stopped, however. Many people saw real trouble ahead with all this individual empowerment. And some of the unlikeliest pessimists were among the most concerned. I was prepared for the Russian and Middle East governments to have objections. I was not prepared for many of the others.

One of the first eye-openers was in, I still think, an unlikely place. On a cold winter morning I climbed up the incline to the European Parliament building off Place Gare de Luxembourg in Brussels. After being greeted by a staffer, I was led through a veritable labyrinth of corridors. We finally reached the room for the breakfast meeting. The attendees were there to discuss the Internet. I had been brought in as an outside speaker to talk about the larger global trends. Only a relatively short presentation on the NIC's *Global Trends* project would be required, and they would be sure to get the point about the world being at an inflection point where the balance between individual and state was fundamentally shifting. No sooner had I finished my pitch for how the Internet had opened up untold opportunities for untold millions than a woman's hand shot up. She introduced herself as a member of the European Parliament and dove straight into exclaiming how "hyperconnectivity" had ruined her life. I must have looked puzzled, because she went on to describe the unintended and, in her mind, harmful results of the Internet revolution. Constituents were overly demanding and relentless; it had become a 24/7 world where longer-term goals could no longer be worked on. On and on she went as I tried to grapple mentally with the oddity of all of this flowing forth from a roundtable with the stated mission of furthering technological development in the European Union (EU).

It was clearly a trend. Everyone agreed with my judgment that individual empowerment was the number one megatrend and the right starting point for looking at the future. However, more and more voices sounded the alarm. In Kenya, one speaker warned that "individual empowerment comes at a high risk. Ethnic affinity is a reality of life, but can be politicized and become a weapon for conflict. Populism that's antimarket, antiwelfare, antigovernment is on the rise." She ended by voicing her biggest fear: "I am not even sure Kenya will be a united country 20 or 30 years from now." She attributed that to growing fragmentation that comes with individual empowerment.

In democratic Brazil, a former liberal minister in the Cardosa administration derided individual empowerment: "The politics of identity leads to fragmentation. This does not lead to convergence of values because the politics of identity is to differ with others rather than find common ground." He said, "The world looks more like Hobbes than Kant to me."

Thomas Hobbes was the seventeenth-century English philosopher who lived at the time of the English Civil War and authored the famous treatise on the state called *Leviathan*. Much of the book is occupied with demonstrating the necessity of a strong central authority to avoid the evil of discord and civil war. Immanuel Kant lived a century later, and he believed that one ought to think autonomously, free of the dictates of external authority. He was enthusiastic about the French and American Revolutions and Irish efforts to fight the British for greater autonomy. A man of very regular habits, he only deviated from his routine of a daily walk on the day he heard that the Bastille had been stormed by the people of Paris, which started the French Revolution.[1] He was also known for his treatise on *Perpetual Peace*, believing peace was possible in war-torn Europe so long as the state was based on the rule of law.

I never thought my university courses in philosophy would come in so handy for thinking about the future, but it became a leitmotif throughout the drafting of the NIC report. Were we facing an optimistic or pessimistic future? What did individual empowerment mean for the state? Were we entering a new period of chaos, with echoes of Europe's bloodletting in the seventeenth and eighteenth centuries?

The struggle between authority and the individual is endless. But we are at a point in history when the pendulum has swung much more in the direction of the individual. I expect it to swing back eventually, but not for some time and not completely. I am reminded here of the invention of the Gutenberg printing press in the mid-fifteenth century and the multiple repercussions that flowed from that technological change. The power of political and religious authorities was threatened, bolstering dissent and the flow of ideas across borders and giving a lift to the emerging Protestant middle class in Western Europe. In strengthening Protestant dissent through the wide dissemination of the Bible and Protestant tracts, the printing press revolution set in motion the social and political divisions that led to the religious wars that racked Europe in the sixteenth century. The printing press, too, eventually became an ingredient in the Catholic Church's Counter-Reformation, which upgraded the education of priests and proliferated the printing of devotional works to aid in the missionaries' work in Spain and Portugal's New World empires.

An equally complicated dynamic is at work with today's empowerment of the individual. Like the Gutenberg Bible, today's Internet and social media have set in motion a long-running revolution. The direction of these changes is not linear but more crablike in movement, spinning off other consequences, many times unintended. The nation-state—although deeply challenged—won't go away. Other nonstate bodies, including the individual and civil society, however, are growing more powerful and contesting governments' authority and legitimacy. The changes favoring individual empowerment are so powerful that they constitute sea changes.

The current technology revolution is a huge factor in tipping the balance favoring the individual and allowing those left behind by earlier revolutions to leap ahead. Mobile subscribers have been doubling every year since 2002 in Africa and increasingly with smartphones, which enable Internet connectivity. Now Africa has twice as many cell phones as there are in the United States. The rapid spread of telephony in Africa is an example of mobile technology overcoming the lack of landline infrastructure to spur communication and connectivity. The less developed are sprinting ahead in some technologically enabled areas such as mobile banking, partly because the brick-and-mortar institutions are less prevalent and mobile banking fills in the gap.

Individual empowerment remains a complicated process, and the end results will be both positive and negative. Hopefully the former outweighs the latter, but in the short to medium term—just like in the fifteenth and sixteenth centuries—the rise of the new middle classes empowered with new technologies could be very disruptive. I will explain more as we peel back and examine the forces favoring individuals and the broader impacts, both expected and unintended.

The most obvious symptom and means by which individuals are becoming more powerful is by growing prosperity. This growing prosperity is manifest in the increasing global middle class, which constitutes a tectonic shift. I can't emphasize too much how important this growth is to understanding the coming new era. Over the next couple of decades, a majority of the world's population won't be impoverished, and the middle classes will be the most important social and economic sector—not just in the West but in the vast majority of countries around the world.

How should we define middle class? The usual way is to talk about per capita consumption. The international futures model I have used to estimate membership in the middle class defines it as per capita household expenditures of $10–$50 per day at purchasing power parity (PPP) rates. Goldman Sachs—which did a study—used a comparable gross domestic product (GDP) per capita of $6,000–$30,000 per year.[2] Depending on the specific income or consumption levels, you can arrive at different numbers for individuals in the middle class. A rise of the current 1 billion or so to over 2 billion is a conservative estimate. Others forecast 3 billion people or more in the global middle class by 2030. An EU report claims that over the last decade, over 70 million people per year joined the ranks of the middle classes. The report estimates "by 2030 just above half the world population" could be middle class.[3] The world's population in 2030 is expected to be 8.3 billion, which would mean over 4 billion would be in the middle class.[4]

The most rapid growth will occur in Asia. The European and American middle classes will shrink from 50 percent of the global total to just 22 percent, with 2015 being "the first time in three hundred years, the number of Asian middle class consumers will equal the number in Europe and North

America."[5] If China achieves its target of increasing household expenditures at least as rapidly as GDP, the Asian Development Bank has estimated that the size of its middle class will explode, with "75 percent of China's population enjoying middle class standards and $2/day poverty will be substantially wiped out."[6]

One study found that while accounting for only 4 percent of the middle class in 2010, China "could catapult to become the largest single middle class market by 2020, surpassing the US."[7] But China might be overtaken in the following decade by India, thanks to that country's more rapid population growth and more even income distribution.[8]

Goldman Sachs in its study underlined that not even counting China and India, "New entrants to the middle class would still be larger than the world has seen for many decades."[9] Multiple studies project that the rate of growth in the size of Africa's middle class will be faster than elsewhere in the rapidly developing world, but the base it is starting from is very low.

Much of this global middle class will be lower middle class by Western standards. Growth in the numbers in the top half of the range of this new middle class—which is likely to be more in line with Western middle-class standards—will still be substantial, rising from 350 million in 2010 to 679 million in 2030.[10] The next generation of leaders in the developing world will most likely come from this segment.

Poverty won't disappear, and the fear of slipping back is likely to haunt many in the new middle classes. One Kenyan official worried, "The middle class is still really close to the lower class. They are vulnerable and prone to go back to the poverty level." Today about 1 billion people globally are living in extreme poverty, earning less than $1.25 a day, and 1 billion are undernourished.[11] The number of those living in extreme poverty globally has been relatively stable for a long time, but the rate has been declining with population growth. Significant numbers of people have moved from well below the poverty threshold to relatively closer to it due to widespread economic development. Absent a global recession, the number of those living in *extreme* poverty is poised to decline as incomes continue to rise in most parts of the world. The number could drop by about 50 percent between 2010 and 2030 but could still remain substantial—nearly 300 million in Africa alone in 2030, with many being undernourished.[12]

The number living in extreme poverty in East Asia, notably China, has been reduced substantially and will drop further, owing to rapid economic growth. The numbers are expected to drop rapidly in South Asia and the Middle East. In sub-Saharan Africa, however, the average person living in extreme poverty will be much poorer than the average poor person in South Asia.[13]

Under most scenarios—except the most dire—important advances in eliminating extreme poverty will be attained by 2030. However, if a prolonged global recession happened, as many as 300 million more people would remain in extreme poverty and experience malnutrition.[14] Under low-growth scenarios, the extreme poverty rate would not see the big reductions that have occurred in the past couple of decades, and fewer new entrants would join the middle class.[15]

This means that under any scenario, there will still be plenty of poor people; the problem of poverty has not been solved and may be harder because many of these people are concentrated in countries—such as the landlocked countries in Africa—with few inherent sources of economic opportunity.

We are also seeing a lot of progress in health, which is a critical ingredient in the individual empowerment story. Like rising per capita income levels, improvements in health show the same pattern of the developing world catching up with the rich advanced countries and the life expectancy increasing everywhere. Deaths from infectious and communicable diseases are now falling for everyone. For centuries infants and young children have been vulnerable to diarrheal and respiratory infections, plus HIV/AIDS and malaria remain significant problems in sub-Saharan Africa. Despite the HIV/AIDS epidemic, there has been a rapid shift for several decades from communicable to noncommunicable diseases. In 2010, 7.2 million Africans died from communicable diseases and 3.5 million from chronic diseases. The trend in African deaths from the two causes is projected to cross in 2025, with more Africans dying from chronic diseases in the future.[16]

Out in the field, several nongovernmental organization (NGO) health experts were more cautious about Africa getting to that point and whether we will see it by the projected 2025 date. One medical worker told me that even with the free prenatal care and extended health immunization program, it was hard to get mothers into the clinic for more than one visit. "The challenge is that a lot of women just go for one visit, figure out the baby is fine and don't go back for the three follow up ones.... Hospitals are there, we have staff, but we need to get mothers into the clinic. You need to make mothers see that health is critical for her and her baby's health. You also need to factor in salary loss for the day they go to the clinic and get rid of the perception that older generations gave birth at home which means they will be all right without a lot of treatment.... A lot of it is word of mouth among villagers, so social networks are the ones through which you want to spread your message."

Still, despite the obvious uphill struggle and absent a major pandemic, *global* deaths from all communicable diseases—including AIDS, infectious diarrhea, malaria, and respiratory infections—are projected to decline by nearly 30 percent by 2030.[17] AIDS appears to have hit its global peak—around 2.3 million deaths per year—in 2004.[18] Enormous progress has been made toward wiping out malaria, but past advances have slowed many times due to donor fatigue and growing disease resistance to medicines. There's still likely to be a significant health gap between rich and poor countries even by 2030, but it will be shrinking and everyone's health will be improving.

The rapid growth of increasingly healthier and more prosperous middle classes has important implications. Most of the Western studies have focused on the new markets for consumer goods, such as cars, which rise sharply with the growth of the middle class. Large US and Western businesses are growing more and more dependent on those becoming thriving marketplaces, drawing an increasing proportion of their profits from overseas.

More importantly for the countries involved, the growing middle class will be an engine of growth. History tells us that those in the middle have in the past vigorously accumulated capital, be it physical—plant, equipment, or housing—or human—education or health.[19] But past examples also show that differences matter in how the middle classes consolidate. Brazil and South Korea both had similar income levels and rates of growth in the 1960, but Brazil's high levels of inequality are reckoned by many to have retarded its economic development. Brazil's middle class made up only 29 percent of its population, in contrast to Korea's 53 percent in the 1980s. Brazil has now caught up with over 50 percent middle class in the population, but its per capita remains substantially less than in South Korea.[20]

In preparing the NIC report, I spent time in Brazil studying the state of its middle class. Many Brazilians are in fact very proud of the growth of their middle class. A Brazilian social scientist told me that "we see inequality falling faster than expected." The main symbol of the new middle class has been the explosion in formal employment—workers with a formal employment contract rather than a cash-only arrangement. During the 2000s, formal job creation outpaced informal job growth by a three-to-one ratio. There was a big jump in people taking educational courses. And many Brazilians were pleasantly surprised that the rise of incomes did not translate totally into increased consumption. "The Brazilian rise was more sustainable than I thought," said an economist I spoke to, because the population was "not just consuming" but also investing in their future. The growth rate in education was very high. According to experts I consulted, "the quality of education, not just the quantity of growth" is getting better in Brazil but has a long way to go.

"Social mobility and decreasing inequality should be celebrated," a Brazilian expert on inequality told me. But he said one needs to be careful with "international comparisons." "No one in Brazil has the kind of public services that are available to the poorest person in Belgium. It is very difficult to compare groups on the basis of income if we do not include services." Middle classes also include very disparate groups. There is a big difference between public and private sector workers. The first have permanent jobs, whereas many have much less security in the private sector, which includes a big informal sector "that if they paid all the taxes they were liable for would not survive."

"Middle classes in Brazil pay a major part of their income to the state, but don't receive that much from it. Poorer classes get much more from the state than the classes paying for those services. Increasing indebtedness [is a way] to keep one's quality of life." I heard this from several experts at a conference we held at the Instituto Fernando Henrique Cardoso in São Paulo, a year before the outbreak of demonstrations in Brazilian cities to protest the lack of public services—particularly education and health—and too much money going to preparations for Brazil holding the World Cup games in 2014. It underlines a key point about middle classes: the insecurity about staying middle class.

What the state does or does not do is evermore under scrutiny with the rise of the middle classes, which is why all the government officials I talked to saw the state as under increasing pressure.

In that vein, corruption is a big issue for the middle class everywhere you go, and I heard endless complaints. Still, a former Brazilian official told me at the conference, the "Brazilian poor think corruption is not that bad, as they don't perceive it affecting them."

In Kenya, government officials and academic experts had different views on corruption. They worried about a receding Western interest in Africa that would harm the fight against corruption. One told me, "We are seeing differences between Western views and Chinese and Indian views of governance. If the West no longer has the same resources of aid on governance and rule of law, there will be big problems for Africa. Governments all over Africa will turn to China for aid and forget the West and its strings [conditions] on democratic governance and human rights and anti-corruption measures."

They rightly saw too that Africa's natural resources could be a source of corruption or of broader strife. A former senior Kenyan official told me that "there are too many deals in Africa that are dirty and not transparent. The Chinese are especially contributing to this. I don't think we are prepared in Kenya for the oil find.[21] We have not put into effect laws and regulations necessary for resource exploitation. This problem is not only about oil and gas, but other minerals and natural resources. This has been left to a few bureaucrats and not opened up to proper debate. Key decisions have been made without proper consideration."

Another expert at the conference that Kenya Institute for Public Policy Research and Analysis (KIPPRA) sponsored on global trends saw more "interstate conflict over resources." For him, a country that cannot manage the exploitation of its resources without massive corruption is "doomed." He also worried that the lack of proper oversight was endangering the environment. Corruption is particularly insidious, particularly when institutions like the judiciary fall prey, which makes it all the harder to root out. Unfortunately, we know that, historically, rapid economic development often fuels corruption and organized crime. For people in the developing world, in survey after survey, publics cite it as one of the top issues to be solved.

Going around and briefing *Global Trends* in the United States or Western Europe—particularly the bit on the rising middle classes—was, let's say, daunting. Many stared in disbelief at the idea that the middle classes could be thriving. They talked instead about their fears of a middle class that was disappearing or shrinking. Of course, median incomes— even stagnant ones in many Western countries—are above and will remain well above middle-class incomes in the developing world for a long time to come, even with higher growth elsewhere. But there is something to the fears of Western middle classes.

The World Bank's Branko Milanovic has recently accomplished a remarkable feat in tracking global inequality. His conclusion is that there has been the "profoundest global reshuffle of people's economic positions since the Industrial Revolution." The poorest haven't escaped their dire state, but the rest of the poor are now better off, with many escaping absolute poverty. His research shows the new global middle classes have seen substantial real income rises of 3 percent per capita annually. In contrast, the Western middle classes—which still remain in the upper quartiles—have largely stagnated while the top 1 percent have done extremely well, the top 5 percent somewhat less so. His conclusion is that globalization created polarization among the richest quartile of world population, allowing the top 1 percent to pull ahead of the other rich and to reaffirm the public perception of the wealthiest being biggest winners.[22]

So the perception among Western middle classes of stagnation and even decline is not far off, even if they are still better off than the emerging global middle classes. Middle classes everywhere expect to be always doing better. This is a universally shared value (and my definition, at least) of what it is to be middle class. This is why the leveling off of income growth among Western middle classes—which has many causes—is so distressing, particularly when others seem to be doing better. The share of global middle-class consumers from the United States will decline and be dwarfed by the wave of new middle-class consumers in the developing world. Slower economic growth among many Western countries will further ingrain the perception of a struggling Western middle class that faces greater competition from an increasingly global employment market, including competition for jobs requiring higher skills. Some estimates, for example, see middle-class consumption in North America and Europe only rising by 0.6 percent a year over the next couple of decades. In contrast, spending by middle-class Asian consumers could rise 9 percent a year through 2030, according to the Asian Development Bank.[23]

The education sector will be an increasing social and political battle-field. Education will be both the driver and a beneficiary of the expanding middle classes. It may be a way too for the Western middle classes to regain their momentum. The economic status of individuals and countries is likely to depend even more on their levels of education. The good news is that there has been a massive global expansion of enrollment rates at all levels of formal education since 1960. Between 1960 and 2000, gross enrollment rates increased 50 to 70 percentage points at various different levels of education. Experts who have studied the education transitions in developing countries today say that they are proceeding "much faster" than those in industrialized countries in the nineteenth and early twenti-eth centuries.[24]

Obviously there are regional variations: completion of the transition to universal primary education for girls and boys remains a problem for sub-Saharan Africa and a small number of other countries, including Pakistan, Afghanistan, Iraq, and Yemen. The lack of educational attainment at lower levels in these countries is very disquieting. Outside of this cluster, the criti-cal struggle is to raise enrollment rates at the secondary level. Countries in the Arab states and the poorer countries of East Asia and the Pacific have the steepest climb, but Latin American and Caribbean countries are also behind the advanced economies in enrollment rates at the secondary level.

Overall there is strong convergence between advanced and developing countries. "In 1960, the relative distance between the region with the high-est average education years and the region with the lowest was a ratio of over 7-to-1 for North America and Western Europe compared to the Arab States. In 2000, the greatest distance was a ratio of 4 to 1 for North America and Western Europe compared to sub-Saharan Africa."[25] The Middle East and North Africa is a region that has lagged others, but even here the aver-age years of completed formal education are likely to rise from about 7.1 to more than 8.7 years over the next couple of decades. Moreover, the level for women in that region could rise from 5.0 to 7.0 years.[26]

Women throughout much of the world are steadily narrowing the gap with men in years of formal education and have moved ahead in enrollment and completion rates in upper-middle and high-income countries. By 2005 most regions had reached gender parity except for the Arab states, South and West Asia, and sub-Saharan Africa. But even in these laggard countries, significant progress had been made compared to the situation in 1960. At the secondary level, progress has been dramatic, even in countries with disappointing gender enrollment parity at the primary level. Progress was most significant in the Arab states. At the tertiary level, enrollment rates are substantially higher for men in South and West Asia and sub-Saharan Africa, but the rate for women exceeded men in Latin America, North America, and Western Europe.[27]

Obviously, quality of education is something that can't be measured easily. It was the topic of many discussions I had in exploring the future with groups all around the world. In a discussion in South Africa in 2007, there was a general worry that standards were falling. A South African professor told me, "South Africa has the highest level of access to schooling in the developing world, but so what? We need to work on excellence." This was a universal theme throughout the developing world, that their educational systems did not match those found in the rich world. But the latest university rankings show Asian universities gradually gaining over Western ones.[28] China, Brazil, India, and South Korea have also increased their scientific output of papers 20-fold over 30 years from 1981 to 2012. Lower-income, smaller economies grew their scientific output faster than larger systems.[29]

It is also a big issue in the United States and Europe. McKinsey Global Institute, the research arm of the global consultancy firm, sees the mismatch between the skills being taught by the French educational system and the new jobs in the knowledge economy as behind the structural youth unemployment that France has suffered for decades and will continue to suffer without major educational reforms.[30] Equally McKinsey has studied the US system and found it very wanting in terms of maintaining standards and training workers for the future employment opportunities: "The United States, which once had the best-educated workforce in the world, has lost its competitive advantage in this area."[31] The proportion of Americans with bachelor's and graduate degrees remains at 41 percent, not substantially changed for decades and barely above the Organization for Economic Co-operation and Development's average and far from leading countries such as South Korea (63 percent), Canada (56 percent), and Japan (56 percent)."[32]

Education rates higher than "identity" for some in the new middle class— their ticket to a more prosperous and more secure future. I am reminded of a project I participated in with the Stimson Center, a Washington think tank, called Regional Voices. Members of the Stimson Center went out and listened to how people in the Middle East and South and Southeast Asia saw their future. This effort was unusual in that we did not talk about abstract ideas or high politics, but used focus groups to talk about the more immediate and day-to-day concerns of groups living in those regions. One of the most interesting studies was on Indian Muslims, which ended up focusing a lot on education. "The issue that recurred most prominently in every focus group and almost every conversation was that of the need for quality education and the need for Muslims to embrace that as a strategy for advancement. In almost all cases, education was identified as the single most important Muslim concern in India today." What made this somewhat startling is that the education focus is at odds with the general "non-Muslim perception of a community inordinately concerned with issues of religious identity." Quality education was seen as "essential for building effective Muslim leadership, and for arriving at intellectual vision and clarity of purpose." A leading Muslim journalist put it succinctly: "Modern education is essential to the development of a Muslim middle class, and a middle class is essential to the development of effective leadership for Muslims." Better vocational education is seen as essential for the advancement for poor and working-class Muslims, but the Muslim community also wants better-quality English medium-education and education in information and other technologies, seeing in that education the key to unlocking the entry route to the middle class.[33]

With education so much in the forefront, countries are competing to build up their educational institutions, and that means luring more foreign students not only as a mark of prestige, but also to help fund the expensive new graduate programs they want to establish. According to UNESCO, over 2.5 million students are studying outside their home country, which they see rising to over 7 million by 2020. The main centers have been traditionally

G-7 or advanced countries: United States, United Kingdom, Germany, France, and Australia. Chinese students have been particularly attracted to US universities, accounting for more than 18 percent of the total number of international students in the United States. Nevertheless, UNESCO, OECD, and other studies have noted the erosion in the United States' share with Asian, Middle East, and smaller European universities attracting increasing proportions of international students.[34]

Interstate competition in the education field is not the only result of the focus on obtaining better education. The competition inside educational institutions has heated up or even overheated.

Some years ago, when I attended a conference in Stockholm that brought big thinkers from around the world to review the *Global Trends 2025* draft, a Peking University professor pulled me aside to tell me privately about the cutthroat competition and corruption in even the best Chinese universities. The competition was so intense that professors were bribed and threatened by the parents if they did not give good grades to their children. Party members were the worst. Most times it was an offer of a bribe, but he had been threatened physically too.

More recently, the *Washington Post* substantiated the claims made by the professor, publishing an article that detailed the bribes needed to get into Beijing's better schools. The article detailed how Chinese parents "shower teachers and school administrators with favors, presents and money." One even bought a new elevator for a top school so his child could be admitted.[35]

The cutthroat competition has lasting psychological and social consequences. Sometimes the upward mobility and increasing prosperity, instead of producing greater security, actually has the reverse tendency of creating more insecurity. The personal stories are perhaps the most illustrative of the internal tensions that the sudden burst of new opportunities has created. Many of them could serve as foundations for novels. A favorite of my own, though poignant, is one that I encountered in China. It's the story of a very talented young Chinese woman who was torn between following her own ambitions and the gratitude she owed her parents. Her family had sent her to Shanghai, a colossal city of 23 million rimming China's eastern coast, in hopes that their daughter could get an education. When I encountered her, she was attending a college of rising prestige and was very conscious that she was expected to make a success of herself.

She took the job seriously, absorbing a full load of classes into her week and only occasionally wedging in time with friends. She was supposed to be her family's engine, not its caboose. In China and across the developing world, the goal is to build a vast, prosperous middle class, and she was one small piece of that plan. Her vision of that new life was to graduate and head back to teach in her rural village.

Only that wasn't her parents' plan. They were a family of small shopkeepers, and for much of their lives they have saved to send her to school. Once she gets out, she is to stay in the city and send money back home to support those she left in the village. She owes them. She is their only child, and their only hope. So once she settles into her life in Shanghai, she is to begin looking for a husband, one with good professional prospects. In the end, she did what was expected and started looking for a husband in Shanghai, although it was psychological torture for her.

If this Chinese woman's story tells us anything, it is that change rarely glides in calmly. Even with growing prosperity, the cultural shifts can still be wrenching.

There is also the question of the political outlook that is fostered by becoming middle class. Samuel Huntington, the late Harvard social scientist, and other academic theorists have talked about "the middle class [that] tends to be born revolutionary and becomes conservative by middle age."[36] Middle classes are defenders of the social and political order, but only if it serves their interests. In this day and age, that means the state must provide good public services. The discussion with Brazilian social scientists pointed to growing resentment well before the 2013 demonstrations because the middle class did not see their taxes translated into better services, especially in the health and education sectors.

Obviously, there is a trade-off between stability or physical security and getting one's expectations met. Given the upsurge in the size of the middle class, there is not as much revolution as one would have expected. And even in those places—like the Arab Middle East—where upheavals have occurred, we're seeing political order and security trump democratic aspirations—in Egypt, for example. In the *Global Trends* reports, we raised this issue about countries with democratic deficits. A democratic deficit is said to exist when a country's economic developmental level is more advanced than its level of governance. In theory, countries with democratic deficits are tinder that might be ignited by various sparks.

The extrapolations we did—based on the International Futures model—highlighted many resource-rich and relatively prosperous countries that are or will be in democratic deficit over the next decades if they continue to develop. Many are in the Gulf, Middle East, and central Asia—Qatar, the United Arab Emirates (UAE), Bahrain, Saudi Arabia, Oman, Kuwait, Iran, Kazakhstan, Azerbaijan—and Asian countries such as China and Vietnam. This set of countries is very different from the "usual suspects" lists of states on the verge of fragility or failure. Standard indications of state vulnerability do not usually include any measure of repression and instead focus on internal conflicts or lack of economic viability. These countries with high levels of democratic deficit, such as China and Gulf countries, present great risks—should they suffer severe political crises—due to their importance to the international system.

So why haven't some blown up? This is the question a lot of us who think about the future ask ourselves. But more importantly, it is also what many authoritarian regimes worry about. It may be due to the type of middle class that is being generated. Because of a high level of energy revenues, several Gulf and Middle Eastern countries are able to provide a level of economic well-being sufficient to hold back pressures for political change. Nevertheless, even then, the pressures are rising for fairer and wider opportunities for the middle classes. Senior UAE officials told us of their worries about satisfying growing expectations for democracy rights despite the high standard of living. They worry that the work of Western NGOs interested in advancing democratic and human rights could prey on this sense of public dissatisfaction with the lack of rights and increase the level of political discontent. They also see religious extremism as a symptom of growing dissatisfaction and link any outside effort to bolster democracy and human right groups as helping religious extremists.

In Russia, the prodemocracy rallies in 2011 and 2012 pointed to a budding middle-class movement calling for fair elections and reform of the political system. But Russia's middle class is quite small and fractured. As little as

20 percent of the population are in the middle class, with the overwhelming majority living in or near poverty and 10 percent who are very well off and above the middle class. Many in or near poverty rely on the modest social welfare benefits that are provided. The costs of social welfare are rising but have been met by the extensive energy revenues the state collects. Many in the middle class are state officials, security officers, public sector managers, and employees of state-owned companies who depend on the state and value stability.[37] They aren't going to bite the hand that feeds them.

Age structure may have something to do with whether middle classes take the democracy plunge or worry more about physical security. In 2008, two years before the Arab Spring, I saw the potential for regimes, such as those of Egypt's Hosni Mubarak and Tunisia's Zine El Abidine Ben Ali, to come under increasing pressures for change. Declining birth rates and a shrinking proportion of very youthful populations provided an opening for democratization. Social scientists have found that as the middle classes grew in formerly authoritarian states like South Korea and Taiwan in the 1960s and 1970s and more young adults were integrated into the work force, pressures for political liberalization increased. An important cluster of North African countries—including Libya, Egypt, and Tunisia—has been getting near that point from 2000 to 2020.[38] However, any transition was bound to be a lot more difficult in the Middle East. South Korea and Taiwan had better economic prospects, which helped to ease any transition to democracy. Egypt is still more youthful than states that consolidated their democratic revolution and became stable. Much of the youthful population, even the more educated, is struggling to find employment. East Asian economies prospered because of sustained government efforts to rapidly improve the quality of the work force through universal education and by developing export industries. In the Middle East, education systems need to produce a more technically skilled work force and encourage citizens accustomed to public sector jobs to accept the demands and volatility of the private sector. It was perhaps inevitable that a faltering economy combined with growing strife between secular and religious forces would push Egyptian middle classes toward opting for order over democracy. As with the failed 1848 democratic revolutions in Europe, democratic pressures will no doubt break out eventually, but when?

China is the big test case. If it would go democratic, it would probably
end the argument about whether democracy is solely a Western or universal value. It would also set off another wave of democracy similar to what
happened after the end of the Soviet Union. Under most economic growth
scenarios, China is slated to pass the threshold of US$15,000 per capita[39]
in the next five years or so. The US$15,000 per capita income level is often
a trigger for democratization, especially when coupled with high levels of
education and a mature age structure. Growing per capita income translates
into a bigger middle class: the Chinese middle class is now conservatively
estimated at about 10 percent of China's population and could be 40 percent
by 2020. As with the other middle classes, however, many Chinese middle
class are up-and-coming entrepreneurs who pulled themselves up by their
bootstraps. But there are also many managers and professionals in China's
large state-owned sector who are in the middle class and are indebted to the
state for their rise.[40]

Certainly there are increasing signs of discontent. Chinese political scientist Cheng Li, in his recent book *China's Emerging Middle Class*, finds "a
raft of mounting evidence from Chinese scholars" of a rising dissatisfaction.
Compared to poorer and richer cohorts, members of the middle class, Li found,
were more skeptical of the government's performance.[41] The sociologist Zhang
Yi found that the new middle class was acutely sensitive to feeling silenced and
to efforts to deprive it of information.[42] A leading pollster, Yuan Yue, found
in 2008 that urban residents were also "far more dissatisfied with the central
government's performance than are residents of small towns or rural areas."
This was especially striking because, historically, people were quick to criticize
local officials but generally complimentary of the central government.[43]

Democracy is a goal for many Chinese, including, oddly enough, some
in the Communist Party. The Party School has held conferences on democracy. It's not a matter of if, but when. The problem is that no one has an idea
of how to undertake political reform without major disruption or disorder,
which all want to avoid. In our meetings in China to discuss the preliminary
report, the Chinese lauded the stress on individual empowerment, agreeing
that individuals "will be more important in determining the future." At the
same time, they saw the rising middle classes as a "destabilizing factor" in
the rich countries as well as developing countries. In the rich countries, the

competition from globalization had made the middle classes a lot more dis-satisfied, while in China and other developing countries individual empow-erment and the rising middle classes had "created new problems" of growing demands and higher expectations of government.

Information technology has proved a great democratizing force. Networked movement enabled by IT demonstrated the capacity for disrup-tion, such as during the Arab Spring when social media was used to organize protests and demonstrations before security forces could intervene. IT pro-vides activists with a tool for quickly drawing global attention to their case for political and social change. Individuals can organize movements around shared beliefs in the virtual world and develop plans for mounting action. The exponential increase in data, combined with quickly growing capabili-ties to analyze and correlate it, will give unprecedented advantages to indi-viduals and networks all over the world. Formerly it was only big businesses that could afford to store and sift through mountains of data to help them fuel their operations. That capability will be available to everyone through big data stored in the cloud.

The use of IT will accelerate because of a number of trends already in train: a 95 percent drop in computer memory costs, a reduction in raw data storage costs to one-hundredth of the current price, and the fact that network efficiency will increase by more than a factor of 200 over the next decade and a half. The shift to cloud architecture will put increased com-puting capability and meaningful analytics in the hands of 80 percent of the world's population. Mobile devices will become increasingly rich sensor platforms, making it easy to track and analyze at a fine level of detail. Nearly all data will be archived indefinitely due to cheap digital storage. Finally, information will be "smart" about itself—indexed, categorized, and richly tagged upon collection—allowing it to be easily analyzed at a later date.

But these same technological developments could tip the balance toward more government power. New solutions for data storage and pro-cessing could help policy makers address difficult economic and governance problems, enable more intuitive and humanlike interaction with computers, enhance the accessibility of usability of knowledge, and greatly improve the accuracy of predictive models. On a visit to Google, we were given a demon-stration of their ability to construct a consumer price index tool that shows the inflation rate in real time and the rate variations in specific locales. Every 30 days the Bureau of Labor Statistics in the US Department of Labor sends out shoppers across a number of cities to collect a "shopping basket" of representative goods—such as various food items—that US households buy every month. From this data they determine the changes in the consumer price index.[44] Because the Internet market has grown so large, Google can track the changes in prices in real time and narrow it down to specific locales. This kind of new data will help to make the government more efficient and targeted.

Current applications of data solutions are already important to commerce and large-scale scientific efforts in addition to government. Large retailers use "big data" to fuse information about their customers' in-store spending habits, credit histories, web-surfing histories, social network postings, demographic information, and so on. From such fusion, data solutions allow retailers to extract valuable insights about their customers' preferences, allowing for very precisely targeted advertising.

The collection of so much data—or "digital bread crumbs" as Massachusetts Institute of Technology professor Alex Pentland has labeled it—means that we are for the first time in a position to be able to predict behavior. Pentland's research shows that from all data provided by social media, such as Facebook, and cell phones with global positioning system (GPS) capabilities, "my students and I can tell whether you are likely to get diabetes by examining the restaurants where you eat and the crowd you hang out with.... We can use the same data to predict the sort of clothes you are inclined to buy or your propensity to pay back."[45]

This isn't necessarily nefarious. Pentland explained that the analysis of big data can be put to good use, bettering society and making governments smarter. In May 2013, 90 research organizations from around the world reported hundreds of results from data analysis of the mobility (as registered through the GPS on cell phones) and call patterns of every citizen in the whole Ivory Coast. They mapped poverty from the diversity of cell phone usage. "As people have more disposable income, their pattern of movement and pattern of phone calls becomes increasingly diverse." The data was used to help improve the transportation system. And finally they analyzed the data for the spread of diseases. The research groups "showed that small changes in the public health system could potentially cut the spread of flu by 20 percent as well as significantly reduce the spread of HIV and malaria."[46]

The new expanding IT architectures and their use—whether by individuals and networks or states—are not deterministic. As we've seen with the example of the printing press, technology is dual use. Used by the individual to widen its capacities, new IT technologies can be used to counter that shift too.

Connective technologies will give governments—both authoritative and democratic—an unprecedented ability to monitor their citizens.

Can dictators shift the balance in their favor? Most likely not over the longer run, but they are getting smarter, and IT is a powerful tool in their hands if used deftly. China maintains the world's most extensive and sophisticated system for Internet censorship, employing tens of thousands of people to monitor and censor material that the regime sees as threatening.[47] At the same time, a RAND study that examined the use of the Internet by dissidents found that the government believes that "future economic growth in China depends on the country's integration with the global information infrastructure."[48] This means it can't clamp down too much for fear of denting economic growth or innovation.

Some of this schizophrenia played out in the tussle between China and Google over Google's effort to make available for its users an unfettered search engine free from government interference. Close observers of China's censorship strategies believe that the government does pay attention to how the country's business elites will react. One such observer "believes Beijing's current strategy is to block new Google services as soon as they become available, well before they develop any meaningful Chinese following. . . . For example, the only reason why Gmail remains unblocked in China (although it is sometimes disrupted) is because too many business and government elites have come to depend on it to communicate with friends, family, and colleagues around the world."[49]

The RAND study of government efforts concluded that Beijing had been "relatively successful" in "controlling dissident use of the Internet," but this was not guaranteed for the future: "The scale of China's information-technology modernization would suggest that time is eventually on the side of the regime's opponents."[50] While the regime is becoming increasingly sophisticated, it is nevertheless up against the growing use of the Internet within all sectors of society and increasing importance of the flow of information. Dissidents get support from the growing international NGO community abroad intent on advancing human and civil rights in China and elsewhere, and they have also become increasingly wily in using the Internet. With 300 to 400 hundred million Chinese already on the Internet, using Chinese versions of social networks like Weibo and WeChat, "it will be difficult to suppress legitimate speech," according to Google CEO Eric Schmidt.[51] Moreover, new software tools—one called Tor—can help shield dissidents from surveillance. According to Schmidt, "The Internet is becoming easier to use, and the same goes for circumvention technologies—which means that activists will face less of a challenge getting online securely."[52]

Other factors—such as growing middle-class frustration with corruption, pollution, inequality, or diminishing economic opportunities—are equally important in thinking about the strength of opposition and regime vulnerabilities. As shown in the Arab Spring, the Internet and social media are superb organizing tools that no authoritarian government can completely control or extinguish. However, more traditional forms of organization and strong institutions are also required, as shown by the Muslim Brotherhood and the military's eventual success in spite of IT-strengthened democratic forces.

We should pay some attention to whether the Internet could reinforce nationalism and racial, religious, or ethnic distrust. The RAND study on the political use of the Internet in China noted that under-30s, which is the largest age group of Internet users, was also the cohort that "is becoming highly nationalistic in outlook.... Only slightly more than 20 percent of the information viewed by Chinese Internet users is in languages other than Chinese."[53]

These trends toward greater nationalism and a deepening of religious or religious identities struck me as the more likely to be the short- to medium-term ideological implication for individual empowerment. The economics of globalization have spread the West's ideas of scientific reason, individualism, secular government, and primacy of law to societies seeking the West's material progress. But many citizens in these rising states are reluctant to sacrifice their cultural identities and political traditions. Religion is likely to be at the center of these ideological debates within and across societies.

Islam especially has strengthened owing to global increases in democratization and political freedoms that have allowed religious voices to be heard, and owing as well to advanced communications technologies and the failure of governments to deliver services that religious groups can provide. A 2013 Pew poll underlines the *overlap* between a strong belief in democracy and the desire by Muslim publics for religion to play a prominent role in politics. The Pew survey found that large numbers of Muslims in Southeast Asia, South Asia, the Middle East, and North Africa say religious leaders should have influence over political matters.[54]

The ability of religious organizations to define norms for governance in religious terms and to mobilize followers on economic and social justice issues raises the prominence of religious ideas and beliefs in politics. The channeling of political dissent into Islamic discourse and government efforts to manipulate the Islamic current will reinforce the religious influence, especially in Middle Eastern politics. Religious activists can draw on sacred texts and a long historical tradition to frame popular grievances in terms of social justice rhetoric and egalitarianism. In this new era, religious ideas, actors, and institutions will be increasingly influential among publics and even elites.

Nationalism is another force that is intensifying, particularly in regions—such as Eurasia and East Asia—where there are unresolved territorial disputes and countries' fortunes may be rapidly changing. A 2012 Pew survey found "roughly half of Russians agree that their homeland should be for Russians only with only four-in-ten disagreeing." The public voiced a similar degree of ethnic chauvinism in 2009, when 54 percent said "Russia should be for Russians." In contrast, when the Soviet Union was in its last throes in 1991, 69 percent disagreed and only 26 percent agreed with the notion "that Russia should be exclusively for Russians."[55]

Earlier research by Pew showed that beliefs in moral and cultural superiority are strongly held everywhere. In the United States, eastern Europe, and throughout most of Africa, Asia, and Latin America, majorities (according to the 2013 Pew survey) believe that their culture is superior to others. This sentiment is particularly strong in a number of developing nations. Fully nine in ten respondents in Indonesia and South Korea and more than eight in ten in India are strong boosters of their own culture. Looking forward, many developing and fragile states—such as in sub-Saharan Africa—face increasing strains from resource constraints and climate change, pitting different tribal and ethnic groups against one another and accentuating the separation of various identities. Ideology is likely to be particularly powerful and socially destructive when the need for basic resources exacerbates already-existing tensions between tribal, ethnic, religious, and national groups.

The move to the city, which is a sure and quick route for many rural inhabitants to increase their economic prospects, is leading to increased expressions of religious identity. Immigrants to cities—mostly Muslims in Europe and Russia, for example—are coalescing along religious lines. Urbanization is driving demands for social services provided by religious organizations—an opening that Islamic and Christian activists have been effective in using to bolster religious cohesion and leverage.

Over time, we would expect some of these differences to iron out as middle classes everywhere share many similar interests. A 2012 European Union study on the global middle class showed that "around four in every five people worldwide believe that democracy is the best available system of government." A 2009 Pew study found that middle classes in 13 countries (Chile, Ukraine, Russia, Venezuela, Poland, South Africa, Malaysia, Mexico, Brazil, Egypt, Argentina, India, and Bulgaria) attached increasing importance to individual liberties and were less inclined to accept gender discrimination.[56]

THE MOST RECENT *GLOBAL TRENDS* REPORT was published before the Snowden revelations showed the extensive scope of the US intelligence community's capabilities to monitor global communications, but I anticipated in the work that "privacy" would become an increasing issue for democratic governments, bearing on the notion of individual empowerment. Was the large-scale secret collection of personal data compatible with democracy, and was big data a strong counterforce to individual empowerment? To my mind, big data is needed more than ever if we are to get a handle on the big challenges of running megacities; efficiently use critical resources such as food, water, and energy; and make new headway in combating chronic diseases. At the same time, privacy is not a trivial issue: fear of the growth of an Orwellian surveillance state is a real possibility. The World Economic Forum noted well before the Snowden revelations that "individuals are beginning to lose trust in how organizations and governments are using data about them."[57] Similarly, it's not just worry about governments' use of individual data, but it's also about the mountain of data that companies are accumulating on our tastes, interests, movements, and the general patterns of our daily lives. I can easily see that individuals' distaste for overly intrusive advertising in coming years will spark a sudden backlash against commercial uses of data solutions. Although individuals see huge advantages in the Internet and social media for themselves, it's natural that they don't want those same tools to be used against them.

Governments, private sector economists, and data specialists are only just beginning to think about how to square this circle. I believe it is doable, but time is running out. Public trust will need to be rebuilt with greater transparency and accountability and even curbs on the kind of data that is collected. The crisis triggered by the Snowden revelations provides the US and European governments, especially, with the ability to put large-scale data collection on a more solid, transparent, and sustainable footing. I believe clear-cut restrictions on government collection and use of data will be needed to reestablish public trust. The worst possible outcome would be a balkanized Internet in which data would not be shared widely for fear of its misuse by the United States or other governments. US national interests benefit enormously from having engineered a universal Internet and from US-based companies being on the commercial forefront of the technological change. A loss of public trust and the end of a universal Internet are not remote possibilities and should not be taken lightly.

It is critical that a comprehensive solution be found to protect individual rights and well-being while at the same time ensuring adequate levels of security. As will be discussed later, the threat posed by individuals and small groups doing enormous harm is part and parcel of the same overall trend of individual empowerment. Through new technologies like biotech and cyber, individuals have the ability to do harm on a scale formerly reserved for states. The ability to discover and track those individuals is an impossible task without big data collections. For some time, government officials have talked about only playing defense, saying it will be some time before they can get out in front of the threat. Big data provides opportunities for authorities to identify and anticipate the most threatening illicit activities and go after places and organizations that support them. However, trust has to be built that such uses of big data are for the general good and not weapons to undermine human rights.

The World Economic Forum and others have thought about the mechanics of protecting personal and proprietary data in the commercial sphere and see a working solution in the development of trust networks. Trust networks keep track of user permissions for each piece of personal data and what can and cannot be done with the data. Many worry such trust networks could be too costly and cumbersome to administer, both for commercial enterprises interested in freely using the personal data and for the individual who has to decide which data to share and with whom. One of the World Economic Forum recommendations is for the establishing of "living labs" where there can be a testing of potentially new regulations and rights and responsibilities of the individual. In all likelihood, it will be hard to develop new models of governance that don't go too far one way or the other in protecting or divulging data. Wherever the line is eventually drawn, privacy will become an enduring concern for individuals as more and more potentially sensitive data, such as medical information, is digitalized and potentially compromised.

Worries about data collection and privacy are beginning to merge with concerns about the economic implications of the Internet revolution, particularly going forward. McKinsey did a study a couple years ago that showed that the Internet is becoming a more critical part of economies in both advanced and developing countries. Their simulation showed that it was likely to create an increase in real GDP per capita of $500 on average during a 15-year period. It took the Industrial Revolution of the nineteenth century 50 years to achieve the same results.[58] In many cases, the research found that the jobs created have so far vastly outnumbered the ones destroyed. In the future, however, it looks like the economic benefits of Internet-based technologies like robotics and artificial intelligence could be more unequal, favoring certain skill sectors and displacing many more workers. A recent study showed that "digitization"—the mass adoption of connected digital services by consumers, enterprises, and governments—provided a $193 billion boost to world economic output and created 6 million jobs in 2011, but developed countries experienced less employment growth compared with the developing countries: "East Asia, South Asia, and Latin America received the most employment growth of all regions, with more than 4 million jobs created as a result of these regions' digitization improvements. Conversely, digitization provided little employment growth in North America and Western Europe." The reason for the relative lack of employment benefits in developed nations is because as digitization increases, productivity improves, and technology replaces skilled jobs; less-skilled jobs go overseas to where labor is cheaper.[59]

Related, too, is a growing concern about the technology revolution aggravating inequality. After decades of decreasing US income inequality, it began to reverse in the 1960s and is now at the level of the Gilded Aged one hundred years ago. Inequality usually expands when countries are developing rapidly, but the new technologies such as the Internet and robotics may be contributing to those working getting a smaller share of growing national income. The few who have the skills to excel at the new technologies, along with corporate managers and owners, will be the big winners. Over time, this will be an increasing source of discontent if the education and training needed to succeed are not readily available.

INDIVIDUAL EMPOWERMENT IS PART OF a broader trend of diffusion of power. It is both cause and effect. Many of the effects of the Internet-based technologies, for example, have been to favor the individual, putting capabilities into the hands of individuals that even governments did not possess two decades ago. At the same time, there is greater insecurity because the churn is continuous. It's not as if anyone can feel secure—from the worker being displaced through Internet-driven automation to the CEOs and political leaders who now have markedly shorter careers than their predecessors. The next chapter will show how the disruptions at the empowered individual level—which fuel a prosperous and tech-savvy, albeit insecure, global middle class—is increasingly disrupting the international system of nations, many of which thought they had witnessed the End of History with the fall of the Soviet Union.

CHAPTER 2

# A Splintered World

IN 2003, THE BRICS CONCEPT EMERGED. THAT WAS WHEN GOLDMAN SACHS HIGHLIGHTED the rise of Brazil, Russia, India, and China (BRIC) as emerging economic powers. Ten years later it is G20 that best symbolizes the challenge to Western dominance or an array of developing states—still including giants like China and India—that collectively are altering the political and economic landscape. I prefer to think about it as part of the overall trend of diffusion of power, which we began to discuss with individual empowerment in the first chapter. Most works about global trends begin with a discussion of the state, and there is a sweepstakes element—which states are going up or down—that attracts a lot of media attention.

Underlying the rise of new states is perhaps a bigger structural change, that is, the changing nature of power—its diffusion. And the biggest change-agent connected with power diffusion is not states but empowered individuals. States feel the effects, but they are not the underlying cause. The cause is the bottoms-up dynamics of millions of individuals who are joining the middle classes and empowered by the new technologies. All governments—even the rising ones—are increasingly under siege with their publics demanding more and better services and greater economic, environmental, and physical security than they can ever deliver. So let's continue the discussion in that same vein by seeing what is happening with states as a part of that overall "diffusion of power" trend.

The state won't disappear. In fact, we could see some strengthening of state capacity among developing states. There is public demand for better services, and some states will have increased tax revenues to work with from their growing prosperity. China would be the key test case, in which there are increasing calls for a social safety net. By contrast, the state in the most developed and high-income countries could see weakening, being overstretched as they are in keeping up with current demands for social spending.

For the international system, the diverse array of states—not to mention growing importance of NGOs, multinational corporations, and superempowered individuals—makes it difficult to build a cohesive world order. By default, the state will remain the foundation of the international system—certainly in the global institutions. I can't see how you would organize the United Nations Security Council (UNSC) around such a diverse array of new actors like NGOs, multinational corporations, and superempowered individuals. Certainly they all play increasing roles in the UN system. But we already have a problem gathering all the most important nations around one table, so how would you be able to accommodate all the important nonstate actors and have a prayer of making the UNSC work?

Societies in both the developed and developing worlds are less cohesive, whether it is through fragmentation along ethnic or religious lines or across partisan political divisions. Many states face new environmental challenges from climate change (more about this in chapter 4) and potentially increased security threats from terrorism or war. States therefore need the cooperation of other states more than ever for dealing with transnational threats, but such cooperation is oftentimes hard to get. Greater interdependence that has come with globalization has boosted global growth but has been a challenge for government. Citizens look to government for help from the negative impacts of globalization, and most often, governments can't provide a solution. Lower labor costs in China or Southeast Asia are not something governments in high-wage economies can change even though many jobs held by workers in developed countries have been outsourced.

Developments in one place increasingly have boomerang effects. The 2011 Pacific earthquake and tsunami had profound political and economic effects not only in Japan, but also in the United States, where auto factories came to a halt because they lacked auto parts from Japanese factories. In Germany, the nuclear energy industry was given a death sentence because of fears of an accident happening there. Pandemics are one of the worst nightmares for governments to deal with: outbreaks are largely random events, but once viruses evolve to become transmittable from human to human, they spread quickly because of the ease of international travel.

In the face of these mounting uncertainties and the possible contingencies, most governments feel a loss of control. Many officials with long careers behind them believe that we have seen a sea change in the challenges facing government. It's the first thing they mention when you talk to them about the future. It is a lot harder for government to do its job. And they identify the trend toward greater power diffusion as a key challenge.

How has this come about? At the international level, there are more actors, starting with more states that are important. When I lecture, I say we live in a G20 world. Several decades ago after the end of the Soviet Empire, it was a G7 world. The G7 countries—United States, United Kingdom, France, Germany, Italy, Canada, and Japan—were political and economic powerhouses. Power was concentrated in that world, particularly because G7 countries shared much the same outlook or set of values.

Now all of that has changed, and changed dramatically. By 2030, Asia will have surpassed North America and Europe combined in terms of global power, based upon measures of GDP, population size, military spending, and technological investment.[1] China alone looks like it will become the largest economy sometime in the 2020s.[2] This rise of Asia, particularly, restores Asia's weight in the global economy and world politics, reversing what had been European and Western dominance since the eighteenth century.

However, just as important as the rise of the large emerging countries like China and India will be that of other non-Western states such as Colombia, Indonesia, Mexico, Turkey, Brazil, South Africa, Nigeria, and even Iran, Egypt, and others who we may see prosper in the next decade or two. Individually, most of these countries will remain second-order players because their size does not approach China or India. However, as a collective group, the rapidly developing states—many of which we categorized in a broad-brush way not so long ago as "the Third World"—will surpass

Europe, Japan, and Russia in terms of total global power by 2030.[3] This group of emerging middle-tier countries will collectively overtake the 28 European Union members in the combined four measures of global power by 2030.[4] When this middle tier is combined with the non-Western giants of China and India, the shift of power from the West to the emerging or non-Western world is even more striking.

The enormity of this shift in national power is reflected in the number of regional power transitions that will be ongoing in the next couple of decades. China is already consolidating its regional position. In 2030, China's GDP, for example, will be about 140 percent larger than Japan's. As the world's largest economic power in the future, China will remain ahead of India, but the gap could begin to close in the next couple decades as China's growth rate falls. In 2030 India could be the economic powerhouse that China has been over the past couple of decades. One would expect that China's current economic growth rate—7 to 8 percent—will be a distant memory by 2030.

The total size of the Chinese working age population will peak in 2016 and decline from 994 million to about 961 million in 2030.[5] By contrast, India's demographic profile looks more promising: its working-age population is unlikely to peak until about 2050. This provides a potential long-term boost for economic growth so long as the needed structural reforms are put in place, including greater economic liberalization, vastly better infrastructure, and a widening and deepening of better-quality education for its burgeoning youth population. Also of significance, India will most likely continue to consolidate its power advantage relative to Pakistan. India's economy is already nearly eight times as large as Pakistan's and could easily be more than 16-to-1 by 2030.

Despite the growing gap with China, Japan can maintain its status as an upper middle rank power, but only so far as it undertakes major structural reforms. Domestically, Japan's political, social, and economic systems will need to be restructured to address its demographic decline, an aging industrial base, and a more volatile political situation. Japan's decreasing population could force authorities to consider new immigration policies, like a long-term visa option for visiting workers. The Japanese, however, will have difficulty overcoming their reluctance to naturalize foreigners. The aging of the population will spur development in Japan's health-care and housing systems to accommodate large numbers of dependent elderly. The shrinking work force will put a major strain on Japan's social services and tax revenues, leading to tax increases and calls for more competition in the domestic sector to lower the price of consumer goods. I anticipate there will be continued restructuring of Japan's export industries, with increased emphasis on high technology products, value-added production, and information technologies.

The working-age population in Japan, declining in absolute numbers, includes a large number of unemployed and untrained citizens in their late teens and 20s. This could lead to a shortage of white-collar workers. At the same time, the government's effort to boost women's increased participation in the workforce—including in the upper reaches—could help make up some of the shortfall so long as it does not lead to an even lower birthrate. Balancing work with marriage and a family is difficult in Japan, where traditional marriages with mothers staying at home remain the cultural ideal. Female participation in the economy is not as bad as widely assumed. At 61 percent for women, it is not far behind the United States (62 percent), the United Kingdom (66 percent), and Germany (68 percent). The *Financial Times'* Martin Wolf believes it might be "possible to raise female participation further to levels found in US and other Western states, but this would not transform the growth outlook."[6]

The next 15 years will probably see Brazil bolstering its position despite the recent slowdown. It overtook the United Kingdom in 2011 to become the world's sixth-largest economy (measured in market prices), but has since fallen back to seventh place. The Centre for Economics and Business Research (CEBR), a London-based economic consultancy, believes Brazil will surge again over the next decade, re-overtaking the United Kingdom and Germany by 2023. CEBR attributed this to Brazil's strong agricultural trade.[7] Mexico, Colombia, and Peru also look set to be regional economic powerhouses over the next couple of decades.[8]

The International Futures model that I used in the *Global Trends* report shows that Europe declines relatively as regions with more rapidly growing states begin to close the gap. Many European countries will be burdened by aging and, in some cases, declining populations. They face the possibility of slower aggregate GDP growth. Germany will remain the leader for the time being of the other EU countries because of its economic growth prospects, but it has a ticking demographic time bomb with its low birthrate and aging population. By 2050 both France and the United Kingdom—which are now smaller in population than Germany—may have larger populations than Germany because immigration has been greater in those former countries. The latest CEBR forecast believes the United Kingdom will overtake Germany to become the largest Western European economy around 2030, based partly on the United Kingdom's more favorable demographic picture.

These "post-mature" states, with median age over 45 years—many of them in Europe—will need to muster funding to adequately support needy retirees while maintaining the living standards of those families and taxpayers who support them. The retreat from pay-as-you-go pension and health-care systems to more securely funded systems is creating a political backlash as governments seek to reduce beneficiaries and benefits, increase workers' contributions, and extend the required number of working years.

By 2030 Russia faces a steep population drop, about 10 million people, a greater decline than any other country during that time frame. Its problem is not just low birthrates, but also the early deaths of men in their 50s due to excessive tobacco, drug, and alcohol abuse as well as high levels of HIV, tuberculosis, and other debilitating diseases. Nevertheless, the International Futures modeling I used in *Global Trends* shows the potential for Russia to defy its demographic destiny and remain powerful. Even though its population will have a rapid decline, it will be large by European standards—more than half again the size of Germany's population.

However, to remain a great power and not a rapidly declining one, Russia needs to live up to that potential, and the recent news is not encouraging. In spite of 7 percent annual growth early in the twenty-first century, its economy has never rebounded from the collapse of communism and remains handicapped by its heavy dependence on energy exports. The 2008 Great Recession dealt a serious blow to Russia because of the collapse in high oil prices, which forced the regime to draw down on its reserves to maintain its welfare programs. Depending on its eventual production levels, the shale revolution could be a further blow, particularly if US exports lessen European dependence on traditional Russian gas and force Gazprom, Russia's biggest company and largest extractor of natural gas, to lower its price.

A team of economists from the liberal Gaidar Institute for Economic Policy believes Russia is already facing serious fiscal challenges that will grow worse as pensions and social spending climb and the economic growth rate plateaus. Government forecasters project an average growth rate of 2.5 percent each year through 2030, below the global average of 3.4 or 3.5 percent. The liberal economists believe Russia faces a shortfall of $28 trillion unless the growth rate picks up.[9]

Russian leaders are seeking to reinvest in technological innovation, but most experts see major difficulties—not least being the pervasive corruption and lack of freedoms—in Russia rebuilding what was a formidable science and technology sector under Soviet rule. However, should it spur diversified economic growth other than energy, its pivotal and vast geographic position between East and West combined with its remaining military power will give it a chance of rebuilding its great power status.

The United States is the other great power so far not mentioned. There will be a longer discussion about the United States and its future role in the global system in chapter 8. The United States shares many of the challenges faced by its G7 counterparts, such as budgetary pressures from increasing costs of its entitlement programs and health care. Partly because of its reemergence as a large-scale energy producer, the United States is in a better position economically than its G7 partners. Nevertheless, like them it faces relative economic decline with the rise of China, India, and a collection of smaller, rapidly emerging middle-tier powers.

I used two sets of measures or "indexes" of national power in *Global Trends 2030* to plot out exactly when the United States and other G7 countries would be surpassed by the emerging powers. In the first power index, there were four measures mentioned earlier—GDP, population size, military spending, and technology—weighted and modeled out to 2030. Using this four-component power index, China surpasses the United States in the early 2030s. The European Union is overtaken by China between 2015 and 2020, and by India around 2030.

A second power index incorporated a broader array of elements and is arguably more relevant to twenty-first-century power, including how healthy or educated or well-governed a country is. Using this index, China's and India's shares of global power increase, but at a slower pace than projected by the other index. This is because health, education, and governance have so far not been high priorities for them. China still surpasses the United States, but a decade later in the 2040–45 period rather than around 2030 as predicted in the first power index. Using the new, broader, "softer" power index, Europe ranks much closer to the United States than in the first index.

Does the recent economic slowdown for the developing states change that calculation? My answer is not much, if we are looking at the *long term*. Long-term structural trends are driving the developed and developing world toward convergence. We always knew this would need at least several decades for convergence of per capita incomes to be accomplished. The GDPs of China, India, Brazil, and others will surpass all or most of the rich states in the next couple of decades, but the per capita income gap will extend decades after that. This is a different pattern than the one followed by the rise of Germany or the United States in the late nineteenth century. Then, individual citizens enjoyed the highest standards of living, too. The new rising states' advantage is in having large populations whose standard of living is rising enough to move the country into the top ranks.

Emerging-market growth from 2000 to 2012 was extraordinarily high, with the BRICs growing on average 6.2 percent a year.[10] There are numerous reasons why that won't happen again. Too much success lulled the BRICs particularly into thinking they did not need to push ahead with structural reforms. Growth in the rich economies has suffered since the Great Recession, and that slowdown has affected the developing states, which still look to the West as trade and investment partners. It's important to remember that the BRICs don't encompass the whole developing world. Others—like central and eastern Europe, Chile, Mexico, Peru, and Colombia, who have recently undertaken structural reforms—are now beginning to show great promise. Moreover, China's growth—although down from its height—is still impressive at 7 percent annually, particularly given its size as the number-two economy in the world. Less growth in China today might mean higher income and more balanced and sustainable growth down the road if it can develop a more domestic-consumption-driven economy. It's also too early to count the other BRICs even if near-term growth is going to be disappointing. The middle-class demonstrations we've seen in countries like Brazil could be helpful in forcing the needed structural reforms.

One can sometimes get too wrapped in numbers and not see the forest for the individual trees. I know people who aren't particularly persuaded by extrapolations of economic growth and other numbers and want some concrete sign of a multipolar world. And I completely understand—all of this seems so abstract. But it's hard not be persuaded that something big is happening—that diffusion of power is real—when you look at outer space. It was only a couple of decades ago that there were only two powers—the United States and the Soviet Union—in space. The 1957 Sputnik launch was a pivotal moment in the American psyche because the Soviets appeared to be getting ahead in the military and technological race. Equally, the 1969 Apollo 11 walk on the moon showed that America was up to the challenge and was the leader in space. China plans to have a permanent space station in 2020 and crewed expeditions to the moon by the mid-2020s.[11]

As of late 2013, at least 60 countries on every inhabited continent have acquired, are in the process of doing so, or are operating their own complex and capable space systems—mostly imaging and communications satellites—in support of wider diplomatic, security, and economic interests. Part of the reason is cheaper technology. A number of the key technologies required in construction of satellites have been subject to Moore's Law, that is to say, doubling of their capabilities at least every two years. Microprocessors, sensors, and other components have progressively miniaturized and are cheaper to manufacture, thus making satellites smaller, more capable, and cheaper to build and acquire. The launch of satellites into Earth's orbit is also much cheaper. Furthermore, a growing number of commercial entities have large constellations of communications and imagery satellites that governments and other enterprises can use for modest costs.

In a further twist, illustrative of the individual empowerment trend, we are now seeing individuals send miniaturized satellites or "cubesats" into space using commercial off-the-shelf components for their electronics. The media in late 2013 reported "the first satellite designed and built by US high school students blasted into space."[12] Nanosatellites, like some of the ones designed by those high schools students, crib their technology from "off-the-shelf" smartphones, which are already equipped with features such as fast processors, sensors, GPS receivers, and high-resolution cameras. The result is low-cost and tiny, but powerful, spacecraft. The student-made satellite is just $3.9 \times 3.9 \times 4.5$ inches and weighs only 2 pounds, according to officials with Orbital Sciences, which supported the project. They have limited operational span because they orbit at lower altitudes than other spacecraft. The small spacecraft is outfitted with a phonetic voice synthesizer, which can convert text to voice and transmit those sounds back to Earth over ham radio frequencies.

This is more than a cute experiment. Cubesats have many different uses, according to a NASA official:

"[By] taking the same measurements at the same time in many different places and gathering that information, we may learn a lot of things that we can't learn even with very sophisticated large spacecraft.... It doesn't eliminate the need for big, complex satellites—there's still a need for that type of thing—but this fills another type of role that we haven't really been able to do before."[13] There's also the Vermont Lunar CubeSat, which was built by researchers at Vermont Technical College and aims to help develop the prototype technologies for a smartphone-powered satellite that could one day be launched to the moon. NASA launched the high school–designed cubesat from its Wallops Island, Virginia, facility, but there are now firms offering launches from commercial aircraft over international water.[14]

I dare anyone to say there isn't a profound diffusion of power underway.

The number of emerging countries that the modeling identifies for moving up to the top table is large, which underlines my point on diffusion and a historically unprecedented degree of upward country mobility. The modeling identifies the original four BRICs[15] plus 18 other mid-tier countries, such as Indonesia, Turkey, Mexico, Nigeria, and others, as emerging powers on the regional and global levels. The role that each of these countries plays will obviously vary enormously, but as shown by the inclusion of many of them in the G20, their weight is already recognized. This is quantitatively and qualitatively different than what has happened historically when the international system constituted a relatively small number and most of them were in Europe.

Why haven't more boats risen? At this time of unprecedented upward mobility, I worry as much about the countries that aren't making it and are staying weak and fragile. Can we expect to see an improvement for the poorest countries?

There may be some good news. There is a high correlation between youth bulges and armed civil and ethnic conflict. Chronic conflict is one of the factors behind state fragility. Since the 1970s, roughly 80 percent of all armed civil and ethnic conflicts (with 25 or more battle-related deaths per year) have originated in countries with youthful populations. Currently, there are more than 80 countries that have a median age of 25 years or less.[16] The "demographic arc of instability" that correlates with youthful populations ranges from clusters in the midsection of Central America and the central Andes, covers all of sub-Saharan Africa, and stretches across the Middle East into South and central Asia.[17]

By 2030, this arc will have contracted. With fertility declines already underway, the tally of countries with youthful populations will decline to about 50 by 2030. The largest persistent cluster of youthful states is projected to be located along the equatorial belt of sub-Saharan Africa. A second, more diffuse group of youthful countries will persist in the Middle East—including the Palestinian Territories (West Bank and Gaza) and Jordan and Yemen in the region's south. In the Americas, only Bolivia, Guatemala, and Haiti will retain their youthful populations.

Among the US Census Bureau's projections for South Asia, only Afghanistan will remain youthful by 2030, although its fertility will also be coming down.[18] However, the aging that will occur among the overall population in nearby Pakistan and India hides continuing youth bulges among certain ethnic and regional groups that could remain a security concern. Youthful bulges will persist for most of the next two decades among tribal populations in Pakistan's western provinces and territories. In Pakistan and Afghanistan, the fertility rates are greater than five children per woman among the Pashtun populations. In India, where the southern states and large cities have attained low fertility, birthrates will remain higher in the poorer, central northern states of Uttar Pradesh and Bihar.

Kurdish fertility in southeastern Turkey appears to be stalled at about four children per woman. In Israel, the fertility of the diverse ultra-Orthodox Jewish minority remains above six children per woman. The persistence of high rates of fertility and population growth among dissonant minorities is bound to disturb the political order, particularly as these populations become much larger.[19]

Besides youth bulges, other conditions can increase the prospects for instability in the short run. First, studies have shown that countries moving through a midrange between authoritarian and democratic rule have a proven record of high instability. In the *Global Trends* report, I systematically looked at countries that are rated to be in this awkward midrange between autocracy and democracy. There is a well-known social science measure—the Polity 20-point scale—that is used to determine where countries fall. Those that are not far along and have not achieved attributes of democracy such as openness and competitiveness of executive recruitment or participation by all segments of the population in the political process are considered high risks. Others that are closer in their development to full democracy are less at risk for major instability.

What is striking about the period we are in now and will be in for the next couple of decades is that there are so many—about 50—who fall into that major risk group. In some ways, this is good news. In the 1960s and 1970s before the end of the Cold War, there were many more dictatorships, not just under Soviet domination in central and eastern Europe but elsewhere in Africa and Latin America, and many were stable. But it came at a price to human freedoms. Authoritarian states—by their nature—tend to be more stable, at least outwardly and as a political entity, until they end. Now that many of them have gone, we are ironically in for more instability until full democracy has been achieved.

The greatest number of countries in the midrange between being authoritarians and full democracy in 2030 will be in sub-Saharan Africa—23 of 45 countries—followed by Asia—17 out of 59 total, including 5 of the 11 Southeast Asian countries and 4 of the 9 central Asian ones—then the Middle East and North Africa (11 out of 16). Recent events in the Middle East confirm the region's vulnerability to the governance transition, which is likely to be still playing out in 2030.[20]

The big question for the future is, what is the overall effect of all these difficult struggles up the greasy pole and the impact of greater diffusion of power at the top? What are the consequences of more players for the international system? Can you manage an international system with so many different actors at different stages of development having different values and vantage points? There's no clear answer, but we can make some educated guesses.

First, the governance landscape will be much more complicated in 2030: my guess is that intermediate levels of government, such as megacities and regional groupings, will assume increasing powers, whereas national governments and global multilateral institutions will struggle to keep up with the rapid diffusion of power. Let's look at cities. The role of cities will be an even more important feature of the future as urban areas grow in wealth and economic power. McKinsey Global Institute calculates that by 2025 more rich middle-income households—defined as having an annual income of more than US$70,000 (in PPP terms)—will live in emerging market cities than in Western ones. Urban areas could inject up to $30 trillion a year into the world economy by 2025. The speed and scale of the urban expansion is unprecedented.[21]

Increasingly cities are likely to take the initiative on resource management, environmental standards, migration, and even security because of their critical importance to the welfare of urban dwellers. The C40 partnership, a group of 40 of the world's top cities with the goal of reducing carbon emissions and increasing energy efficiency in large cities across the world, is among the most celebrated of such examples of new subnational entities beginning to grow up. In early 2014, the C40 partnership has over 1,500 initiatives underway in an effort to cut greenhouse gas emissions and reduce climate risks. The "smart city" concept—which is now in use by many cities—is founded on the principle that Internet technologies can be harnessed to dramatically improve how cities work, maximizing citizens' economic productivity and quality of life while minimizing resource consumption and environmental degradation. Architects and engineers, for example, are designing green buildings that use insights from ecology, architecture, and landscape to reduce buildings' energy consumption to zero. Some greentech buildings even produce more energy than they consume.

Reducing buildings' energy needs is important because buildings currently account for perhaps 41 percent of the world's energy demand and 71 percent of electricity use.[22]

The social problems are going to be just as acute. Cities may provide extraordinary environments for technological innovation but can also be incubators of crime. In cities in many parts of the developing world, as many as 60 percent of all urban dwellers will be under the age of 18 by 2030.[23] If cities lack sufficient economic, educational, or social opportunities, the unemployed youth are targets for recruitment by criminal gangs. On a trip to Rio I was shown the ways that city authorities are currently trying to integrate the favelas, or slums, into mainstream city life, including setting up a ski-lift-like transport system that is free to residents in the favelas, which usually are on the sides of the cliffs away from the city center. Now it takes a fraction of the former two hours or so it took for favela residents to commute to work, and they do not feel cut off. There are legions of examples, of course, in which cities have not been innovative and have sowed the seeds of future problems. Many Chinese cities followed the patterns of US and Western cities with their sprawling suburbs and now are finding themselves fighting similar problems of widespread traffic congestion and pollution.

Besides cities, the growth of intraregional trade points to greater regional integration, suggesting the possibility of a world order built more around regional structures. Nearly two-thirds of European trade is within the European Union; the North American Free Trade Agreement (NAFTA) represents more than 40 percent of total US trade; East Asian intraregional trade is 53 percent; and, excluding Mexico, Latin American intraregional trade is roughly 35 percent and growing rapidly, spurring development of the Union of South American Nations (UNASUR).[24]

Asia has made great strides in starting a process of regional institution-building with a more diverse array of regional groups than anywhere else in the world. My guess is that the scope will increase, especially for more functional groupings aimed at dealing with particular problems, such as environmental hazards—rising sea levels—and trade and financial regulations as regional integration advances. It is less clear whether a regional collective security order can be established in Asia. Geographically, some Asian countries are drawn more toward a Sino-centric system, whereas many others strongly and increasingly oppose the expansion of Chinese influence.

This diversity means that it is difficult for Asian countries to agree on an answer to the most basic of questions: What is Asia? The United States remains the key factor in whether Asia will move toward greater integration: the United States has been influential elsewhere in encouraging regional multilateral institutions. At the moment, a rising China appears as a security threat to many of its neighbors, making it difficult to develop a collective security order even if regional economic integration may be accelerating. This could change if China puts a greater effort into being less threatening. Also, if Asians develop greater doubts about the credibility of the United States' staying power, then for many there may not be any other option except to "bandwagon" with China and try to develop a purely Asian security order.

Regional integration elsewhere will progress, but at varying speeds and more for specific functional purposes. I think regions such as South Asia, central Asia, and the Middle East will have a very hard time building out regional cooperation to the point of dealing with difficult regional peace and security issues in the next decade or two, even if they make progress on trade or sharing of valuable resources such as water. There is too much geopolitical rivalry and distrust that will need at least a generation to overcome. European integration—in the sense that Europe has succeeded in pooling sovereignty—will remain the exception.

Even with this greater governance at midlevels, there is still no substitute for states, particularly if we think that global institutions play an essential role in solving the increasing number of global challenges. As mentioned earlier, states remain the foundation for the global institutions such as the UN, World Bank, International Monetary Fund (IMF), and G20. Ways are being found to incorporate more nonstate bodies—everything from NGOs to cities and corporations—in the working of those bodies, but as the key organization-building body, there is no obvious alternative to the state.

This brings me to a discussion of those critical institutions, the vast majority of which will need to be updated if they are to have any legitimacy in the eyes of the publics in much of the world. Besides the large emerging powers like Brazil, India (who are not permanent UNSC members), and

China (which has a veto in the UNSC but no IMF voting rights commensurate with its economic power), many second-tier emerging states will be making their mark and are not well represented as regional leaders in these institutions. My hunch is that just as the larger G20—rather than the old G7—was energized and brought to the fore because of the 2008 financial crisis, crises of one kind or the other will be the only way to trigger reform in many of these institutions. Otherwise they will slowly die, and in many cases we will be worse off.

Are global institutions important for the future? Lots of people have questioned me about this in particular, and my answer has been yes. However slow, bureaucratic, and sometimes corrupt, we can see some clear-cut achievements in how UN peacekeeping efforts have kept down the casualty rates in conflicts. The UN's campaign to eradicate extreme poverty, promote universal primary education, and fight HIV/AIDS among other goals as laid out in the UN's Millennium Development Goals, has focused worldwide attention on achieving development goals. No single member-state—including the United States—would have the legitimacy to mount such a campaign. To my mind, global institutions are needed to ensure that international order remains rules-based and does not return to a balance-of-power struggle where states jockey with each other and we all end up the loser. That would be a back-to-the-future step with a world order resembling the late nineteenth or early twentieth century, when all the great powers competed against one another with horrific results.

But we have to be realistic. It will be tough sledding for global institutions during this period of rapid change. A difficult trade-off exists between legitimacy and efficiency: trying to ensure all the right countries are represented when a decision is taken while at the same time trying to keep the number of countries involved down to facilitate decision-making. The growing multipolarity and diffusion of power will make the process of updating global institutions difficult. However, no reform would mean the increasing loss of legitimacy in the eyes of many publics in the emerging world.

Discordant values among the key players and lingering suspicions will be the norm throughout the transitional period. Longstanding worries by emerging powers about incursions on sovereignty by more powerful Western actors are deeply imbedded in popular as well as elite opinion and will only ease gradually as the emerging powers have to tackle growing transnational problems. I can still remember the outbursts of anger coming from senior Chinese officials in private sessions against Western demands for China to take a greater share of global responsibilities. In Western eyes, China is a still a poor country with loads of domestic problems. We were seen as trying to thrust responsibilities on China to relieve our own economic woes coming out of the 2008 financial crisis. In Chinese minds, they are not prepared and have too many domestic problems to focus much attention on broader global challenges. This won't go away. For most Chinese, they still see themselves as making up lost time from their dramatic fall in the nineteenth and twentieth centuries. This is also the backdrop in the climate-change debate, in which other countries see the industrialized West as responsible for the high levels of carbon already in the atmosphere. In their minds, the richer countries should bear the major responsibility for the $CO_2$ cleanup and damages resulting from extreme weather events.

China and many other emerging powers will remain particularly leery if not hostile to direct interference, including sanctions aimed at forcing changes in other regimes' behaviors. China followed the Russian lead in backing the UN-mandated disarmament of Syria's chemical weapons stock but also opposed any broader regime-changing intervention. A democratic China that would probably be more nationalistic would be equally concerned about ceding sovereignty to others. At the same time, China has showed signs of moving away from strict noninterference toward greater involvement in peacekeeping and a role for its navy in the international military antipiracy operations off Somalia—both of which surprised observers in the first decade of the twenty-first century. Whether it likes it or not, China has increasing global interests—particularly its dependence on imported energy supplies—so it cannot forever ignore its global responsibilities.

Future governance will not be either black or white: advances cannot be ruled out, despite growing diversity and lack of shared values. Prospects for achieving progress on global challenges will not be uniform. Here's my take on whether we will succeed in tackling the key issues facing us—it's not all bleak, but it certainly is not brilliant either.

On climate change, technology and markets will be more important for reducing carbon emissions than efforts to negotiate any comprehensive broad treaty like 1997's Kyoto Protocol. The expanding use of cheaper and cleaner natural gas could overtake coal, resulting in big emissions cuts for the United States and other big emitters such as China. Other technological progress in renewable technologies would also shift the debate on climate change by making mitigation efforts less burdensome on productivity. Such advances would ease possible agreement to reduce carbon emissions, making it more acceptable to developing countries as well as the United States, which all worry that a carbon ceiling would undermine economic growth prospects.

The future of nuclear proliferation—which we will talk more about—hinges on dissuading North Korea and Iran from further efforts to develop nuclear weapons. Iran's success, especially, could be the tipping point for an arms race in the Middle East, undermining the international nonproliferation efforts. If the international community prevails in its efforts to stop both of them, those examples alone would strengthen the Non-Proliferation Treaty. Similarly, use of nuclear weapons by anyone—either state or nonstate actors—would be devastating to the nonproliferation efforts. My hunch is that Iran will develop a nuclear threshold capability but won't test like India or Pakistan. This will be enough to alarm its neighbors and undermine nonproliferation and the Obama administration's goal of a nuclear zero world. (More on this in chapter 6.)

Increased great power convergence in combating the challenges of weak and failing states is conceivable, particularly when the interests of all the powers are at stake. With their large military manpower, emerging powers, including Brazil, India, Pakistan, and South Africa, are already playing important roles in supporting peacekeeping operations.

Coalitions of the willing with the tacit acquiescence of the other powers could get the job done in some cases. Although there is broad international support for protecting populations from genocide, war crimes, ethnic cleansing, and crimes against humanity, the emerging powers have shied away from taking the initiative to avoid the appearance of interference. Of course, this would allow others to take action, including with the use of force. With instant communications and a more engaged global public opinion, the great powers will have increasing difficulty avoiding action for humanitarian relief or suppression of genocide. The 2011

UN-mandated action against Libya's former leader, Muammar Gaddafi, serves as an example of Russia, China, South Africa, and other developing states going along with NATO military intervention, despite later regretting it. By contrast, except for permitting the chemical weapons disarmament, Russia, China, and other developing states have strongly opposed any intervention or strong sanctions against the Syrian regime despite a humanitarian disaster of mammoth proportions.

Internet governance is a fascinating new area where broader civil society groups as well as states are increasingly engaged. Many of the civil society groups argue against a privileged role for states in Internet governance, but states see their interests more and more engaged. Many states— not just Russia and China, who are the strongest proponents—want an expanded state role in Internet governance. These states include many Arab countries worried about the political uses of the Internet and key emerging economies such as South Korea, Indonesia, Turkey, Brazil, Argentina, and Mexico, who would favor somewhat more state oversight. It's actually a smaller group, including the United States, United Kingdom, Canada, Sweden, India, Kenya, and New Zealand, who would argue more for the status quo—although even there they see a state role and want to use the Internet for state purposes. A smaller group comprising global communities of Internet users would be the only ones to opt for a decentralized organization for Internet governance.

Experts see several possible futures, from one of minimalist change from the present to one where there is a breakup into functional blocs— an Internet composed largely of users from OECD member states and another of users primarily drawn from Russia, China, and the Arab world. Communication between the blocs would be limited and subjected to substantial political control. A third set of scenarios would see the Internet as beginning to tip over into breakdown with "hacktivists," cybercriminals, terrorists, and other destabilizing forces. This scenario may shift the balance toward a preference for more state control, even by the currently more laissez-faire-inclined countries.

A lot is at stake in how the Internet is governed, and the stakes are growing. All countries have shared interests—particularly on the economic side— but other factors, particularly fear of growing seditious activities enabled by the Internet, could trump those economic interests for many countries and send the whole Internet down a different path where there would be far less connectivity.[25]

In all these policy realms, the shared interests among the diverse collection of major countries mean that even if the best case is not achievable, multilateral and regional cooperation is unlikely to unravel completely. The example of G20 countries avoiding 1930s-style protectionism—despite the most serious post–World War II recession in 2008 and prolonged downturn, including high levels of unemployment for some Western economies—is a case in point. On the other hand, there is no longer any single nation or even a bloc of countries like the G7 that have the political or economic leverage to drive the international community toward collective action. This all adds up to global cooperation being difficult to forge in the best of times and breakdown becoming increasingly likely.

Before concluding this chapter on a splintered world, one more question is worth posing and trying to answer: Is there an alternative global order out there just waiting to come onto the world stage? In 1919, President Woodrow Wilson's Fourteen Points called for a new postimperialist order based on democracy and self-determination. Soviet communism also posed an ideological as well as military threat to the Western liberal order throughout most of the Cold War. This question about whether we are going to wake up to some new world order proffered by the BRICs or others is endlessly debated by experts. Some have seen state capitalism as so divergent with liberal economics that it can be categorized as an alternative and countervailing system. I think that's questionable in light of recent pronouncements by Chinese president Xi Jinping aimed at curbing the power of the state-owned enterprises, which are the basis for state capitalism. The BRICs are so diverse—some authoritarian, others firmly democratic—and have so many competing interests that they are highly unlikely now or in the future to share a unified vision.

The more likely case is that there is no real alternative out there. Ever since the end of the Cold War, we have yearned for a more black-and-white idea of the global system we're headed into: *multipolar* is a description, but many examples of it exist, both good and bad. We know that the "End of History" did not happen, and many political, economic, and social differences have persisted if not proliferated. There are more divisions and divergences now than ever before; such complexity is difficult to deal with, particularly as there is no sharply defined denouement in sight. This then is more of a splintered world than anything else, with the potential to turn into a dysfunctional and chaotic one if we are not careful.

# CHAPTER 3

# *Playing God*

MOST OF US ARE RELATIVELY COMFORTABLE ABOUT TALKING ABOUT THE RISE AND FALL of countries or even civilizations. That's an age-old story we're familiar with. Being able to change or duplicate human nature, however, has been such a staple of science fiction and related films and television—like *Blade Runner*, *The Six Million Dollar Man*, or *The Matrix*—that it has been easy to dismiss as entertainment or diversion. In the nineteenth century Charles Darwin's theory of evolution shattered earlier conceptions about humans' creation and undermined the literal biblical interpretation and, for some, their faith. People started applying the principle of survival of the fittest more broadly, with mostly deleterious effect. Racism was supposedly justified and war extolled as an extension of the law of nature.

We're at another watershed moment, and it is hard to know the full extent of the change or what will be the total effect. We no longer just study creation, as in Darwin's day; we can now change our fundamental human nature. In other words, we don't have to wait for God or natural selection. At the same time, as Ray Kurzweil, author of *The Singularity Is Near*, put it, "By understanding the information processes underlying life, we are starting to learn to reprogram our biology to achieve the virtual elimination of disease, dramatic expansion of human potential, and radical life extension."[1]

It's not just because biological sciences have advanced to a new level that we are making these discoveries. The convergence and synergies of several broad technologies—particularly nano, bio, IT, 3D printing, artificial intelligence, new materials, and robotics—is what makes this technology revolution different.

This is scary stuff, particularly in the context of the other changes underway, such as superempowered individuals and a splintered world with more and more powerful states that don't agree on values or principles. My intelligence background tends to make me see all the traps and unintended consequences. Before I lay out potential drawbacks, let's examine the major good that could come out of these new capabilities.

One of the first indications that something totally new was afoot was when I was starting work on the *Global Trends* project and went to a conference presentation by a Johns Hopkins doctor about implants and advanced prosthetics that would help returning soldiers who were amputees and paraplegics. A microchip implanted in the brain is used to power a robotic arm. The brain implant picks up the patient's brain signals, decodes them, and then, through a computer cable hookup, moves the robotic arm. Eventually scientists hope the connection will operate wirelessly. Over time, restoring movement of the patients' own limbs—in the case of paraplegics—remains the ultimate goal, according to scientists at the Brain Institute at Brown University.[2]

Jeffrey M. Stibel, chairman of Braingate, a company developing brain computer interface technology, has talked about the progress made in restoring lost vision: "You effectively have a brain implant that hooks to what looks like sunglasses. The glasses are actually processing what you normally would be looking at except this person is blind, and then feeds that information through a computer chip directly into the mind, to give that person the sensation that they are actually seeing something, and it works reasonably." Stibel think there is much work yet to be done to perfect the brain implants, but we are well on our way to a "mind over matter" universe.[3]

Exoskeletons are another invention that is increasing our physical capabilities. They normally consist of an outer framework that is strapped to the legs of a soldier and through a powered system of motors or hydraulics allows soldiers to carry heavy loads—up to 220 pounds. According to press reports, Lockheed Martin is testing a model that would be capable of providing 72 hours of continual use.[4] Over time, as battery storage technology improves, limited electrical power may no longer be a constraint. These exoskeletons are designed to avoid impeding a soldier's movement. Rather, like brain implants enhancing mental powers, exoskeletons can increase physical capacities. Exoskeletons are now being designed to aid upper body strength as well.

Human augmentation will allow civilians and military people to work more effectively, and in environments that were previously inaccessible. Elderly people may benefit from powered exoskeletons that assist wearers with simple walking and lifting activities, improving the health and quality of life for aging populations. Successful prosthetics probably will be directly integrated with the user's body. Brain-machine interfaces could provide superhuman abilities, enhancing strength and speed, as well as provide functions not previously available. For example, signals from the brain could be sent, bypassing damaged sections of the spinal cords, but activating motor control nerves in disabled hands or other limbs.

As replacement limb technology advances, people may choose to enhance their physical selves as they do with cosmetic surgery today. Future retinal eye implants could enable night vision, and neuro-enhancements could provide superior memory recall or speed of thought. Neuropharmaceuticals will allow people to maintain concentration for longer periods of time or enhance their learning abilities. This would be a step beyond Google Glass's wearable computer, which has an optical head-mounted display that allows people to be in instant and continuous touch with the Internet. Augmented reality systems—such as those that would improve IQ or allow night vision—could hugely increase your mental and physical capabilities and agility, making you better able to deal with real-world situations. Needless to say, militaries are interested in the possibilities. A recent study by the Washington think tank Center for New American Security notes that while the US Defense Department has shown some discomfort with "increasing individuals' performance beyond their baseline," "there are some indications that other nations are willing to run programs that the United States is not."[5]

For human enhancement, advances in robotics will also be important, as I found during a visit to Silicon Valley. These can provide much-needed physical and mechanical support in the case of the handicapped. If your best friend's son was paraplegic, and you had the means to help, wouldn't you? This is how Willow Garage, one of the biggest robot developers in Silicon Valley, got his inspiration. I was reminded of how Alexander Graham Bell invented the telephone: he was originally attempting to find a hearing aid for his wife and daughter, who were deaf. In Willow Garage's case, the friend's child was entering adulthood without being able to care for himself. An institution loomed in his near future. Now, a humanlike robot stays at his side, allowing him to live a seminormal life; with the aid of his humanoid friend, the young man can manage on his own. Using a two-way video, he can also direct the mobile robot to navigate around another physical space and interact with other humans at the user's behest.

One of the biggest challenges is actually making the robot more human. Robots have better mechanical capabilities than humans do, making them ideal for routine tasks. Industrial robots have transformed many manufacturing environments: over 1.2 million industrial robots are already in daily operation around the world. But many industrial robots are caged, kept well away from human contact, because a swing of the robot's arm could kill you. They are programmed to do motions at a set speed and with a set purpose in mind. They are expert at working on assembly lines, outdoing humans with the regularity and precision of motions to perform a set job. Caring for another person is a whole different ball of wax. They need to respond to sensory touches, be able to hold cups without smashing them, and be sensitive to the movements of the humans they are helping. In other words, the inventors have to give them all the skills and learning abilities of a human companion. We are a long way from Frankenstein.

Developers are indeed extending the capabilities of robots, crossing that boundary between industrial robots and nonindustrial robots. Baxter is a prime example. Built by Boston-based Rethink Robotics, a start-up company that was founded by Rodney Brooks, Baxter was introduced in September 2012; it costs a modest US$22,000 and shows how robots are becoming more people-friendly. Instead of a motor driving an arm, as is usually the case in industrial robots, the motor drives a spring, and the spring drives the arm. This has the advantage of the arm being able to feel if it hits something and stop. As Rethink Robotics advertises, it requires no safety cages and no programming. Line workers can train Baxter manually. It's so adaptable and intelligent, in fact, that the MIT Media Lab, according to press reports, is training Baxter in late 2013 to perform in a live show alongside magician Marco Tempest. The aim is to show how Baxter can combine predefined movements with computations that allow it to adjust to some variability in Tempest's routine.[6]

Although much development is still required to improve robots' cognitive abilities, many of the building blocks for futuristic and highly disruptive systems will be in place in the next couple of decades. Such robotics could eliminate the need for human labor entirely in some manufacturing environments, with total automation becoming more cost effective than outsourcing manufacturing to developing economies. Even in developing countries, robots might supplant some local manual labor in sectors such as electronics, potentially holding down local wages or putting many out of work.

Health-care and elder-care robots will become particularly important and pervasive as robots become increasingly able to interact with humans. In hospitals, we are already seeing them perform specialized functions such as surgical support, including carrying out robotic surgery under the control of skilled surgeons. The da Vinci System consists of a surgeon's console that is typically in the same room as the patient, and a patient-side cart with four interactive robotic arms controlled from the console. Three of the arms are for tools that hold objects and can also act as scalpels, scissors, or other surgical instruments. The fourth arm carries a camera with two lenses that gives the surgeon full vision from the console. The surgeon sits at the console and looks through two eye holes at a 3D image of the procedure while maneuvering the arms with two foot pedals and two hand controllers. The da Vinci System scales, filters, and translates the surgeon's hand movements into more precise micromovements of the instruments, which operate through small incisions in the body. Da Vinci robots operate in several thousand hospitals worldwide, with an estimated 200,000 surgeries conducted in 2012, most commonly for hysterectomies and prostate removals.[7]

Japan and South Korea are investing heavily in the development of robots able to assist with daily living for the growing number of seniors in their societies. Militaries are expected to increase their use of autonomous systems, including robots as well as drones, to reduce human exposure in high-risk situations and as a hedge against rapidly rising personnel costs.[8] Robots are already used routinely to investigate, and if necessary detonate, disguised packages with bombs in them or to destroy other questionable material. The robots are controlled by a human with a joystick informed by cameras to guide the robot to its target and instruct it when it arrives. Manually positioning robots to remove or detonate the device can be laborious and time consuming. An autonomous robot can speed up the process, with the robot itself virtually instantly assessing the situation using sensors, resulting in far faster assessment and decision making than a human. The shift to unmanned systems will no doubt accelerate with the development of artificial intelligence in robots and drones and the proliferation of sensors in the "Internet of Everything" world (detailed later in this chapter) that we are rapidly entering.

Perhaps in the future, warfare will be conducted by autonomous robotic soldiers, ground vehicles, and drones with little human intervention. There is enough worry about such a future scenario that the United Nations and Human Rights Watch are calling for a ban on killer robots. For the moment, cost is both a driver and barrier to the implementation of robotics technologies. Robots are still expensive to buy, but their ability to repeat tasks efficiently and quickly, reduce waste, or minimize labor costs can save companies money. Manufacturers could lease expensive robots to users, but the cost per unit must decrease significantly before widespread applications emerge. Technology development is the biggest single constraint for nonindustrial robotics, because researchers must overcome major barriers in the development of robots' intelligence, including their understanding of the world around them, coping with unanticipated events, and interacting with humans. Nevertheless, with many enabling technologies now available off the shelf, we are seeing a new generation of developers and enthusiasts construct new robotic products that are more adaptive to their surroundings.

Human augmentation is not the only way in which we seem to be tampering with human nature. The growing longevity of humans is a key part of this story, heightening expectations and reducing limitations. It is not just the length of time we can expect to be alive but also the quality of our senior years that could improve. It's important to recall that the widespread

societal aging is precedent-setting and carries with it some risks and challenges. OECD high-income countries will reach as a group a median age of
42.8 years by 2030, rising from an average of 37.9 years in 2010. Whereas
in 2012 only the populations of Japan and Germany have matured beyond
the median age of 45 years, by 2030, in a tectonic shift, a much larger group
of countries—South Korea and much of Europe—are projected to have
entered this postmature category. The populations of these countries will
feature a large proportion of people over 65 years of age—an unprecedented
"pensioner bulge."[9]

Societal aging and longevity are not, of course, the same thing—fewer
younger people relative to older people can raise the average age, but this
does not necessarily lead to longer life spans. However, we are seeing both.
Much of the aging of society is due to falling birthrates, meaning the usual
population pyramids—a large youthful base to support and perpetuate the
rest of the population—are shrinking. What should be healthy, pyramidlike
age structures are increasingly misshapen with a larger proportion in the
adult and senior years, making the pyramid look distinctly top-heavy.

Also important, though, has been the increasing life expectancy we're all
experiencing in the world. In May 2013, the UN's World Health Organization
released figures showing that "the global life expectancy has increased from
64 years in 1990 to 70 years in 2011," which is dramatic. As Colin Mathers,
WHO coordinator for mortality and burden of disease, stated at its annual
Geneva meeting on health statistics in May 2013: "That's an average increase
in life expectancy of 8 hours a day over the last 20 years." The gender breakdown shows global life expectancy at birth for women was 72 years and
men 68 years in 2011. Life expectancy has only fallen in North Korea, South
Africa, Lesotho, Zimbabwe, and Libya since 1990, the UN baseline year. By
contrast, China and India had seen a seven-year jump in average life expectancy at birth since 1990.[10]

There are several different factors at work. For much of the world,
especially in developing countries, the increase has been due to the rapid
fall in child mortality and improvements in life expectancies in the two
biggest developing states: China and India. However, even in the rich,
advanced world where life expectancies are already longer, there had
been significant increases. Countries that already have the longest life

expectancies—Japan, Australia, and Switzerland—continue to see their populations living longer.

"Presumably there will be some slowing down eventually unless gene therapy and all sorts of new scientific breakthroughs change that," Mathers said. My contention would be that such scientific and technological breakthroughs are exactly what we're in for, and we need to prepare. The biotech revolution is one big thing happening already with huge implications for all of us and, getting back to the overall theme, is utterly transforming the human condition as we have known it.

The cost of sequencing genomes—which is laying the basis for the biotech breakthroughs in gene therapy—has dropped exponentially. The first sequencing of the human genome in 2003 cost more than $1 billion, then the cost dropped to $100 million; now it is about $1,000 for total personal sequences, and it is expected to soon drop further to $200, which will not only help with individual medical diagnosis but also with big data analysis to discover genetic links to specific diseases and disorders by analyzing millions of genomes and crowdsourcing analysis. With falling genome prices we should be able to perform ever-larger studies to correlate genes with medical history.[11] McKinsey Global Institute believes desktop gene-sequencing machines are not far off, potentially making gene sequencing part of every doctor's diagnostic routine: "The ability to genetically sequence all patients, along with the viruses, bacteria, and cancers that affect them, can allow for better matching of therapy to the patient. Sequencing can also help physicians understand whether a set of symptoms currently treated as a single disease is, in fact, caused by multiple factors."[12]

The future accuracy of molecular diagnostics based on such gene sequencing, combined with big data analytics and artificial intelligence, has the power to transform medicine. Today, physicians struggle to differentiate between many illnesses with similar symptoms. Obtaining results from detection tests can take several days, leading to delays in diagnosis that can be life threatening. Consequently, diagnostic and pathogen-detection devices will be key enabling technologies for disease management.

Molecular diagnostic devices will revolutionize medicine by enabling rapid testing for both genetic and pathogenic diseases during surgeries. Readily available genetic testing will speed disease diagnosis and help physicians decide on the optimal treatment for each individual patient. Such personalized medicine will reduce the health-care costs linked with doctors' prescribing ineffective drugs.

In addition, the declining cost of such testing will facilitate the cataloging of many more individuals' genetic profiles, which will lead to a greater understanding of the genetic basis of many diseases. "These advances will facilitate the development of new classes of targeted medicines as well as sensitive and specific diagnostic tests. It is highly likely that the maximum value for these advances will be gained where the diagnostic and therapeutic applications of this knowledge are bought together in the developing field of theranostics."[13] Theranostics "is rapidly facilitating the shift from 'trial and error' medicine to personalized medicine and holds great promise for improved patient outcomes.... This approach has the potential to help improve drug efficacy by understanding which patients serve to benefit the most from treatment."[14]

"Doctor Watson" also is likely to make a huge contribution by scouring, instantaneously, all the latest state-of-the-art information in the current medical literature. Doctor Watson is the IBM robot that beat two human champions at the US game show *Jeopardy!* in 2011. More recently, IBM, together with Memorial Sloan Kettering Cancer Center in New York and WellPoint, a US health company, is using Watson to help oncologists in their diagnosis of cancer in patients. To keep up with the state of the literature would take a human 180 hours a week according to one estimate—an impossible feat. However, it's child's play for a superendowed robot. Watson provides doctors recommendations for treatments based on its surveying of all the available literature and what is in the patient's files. Watson then suggests and ranks several different treatment possibilities, showing the underlying documentation for his decision. The live doctor can argue, speaking into a microphone and asking for more proof for Watson's recommendations.

Obviously it will take time for doctors to get used to robots at their sides. However, studies on human interactions with avatars show that eventually the back-and-forth in question-and-answer sessions between human and avatar becomes very natural. Children particularly make little distinction between an avatar and a human adult. My hunch is that comfort with Watson will be generational, with the young less questioning and the older professionals more grudging in their acceptance. The uses to which Watson can be put are endless, and not just in the medical field. What will be fascinating to watch is how the explosion of knowledge generated by the new understanding of genetics can be quickly exploited and used because of the mental powers provided by a Watson robot in hospitals and doctors' offices.[15]

Advances in regenerative medicine almost certainly will parallel these developments in diagnostic and treatment protocols. For example, replacement organs such as kidneys and livers could be developed and be standard procedures in the next couple of decades. Additive manufacturing or 3D printing, a totally new manufacturing process (discussed further in chapter 6), is already making impressive strides in the bio-printing of arteries, tissue, and simple organs from the patient's own tissue, and over the next decade or so it will also be able to fabricate more complex human organs.

My guess is—given the startling progress and pace of bio and medical breakthroughs—that these new disease management technologies will continue to push forward the frontiers of life expectancy, tipping the demographic profile of many countries evermore toward an older, but presumably healthier, population. However, improvements in disease management technologies could be out of reach of poor people in countries that do not have health coverage or only rudimentary forms of medical care for all citizens.

Cost is a major barrier, keeping molecular diagnostic technologies from being routinely used by physicians despite the falling costs of genetic sequencing. Today the number of known disease-related genes is insufficient to provide mass screening. Computer processing power and big data storage and analysis will be key for being able to exploit the exploding amounts of data gathered by genome sequencing. However, computing technology is unlikely to be a limiting factor with the growing availability of ever-cheaper cloud computing power and ever-more powerful algorithms for data analysis.

Setting clear guidelines for the use of the mass diagnostic testing and gathering of information, which ensures privacy protection, will be critical to getting public buy-in for any large-scale programs. We all worry now that our financial identities can be stolen and our financial livelihoods compromised;

just imagine if your medical identity was at stake. Cybersecurity will increasingly be a concern as more and more individuals' DNA data are loaded onto computers and entered into databases.

There are other broader consequences of societal aging that will need to be resolved. Countries that are rapidly aging may experience slower aggregate GDP growth or stagnation. These postmature states will find it difficult politically to push through cost-saving reforms of their retirement and health-care programs—and muster funding to adequately support needy retirees—while not saddling younger generations who will have to support the retirement programs of their elders. Governments of countries with relatively high median age—in the upper 40s to 50 years old—could be pressured to vastly restrain discretionary state spending and impose a higher tax burden.

Some analysts expect aging societies to be risk-averse and fiscally limited; some European and rapidly aging East Asian states might conclude that they cannot afford to maintain a sizeable military establishment or project their power overseas. European defense cuts over the past decade may then be just the tip of the iceberg. The rapid growth of Asian and African minorities in low-fertility West European states risks increasing erosion of social cohesion and growing reactionary politics.

The truth is, we don't know how this will work out. An aging society may not be the disaster that it would have been if physical labor were still the critical need as it was in many premodern societies. The advances in health care just talked about are likely to improve the quality of life for seniors, enabling them to work longer. And some surveys indicate, in the United States, for example, an interest by the baby boomer generation in continuing to work—though on a more flexible schedule—even if they would financially be able to completely retire and maintain their current standard of living.

I would say so far so good with new technologies enhancing human nature, making us live longer and have a better quality of life. There are a couple of big caveats we have to worry about and try to do something about before it is too late. First, we need to prevent these new technologies from introducing a whole new dimension of inequality. It won't be too long before parents will be able to select the exact traits they want for their offspring. "In twenty to forty years, at least in the developed world, most babies could be conceived through in-vitro fertilization, so that their parents can choose among embryos. That way, the parents or someone else can select among a limited number of embryos with the combination of genes they most want to see in their offspring. It's going to happen," according to Hank Greely, a professor at Stanford Law School and the director of the university's Center for Law and the Biosciences.[16] The problem is that at least in the beginning, not all parents will be able to afford the procedure, so are we going to give one set of parents an advantage based on their wealth and inclination? The second, as Greely indicates, is that "China will have fewer cultural and legal barriers." How you level the playing field across the different cultural barriers would seem difficult to say the least.

Second, some of the enhancements—like command-and-control brain waves for operating prosthetic devices to help us walk again or live ordinary lives if we suffered amputated or paralyzed limbs—may seem a little science-fiction-like. But they still have the humans in charge. The discoveries we are talking about as part of the biotech revolution begin to cross the line, with synthetic biology or designing DNA from scratch to produced desired traits.

I say crossing the line because I think we're opening up a Pandora's box, if we are not careful. The consequences of being able to manipulate one's DNA to avoid diseases or enhance attributes—physical and mental—opens the door to manufacturing viruses with insidious and long-lasting effects. Turning away from confronting the ethical, moral, and security challenges of genetic engineering won't make the issues go away. With prices coming down, parents around the world are increasingly interested in sequencing their baby's genomes for possible diseases. Prenatal sequencing opens the door to manipulating DNA for desirable traits. As with everything, there is good and bad.

Advances in synthetic biology have the potential to be a double-edged sword and to become a source of lethal weaponry accessible to do-it-yourself biologists or biohackers. As costs decline and DNA sequencing and synthesis improve, researchers are laying important foundations for the field's development. Because early commercialization efforts have capitalized on the supply of tools and low-cost materials to academic and commercial researchers, the biocommunity has established an open-access repository of standardized and interchangeable biological building blocks called biobricks that researchers can use. Such advances not only contribute to opportunities for exploring increasingly novel and valuable applications in building designer organisms, such as toxic-waste-consuming algae, but they also raise the risk for unintended and intentional dual-use developments to occur. And here the advances that are opening up opportunities in the medical, agricultural, or energy realms are also raising the risk of "bioterror," which could lead to release of lethal viruses and development of biological weapons for bioterror built on dual-use technology. This will be particularly true as technology becomes more accessible on a global basis and, as a result, makes it harder to track, regulate, or mitigate bioterror if not bioerror. I will go into greater depth on biotech's dual-use implications for security later on in chapter 6.

WE ALSO COULD BE CROSSING THE LINE and losing control in the world of big data. Big data and the algorithms that extract value from big data are increasingly essential to the running of our economies. Big data and IT have fueled the biotech revolution and far-reaching discoveries in other scientific areas. Soon a lot more things will be connected to the Internet; some estimates place the current figure at over 15 billion Internet connected objects (the Internet of Things), everything from our smartphones, laptops, and PCs to sensors monitoring agriculture production, city functions, livestock health and location, whole building systems, medical devices, and even forests and individual trees. The potential is for a huge boost in efficiencies. Just as retailers today fuse together information about their customers—their in-store spending habits, credit, web-surfing histories, social network postings, demographics information, etc.—to better target customers' preferences, city authorities can combine information from sensors and ubiquitous posted cameras to better understand commuters' behaviors and their transportation needs as well as the functioning of city infrastructure. The list goes on for the applicability of big data and the Internet of Things.

Increasingly though, computers will be making decisions too, and this is where we have to introduce some fail-safe measures. In early 2014, there was an announcement that one of the world's largest supercomputers—Japan's K computer—had carried out the most accurate simulation of the human brain ever, taking 40 minutes to process one second of human brain activity. The researchers expect that simulating the whole brain will be possible as even more powerful computers become available, most likely within the next decade.[17] Understanding and being able to replicate how the human brain works has huge medical applications for treatment of Alzheimer's, Parkinson's, and a host of other brain disorders. It will also give a boost to the prospects for artificial intelligence and better applications of big data.

Early artificial intelligence researchers developed algorithms that imitated the step-by-step reasoning that humans use when they solve puzzles or make logical deductions, but human beings solve most of their problems using fast, intuitive judgments rather than the conscious, step-by-step deduction that early artificial intelligence was able to model. Artificial intelligence research has made some progress at imitating brain activity, but the recent successful simulation of human brain activity by the Japanese computer will help to advance understanding. In all of this, the development of algorithms that computer software uses to replicate human brain activity is required. The search for more efficient problem-solving algorithms is a high priority for artificial intelligence research.[18]

A colleague at the Atlantic Council, Dr. Banning Garrett, has explored an algorithm-run world and its risks.[19] He notes that improvement in algorithms has received much less public attention than increases in microprocessor performance—the pace of algorithm advancement far outstripping Moore's Law. While processor speeds improved by a factor of 1,000, algorithm performance improved by an astounding 43,000-fold over the same period between 1988 and 2003. Algorithms and the Internet of Things, which is increasingly referred to as the Internet of Everything, is largely a marriage made in heaven, making important contributions in science, health care, efficient use of resources, and smart cities. However, together, big data and algorithms can facilitate a huge invasion of privacy. More ominously, there is the huge potential for misuse of predictive algorithms. "Already, insurance companies and parole boards are using predictive algorithms to help tabulate risk and a growing number of places in the United States employ predictive policing, crunching data to select what streets, groups and individuals are subject to extra scrutiny," says Garrett.

As Garrett explains, the key limitation of algorithm analysis is that the results are based on correlations, not causality. In their book on big data, Viktor Mayer-Schonberger and Kenneth Cukier have explained that correlations are often good enough and they can be found "far faster and cheaper than causality."[20] But spurious correlations could lead to mistaken judgments of causality and their policy consequences or persecution of innocent individuals based on predicted propensities.

Algorithm-driven decision making can take humans out of the loop with potentially disastrous results. Stanford professor and archaeologist Ian Morris's most recent book, *War! What Is It Good For?*, opens with an incident that could have destroyed much of the world if there were no fail-safe system with algorithms. Stanislav Petrov was deputy chief for combat algorithms at Scrpukhov-15, the nerve center of the Soviet Union's early nuclear warning system. The algorithms that Petrov and his team had helped to write alerted Petrov on September 26, 1983, that the Americans were launching a first strike. Fortunately, Petrov realized it was a false alarm and dissuaded the Soviet General Staff from believing the faulty algorithms. But he had to make a split-second decision and get his military superior to abort a counterattack.[21]

Hopefully there won't be such false positives in the future, but the example of an incident decades before supercomputers and the explosion in the use and development of algorithms, which today have become so ubiquitous in every walk of life and not just for missile systems, points up the dangers.

Garrett rightly warns that no matter how well written or extensively tested algorithms are, there will almost always be real-world exceptions, and these exceptions will occur when algorithms face an unforeseen combination of events or inputs. This means that cybersecurity will be an ever important concern as more and more "things" are connected to the Internet. With new connected things there arises new vulnerabilities, and for businesses that are focused on the added efficiencies in connecting systems, "security is not the first concern in this competitive market."[22] With billions of devices programmed to handle multiple functions autonomously and asynchronously, any node could be an attack vector for the entire system.[23] This is a world, after all, "where machines, enabled with complex algorithms and adaptive behaviors, [now] act as intelligent agents on behalf of individuals. By carrying out tasks ranging from optimized traffic management to monitoring the health of the elderly to nuanced control of energy usage, the Internet of Everything should make the world smarter and our lives easier. It will also make it much easier for hackers to cause real-world damage."[24] There have already been a number of test cases where computerized systems in today's cars and electronic medicine cabinets for hospital prescriptions have been shown to be highly vulnerable to a hacking attack.[25] Given the potential for sizeable damage if not disaster, key systems will need a separate infrastructure to instrument and monitor them.

In a world where machines will be running whole systems without much human intervention, ways will need to be found to keep the systems running to serve their intended aim while minimizing any unintended consequences. One is reminded of the famous Joseph Losey–directed film *The Servant*, starring Dirk Bogarde. In the film, a wealthy young Londoner hires Bogarde's character to be his manservant. At first the two form a quiet bond, retaining their social roles as upper-crust employer and servant, but in the course of the film the roles are reversed. The wealthy Londoner becomes wholly dependent and degenerates completely as his servant increasingly rules the roost. This is a future to avoid.

CHAPTER 4

# An Era of Scarcity or Abundance?

IN JUNE 2012 I WENT TO ABUJA, NIGERIA, AS PART OF THE SWING AROUND THE WORLD TO test out a preliminary version of *Global Trends 2030*. On the face of it, Abuja seemed an unlikely place to find think tanks—a key target in other capitals for sounding out experts. The US ambassador pointed out from his window where Boko Haram, the Muslim insurgent group, had staged a suicide attack against a UN facility, and throughout the couple of days we were in the Nigerian federal capital, we were heavily guarded and escorted by embassy officers to all our appointments.

Fortunately the meetings were well worth it and, in one particular case, eye opening, especially on the current impact of climate change. I can still remember the rather elderly and well-dressed gentleman who leaned across the table and, speaking softly, said, "We are living the climate change that you somehow think is still off on the horizon." He went on to talk about the growing environmental degradation in northern Nigeria after successive years of poor rainfall and frequent droughts. He worried about the migration of communities from the Sahel focused on livestock raising and grazing onto lands occupied by sedentary farmers. He saw an increasing resource competition as population pressures build from both high birth rates and incoming migrants escaping the even more devastating 20-year drought in the Sahel. He went on about his fears of a breakup of Nigeria as Lagos and the south was seeing newfound prosperity. It was an old story—the British had cobbled together Nigeria in part because they wanted to wed the poorer northern states to the more commercially vibrant coastal areas. Tensions had always existed, but now there was renewed talk of fragmentation, and as he said, an important new factor was the environmental deterioration in northern Nigeria.[1]

He was right that a lot of our analysis had characterized climate change impacts as largely in the future. And in relative terms the biggest impacts—assuming there is no significant cutbacks in carbon—would be later in the century. But his point, too, was to put climate change in a bigger context, connecting it with other factors like exploding population growth, pre-existing ethnic and religious tensions, migration, slow growth, and poor governance.

In truth, we had seen climate change as having a "multiplier" effect, amplifying already existing tensions and weaknesses and perhaps tipping over already fragile situations to outright instability. Obviously seeing and hearing firsthand made all the difference. Earlier versions of *Global Trends* paid scant attention to resources except energy. Climate change also got short shrift in the earlier versions. Between 2004 and 2008 we did a lot of work on climate change and resources and started to make the connections with other social and political trends.

The National Intelligence Council brooked some opposition, especially from Republican congressmen, about our even attempting to look at climate change through the prism of national security interests. Our contention, as testified to by then NIC chairman Tom Fingar, in an open congressional hearing was that national security is at stake because countries who were partners and friends would likely to be threatened by climate change over the next several decades.[2] Climate change as a threat to US national security has been a topic included for the last several years in the annual threat assessment that the director of national intelligence gives each year to Congress.[3] And with good reason.

Average precipitation patterns will be in flux as wet areas will become wetter while dry areas will become more so. Much of the precipitation decline will occur in the Middle East and North Africa, as well as western central Asia, southern Europe, southern Africa and the American Southwest. In Algeria and Saudi Arabia, precipitation by midcentury is forecast to decline by 4.9 percent and 10.5 percent, respectively, while in Iran and Iraq, precipitation will fall by 15.6 percent and 13.3 percent, respectively.

Flows in the Nile, Tigris-Euphrates, Niger, Amazon, and Mekong river basins have declined because of persistent droughts over the past decade. These persistent droughts are in line with the expected effects of warming from increased greenhouse gas concentrations in the atmosphere.

A further aggravation is the increasing frequency of extreme weather that we did not fully appreciate initially. We hadn't expected the extreme weather to be so frequent and so widespread at this stage of climate change. In fact, I ended up rewriting these passages in the 2030 report several times, each time stressing more the near-term impact of extreme weather. The impact of these extreme weather events outside expected norms—floods, droughts, tornadoes, glacial lake outbreaks, extreme coastal high-water levels, heat waves—has produced food and water *in*security on top of the high economic and human costs of recovery. Recent scientific work shows that temperature anomalies during growing seasons and persistent droughts have diminished agricultural productivity.

One problem in the analysis of the effects of climate change is the lack of specificity of local impacts. The UN's Intergovernmental Panel on Climate Change traditionally concentrates on regions. While what happens regionally due to climate change is important, policy makers are even more interested in the country level. Also, even similar impacts can have different effects depending on how resilient individual states are. This gets us back to the need for understanding the broader context. And what a difficult task it is to think about how a country will react, adapt, and absorb the changes to its environment.

There are countries like China or even India where we expect parts of those countries to experience major water shortages—partly due to changing climate—but we believe they are likely to manage and could benefit if they manage to successfully deal with the challenge. China is putting a lot of resources into green energies with an eye to satisfying growing energy demands in a carbon neutral way and becoming a technological leader in green energies. For China, necessity may be the mother of invention, and all the challenges will be seen in hindsight as huge opportunities. For many poorer states, the challenges from rising temperatures and changing precipitation patterns may be too much to cope with.

*Scarcity* is a loaded word—conjuring up as it does for some a Malthusian dog-eat-dog world—and its use in *Global Trends 2030* was hotly debated. A lot of people we talked to did not like the connotations, particularly as Thomas Malthus, the eighteenth-century English cleric and early economist, proved to be wrong in the end. Exploding population growth did not outstrip available food supplies in the eighteenth or nineteenth centuries because technology kicked in and increased productivity. I hope the same will be the case in the twenty-first century. And one way of trying to increase those chances is by pointing out the stiff challenges ahead.

It is fair to say we face major scarcities *unless* proactive and preventive actions are taken. An extrapolation of current trends in per capita consumption patterns of food and water show the projected extent of the problem during the next couple decades. Demand for food is set to rise by more than 35 percent by 2030, but for major cereal grains like wheat and rice, average rates of yield growth have slowed from about 2 percent per year in the 1970s and 1980s to about 1 percent per year since 1990. According to McKinsey Global Institute, "Trends in resource prices have changed abruptly and decisively" since 2000. During the twentieth century, prices fell in real terms; since 2000 they have more than doubled, even though commodity prices in the past couple years have eased. They are still close to historic levels.[4] The world has consumed more food than it has produced in many years of the last decade. A major international study finds that annual global water requirements will reach 6,900 billion cubic meters (bcm) in 2030, 40 percent above current sustainable water supplies.

Agriculture, which uses approximately 3,100 bcm, or just under 70 percent of global water withdrawals today, will require 4,500 bcm without efficiency gains by that same time. About 40 percent of humanity lives in or near an international river basin; over 200 of these basins are shared by more than two countries, increasing the dependencies and vulnerabilities from changes in demand and availability of water. Based on current trajectories, the Organization for Economic Co-operation and Development (OECD) has estimated that by 2030 nearly half of humanity will inhabit areas with severe water stress. The world is already farming its most productive land. Given the limited availability of new arable land, boosting crop efficiency will be critical to meeting global food needs.

The case of Africa is particularly worrisome. Agricultural productivity in Africa will need to be boosted to avoid shortages. Unlike South Asia and South America, which both achieved increases in production per capita, Africa only recently returned to 1970s levels. Many African states don't have good enabling environments for agricultural production, including an absence of sufficient rural infrastructure and transportation networks to get seeds and fertilizer from the ports to inland areas, and weak governance. Even a fairly marginal improvement in food supply chain management could mean significant reductions in waste, negating pressures from growing populations.

Wheat will likely continue to exhibit particularly high price volatility. Significant production occurs in water-stressed and climate-vulnerable breadbasket regions such as China, India, Pakistan, and Australia. In general, the countries most vulnerable to food-price inflation will be import-dependent poor countries, such as Bangladesh, Egypt, Djibouti, and Sudan.[5] For this set of countries, the primary line of defense to cope with rising food prices will be to expand existing subsidies on basic foodstuffs. This is a difficult proposition, especially as many of these countries are waging a battle against ballooning budgets.

China, India, and Russia are also vulnerable to higher food prices but are better able to shield themselves. Russia and China are both large grain producers. These countries also have healthier budgetary situations to provide subsidies and, through price controls, deal with food-price rises and spikes. Rich states can also buy foodstuffs on the international markets.

In an interesting twist that is indicative of the increasing concerns, Saudi Arabia, the United Arab Emirates, South Korea, and others have been buying long leases on overseas farming land. Chatham House's "Resources Futures Report" talks about a general "new scramble" for resources that includes minerals in addition to land.[6] The amount of land that was acquired between 2000 and 2010 equals an area eight times the size of the United Kingdom, of which 134 million hectares were in sub-Saharan Africa. While the "land grab" investments represent economic opportunities for the host country, they also show a rising tide of concern about the future availability of food and distrust of the global marketplace in ensuring adequate food supplies at affordable prices. Chatham House research indicated Middle East countries, particularly the Gulf States, accounted for a fifth of reported investment in sub-Saharan Africa.

Of course, just as in Malthus's day, there are solutions to these problems. Technologies exist (which will be discussed more thoroughly in a separate chapter) that can help increase yields. An exciting new find in recent years has been one of the world's largest underground water aquifers in a desert area of Kenya. As reported by the media, the amount of water that can be sustainably exploited per year is estimated to be 3.4 bcm, nearly three times the water use in New York City. Satellite imagery and seismic data were used to discover the aquifers hundreds of feet underground.

During the trip to Africa in 2012, I met with another firm developing and integrating hundreds of before-and-after images and new geospatial maps to accurately provide a basis for the management of lakes and rivers. Dissemination of the data and advice to farmers and property owners was through mobile telephones—wireless connections being particularly critical for Africa because of the otherwise lack of extensive landline infrastructure.

But it's an uphill struggle. Thirty-nine out of approximately 50 African countries are net food importers, which should not be the case for a continent that, unlike most other places on the globe, has available arable land. Reversing the productivity losses in Africa alone would help, but much of this involves difficult political decisions and much more long-range planning, such as changing land tenure laws so the large number of women farmers would have more of an incentive to invest. Roads need to be built so that less food spoils on its way to market. Endemic conflict in parts of central and eastern Africa has also stymied efforts to expand the farming of available arable land.

An added complication for water is that even where supplies exist, infrastructure is lacking for distributing it. During a 2012 conference in Botswana where African technology firms and experts talked about their experiences, one cited the case of western Kenya, where 97 percent of the population has no access to clean water, with a consequence that infant mortality is very high. At a household level, residents had been trying to boil water to reduce bacteria and prevent illness, but there is not enough wood or other local fuel. The solution was a clean-tech water filter and safe storage for water that would last ten years or more. The program has been financed with the help of private sector firms and NGOs in such a way that it was not linked to the irregular flows that come and go with official aid.

The nexus between food, water, energy, and land can't be stressed too much. Food supplies depend on the availability of water. In view of the fact that agriculture uses 70 percent of global freshwater resources and livestock farming uses a disproportionate share of that, water management is critical to long-term food security. However, water management practices—including regulating the price of water, which could incentivize investment and better management—could be politically difficult. Biofuels increase demand for agricultural commodities and ironically have worsened the outlook for food security in some cases. Thirty to 40 percent of the US corn crop is diverted to fuels instead of food stocks in a given year. Producing bio-based energy from nonfood biomass would radically alter world energy markets and could also improve food security.

Unfortunately for many regions, without smarter planning and more technologically sophisticated and innovative solutions, a perfect storm is brewing—if it has not already hit, as in the case of northern Nigeria. For a number of countries in the central belt of the planet across large swathes of Africa, the Middle East, and South Asia, the threat of climate change is aggravated by the exploding population growth, lack of efficient government, and chronic and deepening freshwater shortages. These are all feeding off of each other in a negative spiral to increase the overall challenge of development.

I asked a researcher at the Sandia National Laboratories to help us think about the links among ecological conditions, human resilience, and conflict. For US policy makers, their worst nightmare is not having forewarning of events or developments that will lead to major international crises in which US interests are affected. A number of indices exist that identify current fragile states, such as the Fund for Peace's Failed State Index.[7] The Sandia work attempts to bring in environmental factors such as scarcities of food and water as contributors to state weakness over the next 10 to 15 years.

The Sandia researchers want to identify which countries are particularly susceptible to environmental challenges like food or water scarcities and, consequently, fail. Many countries are threatened by resource scarcities and climate change, but most will have sufficient domestic sources of resilience and be able to survive.[8]

Nothing is foolproof and obviously the exercise needs to be continually updated. But the list highlights several major countries—Nigeria, Pakistan, Ethiopia, and Bangladesh—whose future health is important to us all. Or, alternatively put, the potential disintegration of such large states would be globally destabilizing, involving unprecedented humanitarian efforts that we are unprepared for.

One of the key factors that the Sandia labs looked at in making their forecasts was population growth, and this is probably the most important single variable. The double-digit increase in demand for food and water is directly related to population growth, from 7.1 billion in 2012 to 8.3 billion in 2030. The 8.3 billion in 2030 is pretty certain. Over a longer time frame—such as out to the end of the century—it is much harder to forecast a precise number. The United Nations population division recently revised its projections upward to 10.9 billion, 1.8 billion more than the UN forecast four years earlier in 2008. Deutsche Bank and other experts believe the UN's long-term projections are too large, actually seeing a world of falling populations and a likely 8 billion people total in 2100, down from a 2055 peak of 8.9 billion.[9]

Unlike Deutsche Bank demographers, UN forecasters worry that the fertility rate in sub-Saharan Africa may not fall steadily as it has in other regions as they begin to prosper, urbanize, and grow more secular. Africa is the key variable in trying to determine the longer-range number. And forecasting is particularly difficult for the future African population because of the diversity of the ethno-religious groups. They are unlikely to advance through the normal fertility transition at the same pace. In the past and for other regions, the UN has underestimated the pace at which the fertility rate has fallen. Up until 2013's upwardly revised forecast, it had come under criticism from many scholars for being too optimistic that sub-Saharan Africa will follow the same rapid transition as happened in other fast-developing regions.

This is more than an academic debate. A global population of almost 11 billion could be devastating for the planet, imposing enormous pressures at a time when unfettered climate change could begin to take a major toll. The Chatham House study found, for example, that by 2050 up to 50 percent of agricultural land in Latin America—one of the world's two key production and export centers—may be subject to desertification. Impacts from rising temperatures—which would be severest across the central belt—would be potentially even greater in sub-Saharan Africa.

Whatever the population growth, the rising middle classes—with their appetite for higher protein diets and better sanitation and hygiene—are putting their own pressures on resources. A 2008 Goldman Sachs study that looked at the exploding middle classes worried, for example, that resource constraints are going to be "arguably tighter than they were in late nineteenth century Europe and the US" when the middle classes also made enormous gains.[10] Much of the rising middle class is in urban areas or relocating to them since urban centers are engines of opportunity and productivity. However, urbanization is leading to increases in demands for resources. India's cities will need 94 billion liters of potable water that McKinsey Global Institute and others estimate will not be easily available.[11]

The growth of urban concentrations have, historically, had a devastating impact on surrounding ecosystems, dramatically reducing forest cover, degrading the nutrient content and microbial composition of soils, altering the composition of higher plants and animals—including local extinctions—and changes in the availability and quality of freshwater. By 2030, with the explosion in urban growth, few forested reserves, wetlands, and freshwater sources will be able to survive on the perimeters of large urban areas. Rapidly growing cities will compete to secure water resources and land for housing development, bringing greater prosperity to some nearby farmers but triggering tensions over freshwater rights, water quality, and available arable land.

Not all is bleak in this rapid urbanization process, and in many ways urbanization is part of the solution. Urbanization can help drive down the birthrate, as the move to the cities usually results in smaller family sizes, a greater role for women in the workforce, and higher average education attainment for both sexes. Advanced IT-based management systems could increase economic productivity while minimizing resource consumption. Cameras and distributed sensors could help monitor the health of critical infrastructure such as transportation and power and water supplies. However, the so-called city dashboards that integrate the voluminous data from all the various sources are expensive—which is a big problem for many struggling cities. But there are efforts to find less costly systems.

The stakes are huge for how the rapidly growing megacities decide to develop. Governments around the world, especially in developing countries, could spend as much as $35 trillion in public works projects in the next two decades. To do so in a manner that maximizes sustainability, quality of life, and economic competitiveness, they will need a mix of novel approaches to security, energy and water conservation, resource distribution, waste management, disaster management, construction, and transportation. Some of the world's future megacities will essentially be built from scratch, enabling a blank slate approach to infrastructure design and implementation. Such an approach could allow for the most effective possible deployment of new urban technologies—or create urban nightmares if new technologies are not deployed effectively.

In late September 2013, millions in Dakar, Senegal, were left stranded without drinking water when a pipeline carrying water over 155 miles to city residents burst. Their plight provides a taste of the possible scale of urban disruption if infrastructure is not kept in good repair. As with the Dakar situation, which went unresolved for weeks, the challenges will be on an enormous scale and involve huge costs. According to a Reuters report, groups of protesters took to the streets, burning tires and demanding water, two weeks after the loss of water.[12] An estimated 3 million people who live in Dakar and its suburbs were affected. Management of resources is not just a local issue. Given the scale and rapid growth of urban centers, how city authorities manage will determine not only the future of megacities but also the even larger global battle for more efficient use of resources.

I have not brought up energy even though it shares many similarities with the other resources of water and food. Demand for energy will see a huge rise—about 50 percent—over the next 15 to 20 years due to rapid economic growth in the developing world. However, unlike the case for food and water, there is more confidence about growing energy production to meet the demand. Much of this increased production—and recent opti-mism—derives from unconventional oil and gas being developed in North America.

The scale-up of two technologies, horizontal drilling and hydraulic frac-turing, is driving this new energy boom. Producers have long known about the existence of shale or "source rock"—rock from which conventional oil and natural gas slowly trickled out into traditional reservoirs over millions of years. Lacking the means to unlock the huge amounts of hydrocarbon in the source rock, producers concentrated on conventional reservoirs. Once the industry discovered how to combine hydraulic fracturing (commonly known as *fracking*) and horizontal drilling, the vast gas and oil resources trapped in shale deposits became feasible to tap.

The story surrounding the development of fracking technology is fas-cinating in itself and highlights the serendipity and complexity involved in innovation. It is also a good object lesson for futurologists, underlining the difficulty of forecasting innovations, particularly when it involves already existing technologies for which a new innovative use is found. During the past five years the combined technologies of fracking and horizontal drilling have been an energy game changer in the United States and other countries with large reserves of shale gas and oil.

Fracking technology was first developed and commercialized in the late 1940s. Since then over 2 million fracking operations of gas and oil have hap-pened. A fluid, usually water mixed with a propping agent (usually sand) and a dozen or so chemical additives to control physical characteristics, is pumped into a fracking well. The pressure creates fractures that go through the rock formation; the propping holds the fractures open, allowing the gas to empty through the opened porous formation.

The technology has evolved from its early days. The latest fracturing operations use computer simulations, modeling, and microseismic fracture mapping. For fracking to be most efficient, the technology is coupled with horizontal drilling, a technique that became standard practice in oil and gas wells during the 1980s.

Because of this breakthrough, unconventional natural gas and oil have steadily become a larger portion of the gas and oil production in the United States, reducing the use of coal for power generation and also thereby reducing carbon dioxide emissions. Energy self-sufficiency is not unrealistic for the United States in as short a period as 10 to 20 years. Increased oil production and the shale gas revolution could yield such self-sufficiency, having already exploded with a nearly 50 percent annual increase between 2007 and 2011, sending natural gas prices in the United States into a freefall. The United States has more than enough natural gas for domestic needs for decades to come, and potentially substantial global exports. With the new "super fracking" technologies, recovery rates could dramatically increase.

It is important to underline that production in the United States of shale oil, technically known as light tight oil, is still in its early stages; its full potential remains uncertain, but development is happening at a fast pace. The United States is projected to surpass Saudi Arabia as the world's number one oil producer by 2015 and become energy self-sufficient by 2035.

The greatest obstacle to the proliferation of fracking both in North America and elsewhere is its environmental impact. Poor well construction and cementing, wastewater management, and other above-ground risks will continue to cause accidents. Greater seismic activity around shale producing areas has attracted the public attention in the United States and elsewhere to possible seismic risks. Seismic activity can impact well integrity and construction, increasing the risks of methane polluting drinking water supplies. Many environmental concerns could be mitigated if existing wastewater management techniques and technologies would be followed. A tighter regulatory environment—which is beginning to happen in some US states—could close loopholes and help restore some lost public confidence. More fracking-related accidents could cause a public backlash that could halt the fracking activity in key production areas.

Other regions and countries have significant shale reserves. By various reports, China has one of the world's largest reserves of nonconventional gas—some say double the estimated US reserves. China's relative lack of equipment, experience, and potentially the necessary extraction resources—mainly water—may inhibit or slow down development there.

European leaders are uncertain about the geology, political and public acceptability, environmental impact, and financial viability of shale gas in Europe. For example, national authorization processes vary considerably by EU member-state and are generally stricter than for North America. The

Polish government sees shale gas as an important resource for diversification away from dependence on Russian gas and has been granting exploration licenses, while the French government has banned fracking.

It's perhaps useful to pause here and look back to where we thought we would be with energy several years ago. The *Global Trends* series never was a proponent of the "peak" oil theory that we would run out of fossils fuels before converting to alternative energy. We always thought and continue to think that a variety of technological breakthroughs—including more efficient battery storage, advanced biofuels, and growth in solar energy combined with greater political will—would push us toward a transition out of fossil fuels. My worry has been that in the meantime we would be increasingly dependent on a more limited number of energy producers, and those were concentrated in potentially unstable areas like the Middle East, Russia, and Eurasia.

With the exploitation of shale gas and oil, that restricted energy landscape looks completely overcome by events. In the medium term, we don't have to worry about being beholden to a diminishing number of suppliers. And even though others may make a different decision than the United States as to whether to exploit their shale deposits, others will also benefit from the greater supplies on the market from the increased US production. Experts believe the United States could export as much as 61.7 million tons per year of liquid natural gas (LNG), making the United States the second-largest LNG exporter in the world.[13] Already traditional US gas suppliers like Qatar have shifted their exports to Japan, increasing Japan's energy options. A few years ago Europe looked dependent on Russia for its energy lifeline; growing self-sufficiency in the United States and Canada, however, means there is more gas and oil on the market, making it more a buyer's and less a seller's market, which increases European energy sources. In the wake of Russian aggression against Ukraine, European pressure on the United States for more exports may build at the same time that there could be increasing European efforts—especially in countries like Poland and eastern Europe—to develop their own shale resources.

The potential for more abundant and cheaper supplies of natural gas to replace coal by 2030 would have undeniable benefits for curbing carbon emissions, but one worry is that the relatively cheap supplies of shale gas and oil will dampen the incentives for alternative fuels such as hydropower, wind, and solar energy. The projected level of renewables in the International Energy Agency's baseline scenario for 2035 rises to 18 percent, up from 13 percent in 2011. The IEA see renewables becoming the second-largest source of electricity before 2015, approaching coal as the primary source by 2035, but "two thirds of the increase in power generation from renewables [will be] in non-OECD countries…the increase in China [will be] more than that in the European Union, United States and Japan combined."[14] The IEA's 2013 report concludes by saying that the growth in renewables will depend on large-scale subsidies to facilitate deployment, which in the US case, lawmakers may not want to provide given the expected decades-long supplies of relatively cheap shale gas and oil.

**SCARCITY OR ABUNDANCE? WHICH IS IT?** The shale revolution points to abundant energy resources just needing to be tapped. Solar energy is something that Africa has potentially in abundance. At the Botswana technology conference, I heard from a firm that had designed Butterfly Solar Farms that had simple in-field assembly and panels with double the efficiency of normal ones. It could be used for desalination systems, for crop drying, and to power freezers in slaughterhouses or dairy farms. The firm has a variety of proposed solar projects in Kenya with the idea that the region could become a powerhouse in solar energy. It also designed a "Kyoto Box," or compact kitchen unit, that cooks food in a few hours with no carbon impact. Only 4 percent of farms in Africa are irrigated, so low-cost solar pumps could provide an efficient solution. Also, 50 percent of crops are lost due to lack of preservation, which solar drying could potentially alleviate.

However, most of these good ideas need some sort of government help or facilitation, particularly in building more and better infrastructure. The big problem with the clean and safe cookstoves is the difficulty of distribution across Africa. They're cheap to produce but costly to ship across borders because of the high transportation costs and customs duties. How likely are we to see governments step up to the plate to deal with these big infrastructure challenges in already weak countries? The most likely scenario is that they won't be able to manage it. They are not only coming from behind—not having adequate institutional structures to begin with—but they also face the greatest challenges going forward, including rapid population growth, deleterious climate change, and environmental devastation that hits food and water supplies. For them, without outside assistance, the future does look Malthusian.

There is a broader threat that could turn a challenging situation for many into the bleaker outlook for us all. The Chatham House study warned that competition for critical resources is already acute in many parts of the world.[15] We see this with Middle Eastern efforts to buy up farmland in Africa and China and India to purchase equity rights in foreign oil fields, or in China's case to corner the market on rare earths. That competition could begin to take over, aggravating supply problems.[16]

Foodstuffs are perhaps the most vulnerable to price volatility and shortages. We have seen agricultural producers like Russia and Ukraine clamp down on exports when drought hit in 2010. The 2011 spike in food prices helped ignite the Arab Spring demonstrations. Over 30 countries have used taxes, quotas, and outright export bans to protect supplies of key crops since the 2008 food-price crisis. In actuality, those protectionist measures often aggravate the food situation for all, causing market prices to shoot up. On the one hand, the G20's efforts to counter price volatility in the food sector has been stymied by countries not willing to abjure the use of restrictions and bans, and on the other hand, in the developed world, by major producer countries not giving up on the generous subsidies going to the biofuel and agricultural sectors. The removal of the subsidies by the United States and Europe could help spur development of the agricultural sector in developing states.

To sum up, I learned a lot from my brief visit to Abuja. If anything, I'm more worried that all of us won't be able to avoid a Malthusian future. It's clear many societies don't have the wherewithal to avoid food and water shortages without massive help from outside. And it isn't as if technology per se will solve the problems. There's a nexus—as we've described—between the various resources, but also a broader nexus that is even harder to forge. Tackling problems pertaining to one commodity won't be possible without affecting supply and demand for the others. Agriculture is highly dependent on accessibility to adequate sources of water as well as energy-rich fertilizers and, increasingly, new genetically modified crops. New sources of green energy—such as corn-based ethanol—threaten to exacerbate the potential for food shortages. A continued population explosion in the most vulnerable areas will also need to be contained. With demand growing from a newly enriched global middle class, it doesn't seem possible that the current meat-based Western diet can be sustained without major changes to raising of livestock or widespread introduction of "bioprinted" meat supplies, which applies the latest advances in tissue engineering to meat without requiring the raising, slaughtering, and transporting of animals. There is as much scope for negative tradeoffs as there is the potential for positive synergies. Agricultural productivity in Africa, particularly, will require a sea change to avoid shortages. We are not necessarily headed into a world of scarcities, but we all—government, business, scientists, and the general public—will need to be proactive to avoid such a future.

# PART II

# *Game Changers*

## HOW FRAGILE IS THE COMING WORLD?

Historians oftentimes engage in *what if?* exercises called counterfactuals, in which they look back and replay history as if some great battle ended differently or a different leader was at the helm. If the Battle of Britain was lost and Germany invaded Great Britain, what would have happened to the US and Allied chances of vanquishing the Axis powers? If the North had lost Gettysburg, would Lincoln have been forced to sue for peace with the South? If China had modernized and fended off the Japanese invaders, what then? These are taxing historical exercises, testing our understanding of causation and opening up new vistas of historical enquiry.

The same critical thinking can be applied to the future. We know enough about the broad megatrends to identify key turning points in the future. For example, if China stumbles badly, it will have a huge impact on the rest of us. Or if a major war breaks out, then the ramifications are even more serious.

Four game changers stand out for me: a China that can't manage the next development leap, the growing possibility of war, possible runaway technologies, and a United States that can't stay on top of an increasingly complex world. These represent threats for us all. Negative outcomes in any one of these areas could put global development on a downward trajectory.

Hoping the worst won't happen is not a strategy. Understanding what could happen is a first step to preventing potential disasters. If the European leaders in 1914 really had understood what the coming war could be like and how it would bring many of them to ruin, would they have proceeded? Even the victors lost given the huge human and material costs spent in overwhelming their opponents. A lot is at stake with these game changers.

Negative outcomes can't be discounted, but positive ones too need to be understood. Each of these game changers can turn in welcome directions. What if China's development ends in its assumption of greater global responsibilities? Or what if technology turns out to be the greatest boon humankind has known?

In government decision making, as in ordinary life, we often get obsessed with the small stuff. These are the big questions, and we need to pay more attention to them. We have a lot to lose, but also to gain.

# CHAPTER 5

# *A Revolutionary China?*

IT'S A TRUISM THAT WITHOUT A RISING CHINA THAT THUNDERED ON THE SCENE AND BECAME a global economic powerhouse in such a short time, there would be less concern about the future—at least from a Western standpoint. Certainly China is only one of a number of new powers whose rise has been remarkable and largely unanticipated a couple decades ago. However, China stands out for a number of reasons. First, its mammoth size; what happens can't help make a difference. It has led the pack and economically pulled the others along with its demands for resources. Then there is the fact that it is not democratic, but is growing rich fast. Authoritarian states were not supposed to succeed economically. We were used to a communist bloc whose decaying economies were explained by the fact that they were authoritarian. More than anything else, China has caused us to doubt the universality of Western values. How China uses its newfound power will help make the difference between global peace and prosperity and a total breakdown. China will have a lot to answer for—for better or worse.

China has had a remarkable rise by any standards. China was the world's largest economy in 1820, accounting for an estimated 32.9 percent of global GDP.[1] Over the course of a century and a half, it shrank to around 5 percent of world GDP before starting its recovery in 1979. China's GDP could surpass that of the United States as early as 2017, but most likely in the 2020s, according to most estimates. From 1979 to 2012, annual GDP growth has averaged nearly 10 percent, enabling China to double the size of its economy in real terms every eight years.[2]

Brookings Institution expert Homi Kharas undertook a comparison of China's rise with other countries. In the period from 2000 to 2020, Kharas has calculated that China will increase its share of world GDP by 5 percent per decade. By contrast, the United States increased its share by just 2.5 percentage points per decade during the first half of the twentieth century. In the nineteenth century, the United Kingdom increased its share by under 1 percent per decade; post–World War II, Japan increased between 1 and 2 percent each decade. For many Chinese, however, they are getting back to where they should have been all along.

However, China's per capita income won't catch up with the West anytime soon. Using purchasing power parity, China's GDP per capita was $9,460 in 2012, just 18.9 percent of the US level. The Economist Intelligence Unit (EIU) projects this level will grow only to 32.8 percent by 2030.[3] This is different from the United States' and other countries' rise, which were accompanied by high levels of per capita income. Obviously, China's population is much larger, so that smaller per capita income increase adds up to a very large GDP.

Most ordinary Chinese will still feel like they are catching up even though their country will be much larger than any other. By 2030, China's economy could be a quarter larger than that of the United States, and yet per capita income will be just a third.

This has consequences for us in the West too. As already covered, most Western middle classes feel like they are losing their grip as their incomes stagnate. They look across at the developing world and see many countries there closing the gap. Many blame the competition from the developing world for their stagnant incomes. But the perception among Chinese and others is that they are still making up for lost time in the nineteenth and early twentieth centuries when China sank into poverty. With everybody feeling the loser, conditions are ripe for both sides to blame the other.

China faces a further problem—a demographic one. Like much of the world, China's population is already beginning to age, and the pace will pick up rapidly as it heads into the 2020s. Today 8 percent of the Chinese population is now 65 and older, but in 2030 seniors will exceed 16 percent. Meanwhile, the proportion of China's population in the normal 15-to-65 working age range has already peaked at 72 percent and will fall to about 68 percent in 2030. The proportion of the population aged 15 to 20—now just over 30 percent—will decline to about 21 percent by 2030. Of course, China won't be the only country with a diminishing share of working-age men and women in its population. More advanced economies like Japan, South Korea, and Germany will have far worse problems.

The Chinese government has begun to see the problem. The Chinese Communist Party's recent Third Plenum agreed on possible changes to China's 30-year-old one-child policy. It's unclear how extensive the changes will be. Many demographers question whether China could reverse years of a very low birthrate even if the one-child policy is totally relaxed. Increasing numbers of Chinese live in urban areas that typically correlate with lower birthrates all over the world. Ironically, some Chinese officials still fear a population explosion if the one-child policy is lifted too quickly. I remember asking (before the Third Plenum) a senior Chinese official whether it wasn't time to reconsider the policy. He admitted China had labor shortage problems but thought the consequences of lifting the restrictions would end up in a rush to bigger families that China could not support. As all foreign visitors are told, China has a large population, but not enough food, water, and energy to support it.

Will China grow old before it grows rich? The answer is almost certainly yes, if rich is defined by the West. The G7 economies are set to reach $64,000 per capita in 2020 (when China's demographic crunch will be in full force), more than three to four times China's expected level. The EIU projects China's real GDP growth will slow considerably in the years ahead, averaging 6.4 percent from 2013 to 2020, and to 3.6 percent from 2021 to 2030.[4] The slower growth still ensures that China surpasses the United States in overall economic size sometime during the next decade, but living standards will be improving at a slower pace.

China faces the prospect of being trapped in middle-income status. Many Latin American countries faced a similar situation in the 1980s and were unable to avoid the trap due to income inequality and their inability to restructure their economies. China's leaders want to avoid the middle-income trap by moving China up the value-added industrial production chain. They are promoting science and technology, and China is making progress in sectors such as nanotechnology and stem-cell research. Chinese firms are already starting to go outside China to obtain the next level of technological and managerial innovation. To do so, China is engaging in direct foreign investment in other countries—a logical step at this stage of development and possibly the only way for China to move up the value chain rapidly. The United States is a target, but some of China's efforts at investing in or buying US companies have been met with heightened US suspicion and government disapproval, particularly in sensitive national security areas like communications. The increasing levels of China's cyberattacks can be seen as a part of this effort to extract needed technology intelligence for its effort to become an innovation economy.

How China navigates the many obstacles blocking its way to an advanced economy will be increasingly important to the whole world. China's contribution to global investment growth is one and a half times the size of the US contribution. The World Bank estimates that China will contribute about one-third of global growth by 2025, far more than any other economy.[5] The world's second-largest consumer of oil products now after the United States, China will become the largest net oil importer by 2020. Its appetite for energy and other resources—which many see as beginning to taper off—has helped to fuel economic growth in other parts of Asia, Latin America, and Africa.

China accounts for nearly a quarter of global carbon emissions—the world's highest—and has so far resisted international pressure to commit to absolute cuts. The World Health Organization estimated that air pollution in China caused the death of almost a half million people in 2008, and it has grown worse since. For a majority of the days in January 2013 air quality in Beijing ranged from "unhealthy" to "hazardous." During a few days, the high readings were "beyond the index."[6] This could be slowly changing: the Chinese government recently said it was considering an outright cap on emissions in the 2016–20 five-year plan.[7] China, however, will be living with the health costs over the lifetimes of the people who have been exposed to high levels of pollution.

Many Chinese cities are creating urban sprawl, which is boosting car ownership, higher energy use, and higher costs to provide utilities and transportation networks. China is home to seven of the world's ten most polluted cities. Many of China's coastal cities, like other Asian ones, are vulnerable to the severe weather connected to climate change, which amplifies storm surges and flooding of low-lying areas.

An economically difficult transition could mean an equally difficult political one. Slower per capita growth will increase the difficulty of meeting rising expectations, potentially sparking discontent. A political crisis would make it harder for China to meet its economic goals. A prolonged political and economic crisis could cause China to turn inward, putting the blame on outside forces for its problems at home. Although the leadership and much of the middle class are now wedded to globalization because of China's success during the past 30 years, suspicion of the outside world lingers and, similar to historical cases elsewhere, could become an even more powerful political force if Chinese economic development stalls.

China may be coming to a difficult political transition point. China is slated to pass the threshold of US$15,000 per capita in the next five years or so.[8] We know from other historical cases that this level is often a trigger for political liberalization, especially when accompanied by high levels of education and a mature age structure. A democratic China would probably unleash even more of the nationalism, increasing already rising tensions with China's neighbors. Over the longer term, if rule-of-law institutions become more rooted and the political system stabilizes and is not seen as threatening, Chinese "soft power" could be boosted.

But historically, democratization most often does not proceed smoothly, and we should be prepared for a rocky transition that would make China a difficult neighbor and partner. Key to a smooth political transition would be China's ability to keep on raising living standards, which would avoid the middle-income trap. For most countries, this has been difficult. Of the countries that were middle income in 1960, almost three-fourths remained middle income or regressed to low income by 2009.[9] The majority of those who made it to high income were in Western Europe and Japan. South Korea graduated in the last decade or so to high income, and many credit the toll suffered by South Korea from the 1997–98 Asian financial crisis with forcing the country to make the needed structural reforms to advance. South Korea's economy consequently moved away from the centrally planned, government-directed investment model to a more market-oriented one. A recent study on South Korea and other middle-income economies that made the leap credit a strong social and political consensus behind the successful restructuring and modernization.[10]

The Party's Third Plenum, held in November 2013, called for a more "decisive" market role, though it stressed the continuing importance of the public sector.[11] State-owned enterprises will be subject, for example, to reform, but it is not clear how much and how quickly. Many of the so-called princelings—sons and daughters of the higher-ranking Party officials—are deeply enmeshed with the state banks and state-owned enterprises. If these reforms are fully carried out, their ox would be gored. Ironically, the lack of an economic crisis—in which growth plummets and the Party's hold is put in jeopardy—may make it harder to do what is needed to move China away from a command economy to a more market-directed one.

There is already growing popular discontent. A 2012 Pew opinion survey reported 50 percent of Chinese respondents said that corrupt officials are a big problem, up from 39 percent in 2008. Soon after taking office, President Xi Jinping mounted an anticorruption campaign in response to growing public outrage, but he has also been tightening the censorship on China's vibrant microblogging culture.[12] Many Chinese have used microblogs to voice their opinions on official corruption and environmental degradation.[13]

A lack of rule of law is another huge problem that impedes development. One of the headlines out of the Third Plenum was the need to construct "a rule of law country." China must "accelerate the construction of a fair, high-efficiency and authoritative Socialist judicial system, safeguarding the people's rights and interests."[14] Xi recently reiterated the need for "the establishment of an impartial and authoritative judicial system" but coupled it with reiterating a long-standing emphasis on the priority of Party leadership.[15] It's going to be an uphill battle. One study estimates that between 2001 and 2010, China was the world's largest source of illicit capital outflows at $3.8 trillion.[16] Increasingly, foreign firms complain about the difficulty of doing business in China partly because of the lack of transparency in the judicial system.

The economic modeling I did with the help of McKinsey & Company showed a whopping difference in terms of global prosperity between a world in which China fails and one where it succeeds. If China were to fail, total global income would be $27 trillion less than under the optimistic scenario. Fundamental economic and political reforms would remain elusive in China. Corruption, social unrest, weak financial systems, and chronically poor infrastructures would worsen. Several years ago the Asian Development Bank developed scenarios for Asia in 2050. Unable to overcome the middle-income trap, China and Asia would begin to lose ground, and convergence with Western living standards would be completely out of reach.[17]

In the positive scenario, where China avoids the middle-income trap, the global economy would nearly double. Chinese per capita incomes would continue to grow. And this would be the case for the US middle class: the American Dream returns, with per capita incomes rising $10,000 in ten years.

I'VE HAD EXTENSIVE CONVERSATIONS IN CHINA over the past eight years when showing drafts of the various *Global Trends* editions to Chinese government officials as well as academic and think tank experts. From the start, they have taken a more skeptical view of globalization, obviously seeing the huge benefits accruing to China, but also fearing the resulting political and social fragmentation. Chinese culture is renowned for its emphasis on balance. The famous concept of yin and yang sees opposites as interconnected and interdependent, and they need to be in balance. Otherwise there is disorder. For the Chinese, globalization heightened the yin-yang, or contrary, tensions between countries, but more importantly it heightened tensions inside countries, particularly China itself. Those contrasts are very apparent when one ventures away from coastal areas, where there is still enormous deprivation and poverty.

"I feel we are really in an age of uncertainty, risks, and chaos," said one official who thought such ideas needed more emphasis in the *Global Trends 2030* report. There is resentment too: "Obama said that it would be impossible for the world if China and India had the lifestyle of the United States. But he did not say how we are supposed to stop the public from becoming middle-class consumers." For another, the rise of the middle class in China could "create new problems" because of their "demands for resources and growth."

The draft reports sparked a discussion on the role of the state. All the *Global Trends* editions emphasize the significance of a nonstate sector, whether superempowered individuals, multinational businesses, NGOs, or more nefarious networks like organized crime and terrorism. For the Chinese, the nonstate sector was a difficult topic to get their heads around. A Chinese think-tank expert said, "We Chinese should be careful in talking about the strong state. Among Chinese we think that because we have a strong state and have been successful in the last 30 years, that it is only right for us to respect a strong state. But I would like to challenge this. The state is becoming bigger everywhere but less capable and powerful. We face increasing problems in the world, but government capacity is decreasing and individual empowerment is increasing and challenging state capacity."

There was general worry that China would not be able to take that next step toward building an innovative economy that necessitated dealing with individual empowerment and a strong nonstate sector. One Chinese scholar thought, for example, that I should have added another scenario in *Global Trends 2030*: "What about 'back to the 1990s' in which US manufacturing sectors revive while India and China are stuck in the middle-income trap, perhaps as a result of individual empowerment creating more internal problems." Another worried that real innovation "happens periodically, not consistently." Many worried that even in a decade or two China could not come up with innovations like the iPhone: "In the last couple of years, the United States has not been in good shape, but the United States can still make the iPhone and iPad that no other country can yet make, including China and India."

A prominent scholar and senior government official summed up where China was in his mind: "We still have a long way to go with economic reform first and social reform and then political reform. Economic reform is relatively easy. Now we are focused on social reform—that is eradicating social inequality. Political reform also started earlier in the 1980s but will be the most difficult. Corruption is now at its worst and a great challenge for the Communist Party and the legitimacy of one party rule."

Throughout the discussions, there was a shared concern about the capacity of the international system to deal with all the rapid change. A senior Chinese official said, "We are navigating into uncharted waters with many things new to us." Most were not pessimistic, but cautious. "We hope for international global governance and hope for the positive impact of technology. First we may see some reverse engines and fragmentation, but hopefully this will move toward collaborative efforts."

Their views about future international relations were wrapped up with how China and the United States treat one another. One said, "I am not pessimistic that there will be a new cold war. It will not be a zero-sum competition. But we [the United States and China] are both pursuing a hedging strategy—the worst-case scenario. My concern is that the worst-case scenario is increasing in both countries. We need to downplay the worst scenario and seize opportunities for cooperation."

Others were not so sure it couldn't be worse: "It is a foregone conclusion that there will be a showdown between China and the United States—not necessarily militarily, but one side will enforce its will on the other side. If a conflict occurs, that will be the biggest threat to regional and world security. It seems to me that some Americans believe that China's development will pose a challenge to its relationship with the United States."

One party official thought that "China should look at the US's role in Asia with a less China-centric perspective.... If it is relatively inevitable that emerging powers would be more self-focused and assertive, can the developed countries like the United States learn to better accommodate the interests of emerging powers who are acting from a sense of vulnerability and insecurity?"

No one saw a G2 world—in which the United States and China "ran" the world—as workable. A senior Chinese government official said, "We have a lot of players in the world—how can we get them to work together to get things done? You need a leading role for a group of states, not just the United States and China."

Throughout, there was great concern about where the United States was headed. While many were doubtful that the United States would welcome China at the high table of international politics, the United States still needed to try and manage the international system. "The United States cannot simply stop being the world leader after fifty years....China is not prepared to be in such a high position so soon. We have huge problems at home and need to put our house in order. So in this period, leadership is the problem."

There was general agreement—including from the US participants—that it was more difficult for the United States, China, and others to be "great powers": "For the United States and China, the problem is not just one threat but the scope and variety of threats—this needs to be kept in mind by policy planners in both the United States and China."

Many of these discussions occurred in May 2012. What has changed? Tensions in the neighborhood have increased with Beijing's assertive behavior over the disputed islets in the East China Sea with Japan and with the Philippines, Vietnam, and Malaysia in the South China Sea. It has thrown these countries into the arms of the United States, undermining what would seem to be China's chance of bolstering its regional position. The so-called pivot by the United States to the East Asia region has been as much "pull" from China's neighbors as "push" by a United States wanting to defend its position in the world's growing economic center of gravity. Chinese leaders appear to think that ramping up nationalistic rhetoric will mask the increasing divisions at home and mobilize the population for another economic push. China is nevertheless paying a huge price. All the gains it made from following Deng Xiaoping's dictum that China should maintain a peaceful external environment and not threaten its neighbors are being reversed. If China's ultimate aim is to edge out the United States and be the dominant power in East Asia, its assertiveness over its maritime claims have raised suspicions on the part of its neighbors that will not easily go away.

It's not clear if Xi's assertive policies constitute a very well-thought-out strategy.[18] China still needs others, especially the United States, to help it make the transition to an innovation society. The number of Chinese studying in US universities has doubled in recent years. Many forgo admission to elite universities at home to study in the United States, and there are increasing numbers enrolling in US high schools. China is on course to be even more integrated economically than it is now with its neighbors. Whether or not it eventually joins the US Trans-Pacific Partnership, it has a free trade agreement with the Association of Southeast Asian Nations (ASEAN) and has been negotiating a trilateral free trade agreement with South Korea and Japan. Membership in the Trans-Pacific Partnership could be used by the Chinese leadership as a pretext for undertaking the tough structural reforms it already wants to do.

On the US side, distrust of China at the elite level has grown. In mid-2013, a Pew poll showed that American attitudes toward China have turned sharply negative since 2011. Fifty-two percent of Americans had an unfavorable opinion of China, while just 37 percent expressed a favorable view. In 2011, the balance of opinion was just the opposite: 51 percent held a favorable opinion, while just 36 percent gave China an unfavorable rating.[19] Many policy makers I briefed on the *Global Trends* report were split on whether they wanted a strong or weak China. I don't think there is any contest. It's in US long-term interests to have a strong China. A weak China presents much greater threats to the global economy and East Asian security. Nationalistic attitudes and behavior would worsen even more in the event of a failed economy, potentially increasing US military outlays. While a strong China would mean it would have a bigger budget to spend on its military, it would also mean a China that felt more comfortable with tackling political reform.

The more likely scenario is a China that is neither weak nor strong, but struggles for some time to make the transition. It will continue its drive to become the biggest economy, but popular discontent grows as per capita gains slow and the government battles an increasing array of special interests that are against too much reform happening too quickly. The safety valve will continue to be nationalism, but I don't think we will see a tipping point into any major wars. The big worry is that under this scenario, it will be harder to contain any minor incidents because of the growing nationalism. The government would have a hard time avoiding escalation, particularly if the Japanese are involved. Enmity with Japan is particularly strong because of the perceived lack of Japanese contrition over its World War II record in China.

Will China hugely change the international system? I don't see how it can't due to its size. China, for example, relies heavily on oil imports from the Middle East and will be an increasingly bigger customer than the United States as US production continues to soar. China is building a blue-water navy capable of operating across the deep waters of open oceans, which would enable it to protect the sea lanes that connect the oil export-ing nations in the Gulf to the consumers in Asia. It would make sense that China take more responsibility, but many of its neighbors, such as India and Japan, would fear such a role will increase China's regional dominance. Many Americans would have a problem. Just as China's dependence on the import of vital resources is a persuasive argument by its military for build-ing a blue-water navy, retention of that responsibility is equal justification for a large US military budget. Surrendering that responsibility would be the equivalent, to many Americans, of giving up on its global role. Fitting China into a regional security order, particularly one that has been dominated by the United States, is going to be tough. Chances are it will happen without a major war because of shared interests, but we mustn't be overly confident.

The bigger question may be whether China wants to rewrite the current ground rules for how the international system operates. Although ambiva-lent and even resentful of the US-led international order, I don't think today's Chinese leaders have a vision for a new international order. Along with other emerging powers, they are eager for a greater say in the running of the global institutions like the UN or IMF. But China is more fortunate than most in already being a permanent UN Security Council member with veto power. China stays there in the background except when its direct interests—mainly recognition for Taiwan—are engaged. It hides behind Russia's skirts in opposing sanctions on states like Syria and Iran or efforts to intervene. Where it differs the most with the United States and other Western powers is in putting a greater stress on noninterference in the internal affairs of oth-ers. But even here, China, a country that once criticized UN peacekeeping operations as interference, has now deployed peacekeeping forces to south Sudan and more recently Mali.

I am reminded of a recent exchange with a prominent Chinese professor who teaches at one of the country's elite universities. He said, "Many stu-dents don't want to go abroad, in contrast with ten years ago." According to him, "Strategic thinking is more and more focused on domestic issues and development…the Chinese never had a strong interest in the world outside China. The United States was inward-looking until World War I, and then it became a global power. China is a global economic power, but Chinese leaders are not interested in global security and other issues. Americans think they can change the world, but Chinese don't think you can change the world and are internally focused."

Another of my Chinese interlocutors summed it up well: "China has negative power to say no, not positive power." This presents its own set of problems, particularly for an America that is feeling overstretched and would like partners, but the threat of a rising power trying to radically overhaul the system would appear to be well over the horizon. "China thinks that if we can avoid confrontation, we have achieved the objective, and the Americans are not satisfied and want cooperation and practical accomplishments."

CHAPTER 6

# Will Technology Be a Boon
# or a Curse?

A CASINO RESORT IN GABORONE, BOTSWANA, WAS NOT EXACTLY THE SETTING I HAD
expected for a technology conference. I had come to hear how Africa has
been profoundly changed by technology but was also changing technology.
For once there was a lot of good news and it wasn't a matter of rolling the
dice. One of the key pillars in Botswana's 2016 Vision is to "become globally
connected to broader communications networks."[1] Government officials
told us that Botswana had established an Innovation Hub that could serve
as a catalyst for technology firms to develop Africa's potential. A Microsoft
research center was already slated to come to Gaborone and occupy a new
park development that would be completed in 2014.

The two-day conference was an eye-opener, both for the extent of the
political, economic, and environmental challenges facing Africa and for the
technological progress made in such a short amount of time. On the plus
side, we were told by Alan Boshwaen of the Botswana Innovation Hub that
"the Africa of the 80s and 90s is not the Africa of today.... Smartphones are
outselling computers 4-to-1 in the continent."[2] "There was 65 percent mobile
penetration of the continent" and mobile subscribers have been doubling

every year since 2002 in Africa. Now Africa has twice as many cell phones as there are in the United States." And oh—by the way—Africa has many of the fastest growing economies in the world. The rate of urbanization is ramping up and will be probably higher than Asia's in the next couple years. Still, we were told by the head of Botswana's iHub there was a lot of "white space" that tech firms had to navigate: rules are vague, strategy is unclear, authority is fuzzy, and (government) budgets are nonexistent.

For all the promising change, many of the participants saw it as not enough. One speaker warned, "Bad things can still happen despite technology and better access to information." He was particularly worried about population growth. "There will be around 1.5 billion in sub-Saharan Africa by 2030. Unless you are growing economies at high rates, you will not be able to accommodate the rising population." There is birth control, but culture often dissuades its widespread use.

So here we begin to see the beginnings of a pattern. It is not just a matter of inventing or discovering new technologies or technological devices; what's also critical is the context. Changing social and cultural norms had a lot to do with whether the new technologies would make any difference.

The good news is we often underestimate the speed with which the new technologies have taken hold. The rate at which people absorb technology is rising fast. It took approximately half a century before a quarter of the US population was using electric lighting after its commercialization beginning in the 1870s. For the World Wide Web—invented in 1991—it took a mere seven years. And even more impressive, these accelerating absorption rates for new technology are happening on far less prosperous continents. In Africa smartphones are the prime way people access the Internet and increasingly do their banking. The change is happening from the bottom up.

You can also see it in the spread of research around the world. The case of IBM research labs is a good illustration; like the former British Empire, the sun never sets on IBM research. During a visit to their facility in Brazil, we were walked through how IBM has evolved—"from hardware to services, to integrated solutions, to collaboration for a smarter planet"—and how it has branched out from the United States to the rest of the world.[3] Zurich, Switzerland, was the location of the first foreign lab in the 1950s, followed by Israel in the 1960s and Japan in the 1980s. China and India followed in 1996 and 1998. Brazil and Australia have been major hubs for IBM research from 2010. IBM's expansion seemed to be synchronized with the rise of those countries in the global economies.

It's best to think about innovation as a soup-to-nuts phenomenon, from the inception of the idea to its uses that may not have to do that much with the original inspiration. Scientists are not necessarily good at understanding how their inventions can be used, we were told at the Center for Integration of Medicine and Innovative Technology in Boston, Massachusetts (CIMIT). CIMIT had worked in the medical device field taking smart ideas from the notional level through the whole cycle of innovation to implementation and commercialization. CIMIT executives talked to us about the importance of edging aside the inventors in order to be successful in commercializing inventions. "When we go to the development stage, the academics and clinicians are less important," but rather the entrepreneur becomes the "dominant" player.

The lessons we all learned in junior high or high school about atoms and molecules being in constant random motion, rapidly moving and constantly colliding with one another, is probably a good image for thinking about innovation and technology. We tend to think there are separations between scientific disciplines and even more so between science and law or urban planning or institutional governance—but those divisions increasingly do not exist. Instead, as with atoms and molecules constantly moving and colliding, there is increasing overlap and synergies between the different scientific disciplines and science and other subject areas. Moreover, trying to separate the different areas is a hindrance to thinking about science and technology, particularly now. The successful entrepreneurs and innovators, government officials, politicians, and educators—to name but a few—will need to increasingly have a foot in multiple camps.

The stakes are higher now. I talked earlier about many broad technologies—particularly nanotechnology, biotech, IT, 3D printing, artificial intelligence, new materials, and robotics—being at a liftoff point. The human genome could not have been unlocked without the buildup in massive computing power. The synthetic bioengineering revolution—on which we are only at the threshold—relies on the 3D printing process as well as the breakthroughs on genome sequencing, both of which needed IT advances to get off the ground. Hence, the image of atoms and molecules bouncing around and forming different combinations is a good one. It suggests too that there will be an infinite number of possibilities and uses for all the colliding, combining, frenetic action.

The various combinations heighten the possibilities but also the dangers. Let's begin with the automation and manufacturing technologies. Over time, they will revolutionize the nature of work. The magnitude of the changes we are seeing in the manufacturing technologies constitutes a Third Industrial Revolution.[4] This third cycle may change our world even more profoundly over the next two decades than the Internet has changed us in the last 20 years. Obviously, without the Internet there would be no new wave of industrialization, but this Third Industrial Revolution has a force of its own and goes beyond the Internet, particularly when we consider the magnitude of biotech.

Most historians define the First Industrial Revolution as the application of steam power in the eighteenth century; the second was the invention of the modern assembly line at the beginning of the twentieth century. Just like those earlier industrial revolutions, the third one—which has already begun—is changing the way things are made, where and when they are produced, and how they are distributed. It is reducing the energy and raw materials consumed as well as the carbon footprint of manufacturing. It is changing social relations, creating but also destroying jobs and altering the relationship of people to production. It is moving the world from mass production of standardized items to bespoke products to meet the requirements of individual needs. It is also transforming the global economy, providing new opportunities for the developing as well as developed world, but there will be costs if nations don't adapt.

Additive manufacturing—the formal name of 3D printing—is a group of technologies that allows a machine to build an object by adding one layer of material at a time. 3D printing is already in use to make models from plastics in sectors such as consumer products and the automotive and aerospace industries. It appears to be on the way to replacing conventional mass production, particularly for short production runs or where mass customization has value.

3D machines use computer-aided design (CAD) and a computer-guided laser, extruder, or printer head to construct an object one layer at a time.

The basic 3D printing technology was actually invented some three decades ago, but it reached a takeoff point only when it was combined with CAD. The printers can generate geometrically complex objects with internal cavities or moving parts inside an object, which traditional machines cannot manufacture. With 3D printing, manufacturers can avoid the high initial setup costs for specialty tooling and molds. The CAD file can be a laser scan of the surface of another object or a person or can even be medical data, such as computed tomography (CT) or magnetic resonance imaging (MRI) scans, which makes it possible to build objects in the shape and with the functionality of bones or internal organs.

The 3D printing revolution is happening from both the top down and the bottom up.[5] Leading global manufacturers such as General Electric, Boeing, EADS/Airbus, and Ford are using high-end 3D printing machines to go from rapid prototyping to producing critical parts for airplanes, automobiles, and wind turbines. From the bottom up, a combination of low-cost machines and online stores of 3D object files is democratizing manufacturing and empowering individuals, reminiscent of the early days of the Internet when small companies could make a big impact. It has been driven by the "do it yourself" (DIY) movement, with tens of thousands of users buying personal 3D printers for experimentation or starting their own small businesses. "Additive manufacturing could lead to large numbers of micro-factories akin to pre–Industrial Revolution craft guilds, but with modern manufacturing capabilities. Such local microfactories could manufacture significant amounts of products, especially those for which transportation costs are traditionally high or delivery times are long, and in the process shorten and simplify supply chains."[6]

3D printing could unlock new economic opportunities in countries, especially those in Africa that have not industrialized and rely on massive imports, including basic consumer goods. The cost of establishing a basic 3D printing facility—a computer, printers, materials, and Internet access—is significantly less than $10,000, unlike the more substantial amounts required for a conventional factory. Unlike a traditional factory, the 3D printing facility could produce an unlimited number of products without retooling and making products suited especially for the local market. For some developing countries, 3D printing might be for the material world what the cell phone has been in the digital world, helping them leap into advanced manufacturing.

In developed countries, 3D printing could also bring many benefits, including addressing labor constraints and diminishing the need for outsourcing, especially by reducing the length of supply chains. Nevertheless, 3D printing, which requires highly skilled technicians, could have a similar effect to outsourcing in making more low- and semi-skilled manufacturing workers redundant, which would exacerbate domestic inequalities.

We have already discussed robotics in the context of machines overtaking man in mental and physical capabilities. They have the potential—along with other new automation and manufacturing technologies—to utterly transform the labor market mostly for good, but I fear the immediate impact might also include some ill effects, as it will kill jobs.

First the good. As touched on in the earlier section, robots have better sensory and mechanical capabilities than humans do, making them ideal for routine tasks. Industrial robots have already transformed many manufacturing environments. Home robots vacuum homes and cut lawns; hospital robots patrol corridors and distribute supplies; the US military has thousands of robots operating on battlefields, and a new generation of robots is emerging for service sector applications, including cleaning, office work, and maintenance.

Developers are extending the capabilities of robots, crossing the boundary between industrial robots and nonindustrial robots. Although much work needs to be done to improve robots' cognitive abilities, many of the building blocks for futuristic and highly disruptive systems could well be available and in place by 2030. Such robotics could eliminate whole sectors of the labor market in certain industries, with total automation becoming more cost effective than outsourcing manufacturing to low-wage economies. Even in developing countries, robots might replace local manual labor in sectors such as electronics, keeping local wages down. Foxconn—the maker of Apple products in China—reportedly has plans to replace 80 percent of its work force with robots. Foxconn is worried about rising labor costs and the increasing difficulty of getting reliable workers at low wages. Their retention rate has been going down as other opportunities increase elsewhere and Chinese workers demand a higher wage.[7] Robotics will not be limited to the workplace or home environment.[8] Autonomous vehicles, including the iconic Google self-driving cars, could be on the road in the next decade or so. The long-term impact of self-driving cars and other autonomous vehicles could be a radical change in how we use cars, design transportation infrastructure, and utilize land in cities. There could be a sharp reduction in driving accidents and fatalities, over 90 percent of which are due to human error.[9] The amount of urban space now dedicated to cars, about 60 percent, could be substantially reduced by cars being available on demand, summoned by apps, and in constant use. This would drastically reduce the need for parking spaces as well as the overall number of cars, which as personal vehicles are idle 90 percent of the time.[10] At the same time, such personal-use vehicles may be more efficient than even public transport systems—the personal-use vehicles taking people directly where they want to go.

The self-driving car could thus prompt a redesign of cities and a shift in urban lifestyles. Robotic vehicles, especially if accompanied by a change in patterns of ownership and use, would be highly disruptive to the global economy, especially the auto industry. Some auto manufacturers could benefit (or new ones emerge), but the entire notion of what an automobile represents could change as people view autos more as a utility and less as a status symbol.[11]

How likely is the conversion to autonomous vehicles? Most experts believe the social and cultural adjustments will be harder than perfecting the technology, so the transition could take decades. The more serious impediment to the wholesale and rapid changeover to autonomous vehicles are lingering worries about safety and reliability, even though we know in the case of flying that pilots are more prone to making mistakes than automatic pilot systems.

The conversion to autonomous vehicles may pick up steam in the commercial sphere. Autonomous cargo convoys could be made up of several autonomous trucks driving on the highway with one or two drivers overseeing the fleet from the front or rear. Autonomous vehicles could spawn a new era of industrialization in mining and agriculture, addressing heightened demand for raw materials from developing economies and cutting back on the backbreaking labor that is conducted now by humans and even children in some developing states.

The use of unmanned aerial vehicles (UAVs)—now more often referred to as drones—is common in a military context. Most likely, UAVs will be put to an increasing civilian use in the coming decade. Low-cost UAVs with cameras and other types of sensors could support what is called precision farming—customization of the precise amounts of seed, fertilizer, and water for specific areas under cultivation—or inspecting remote power lines. One could see drones also being used to assess and improve traffic patterns. Like self-driving cars, the key problem for UAVs won't be the many uses that they can put to, but the concern regarding whether such vehicles can operate safely and reliably, especially when operating over populated areas. For this reason, most regulatory agencies worldwide greatly restrict the operation of UAVs in civilian airspace.

More threatening are the software breakthroughs, which can do the work of highly-skilled knowledge workers faster and more accurately. The extraordinary power of search engines, such as Google Search or Microsoft Bing, based on powerful ranking algorithms that far exceed any human capability, can sift through billions of data points to answer information queries. Other powerful algorithms are replacing lawyers with "e-discovery" by scanning millions of legal documents at higher speed, lower cost, and with greater accuracy than humans. Similarly, medical X-rays can be more accurately read by computers than radiologists. Google Translate is constantly improving through massive data mining and advanced algorithms. In short, a large number of jobs and even job categories are being or will be eliminated by software breakthroughs.[12]

This brings us to the serious issue of whether more jobs will be created than lost. In truth nobody knows for sure, but there are rising concerns even among economists whose theories tell us that new job categories we hadn't even dreamed about should be able to arise out of the ashes of those that are destroyed. A recent OECD report revealed some disturbing news: in its study new technologies were blamed for some 80 percent of the 4 percent global decline in the share of GDP going to labor over the past 20 years. Instead, the few that are highly skilled and talented in the new technology sectors—along with corporate managers and owners—have been accruing an increasing percentage of the wealth.

I tend to be a tech optimist who believes whole new job categories will eventually be created, but I worry about the lag and the mounting evidence of increasing inequalities worldwide. The First Industrial Revolution started the process of bringing prosperity on an unimaginable scale, but it also impoverished scores of craft workers and helped entrench the class system in nineteenth century Great Britain.[13] Charles Dickens's novels described the precariousness of life faced by factory and other workers even as the middle class expanded. History stands as a warning against the idea that the situation will automatically right itself in the short or even medium terms. Those dispossessed by the new technologies don't always have the means to acquire new skills. The United States and others are in danger of developing an underclass that won't have the opportunity to succeed.

Besides a negative impact on jobs and compensation, the Third Industrial Revolution is spawning other downsides. 3D printing has attracted the attention of the US Congress and the public with reports that people have printed guns and high-capacity magazines for assault weapons. According to press reports, "the chamber extended a blanket prohibition on undetectable firearms in Washington's latest attempt at grappling with a new and sometimes confusing technology."[14] No doubt other worrisome products such as improvised explosive devices, or IEDs, will be printable and make control of lethal items more difficult. Drones have already proved highly controversial with their ability to target individual terrorists. The United States may have developed and first deployed drones for such purposes, but the technology is increasingly cheap and globally available. Not only states but also nonstate actors have access to the technology to build and deploy their own drones for lethal attacks and surveillance. Robotic weapons systems with the ability to autonomously make "kill decisions" are possible and could extend to robotic soldiers. The "Stuxnet" virus, reportedly developed and deployed by the United States and Israel to destroy Iranian uranium centrifuges, has likely set a precedent for development of other autonomous kinetic algorithm weapons that can be deployed to seek out and destroy physical objects. Hacking of autonomous vehicles—from cars to UAVs and drones—could also result in lethal destruction.

The best illustration of how much good, but also bad, can result is synthetic biology. It has so much potential to do good but also the greatest potential to be extremely harmful. Like other new technologies, the synbio revolution results from a convergence of a wide range of other tech breakthroughs. In this new synthetic biology age, you will be able to edit DNA like software in a computer. Craig Venter, who led the private effort to map the human genome and created the first synthetic organism, has termed this "digital life."[15] "The bioengineered digital file could represent the DNA of an existing organism or an altered form of that organism. It could also be an entirely new organism created from DNA building blocks such as BioBricks. BioBricks are DNA constructs of different functioning parts that can be assembled to create new life-forms to perform specific functions."[16] Venter suggests such genetically engineered organisms can be created for biofuels, water purifying, textiles, and food sources among other uses.

A recent National Research Council and National Academy of Engineering report on synbio explained how this works. According to the report, "Synthetic biologists have the ability to design genetic code to elicit a specific function, pre-test the code for functionality using computer modeling, order the relevant genetic material from a commercial or open-source gene synthesis facility and insert the material into a cell body in order to test real world functionality."[17]

Perhaps even more astounding than digitizing life, this digital life can be transmitted over the Internet and the organism re-created anywhere on the planet. Or, Venter adds, digital life can be used to re-create organisms found on Mars by digitizing their DNA and transmitting the file back to Earth, or to send digital files of life-saving drugs to some future human colonists on the Red Planet. Venter has created biological converters to receive and print the files. In a global pandemic, synbio could cut the time normally required to develop a vaccine and "could send the digitized vaccine sequence around the world to be bioprinted for immediate use."[18]

A new organism can be built from scratch. "The 3D printing process allows the designer of a synbio product to work with preexisting modules of the product. Synthetic biologists can work, for example, with BioBricks that can be bought and downloaded, each with a specific functionality."[19] The building-block-devised design can be sent to a bioprinter that will assemble the genetic material and create the new life-form. The creator of the organism does not need the technical expertise to know how each of the BioBricks works, just as the designer of a 3D-printed object does not have to be a software engineer but only versed in CAD software to design the object and send it to the printer.

Synbio may have a massively transformative impact on the world, just like the Internet and 3D printing.[20] There are huge potentials for sustainability: the word *organic* will be given new meaning as structures will both look more organic and be made of organic materials. Drew Endy, bioengineering professor at Stanford University, calculates that genetic engineering and synthetic biology already contribute about 2 percent of US GDP, and in the near term, a synbio-generated technological and economic boom could happen that would be comparable to the impact of the Internet.[21]

However, the ease associated with bioengineering—and the low cost and wide availability of materials and capabilities—is raising concerns about synbio's potential dangers, especially the ability to alter viruses to become more deadly or to create wholly new lethal microorganisms. Laurie Garrett, global health expert at the Council of Foreign Relations, notes that the "world of biosynthesis is hooking up with 3D printing.... Scientists in one city designing a genetic sequence on a computer [can] send the code to a printer somewhere else. The code might be the creation of a life-saving medicine or vaccine. Or it might be information that turns a tiny virus into something that kills human cells, or makes nasty bacteria resistant to antibiotics, or creates some entirely new viral strain."[22]

So far the policy initiatives have focused on introducing reporting requirements on suppliers of goods, but such efforts could become futile as research becomes more diffuse. Recent trends suggest applications of the technology will continue to advance ahead of understanding all the risks. Absent efforts to strengthen regulatory frameworks to proactively manage risks, the greater access to synbio increases chances of the development and use of bioweaponry by individuals or terrorist groups. There is also the worry that biohobbyists working in their garages could inadvertently release dangerous material.

Part of the problem in tackling the security aspects is a fear that too heavy a hand in regulation could stifle the scientific advances. Keep in mind that amateur hackers and gamers have played a key role in developing the Internet and its applications or apps. The same bottom-up innovations are expected from the biohobbyists. Turning that interest off through regulation—which is probably not possible anyway—could undermine prospects for possibly the most exciting new scientific field. The emphasis therefore has been put by scientists and authorities on developing overlapping self-monitoring communities. I think the stakes are so high that more concerted security measures need to be put in place, however, to ensure the science is not misused.

MANY OTHER TECHNOLOGIES ARE far less dangerous but have other problems attached to them, particularly the need for substantial upfront investment or some sort of government backing to make them commercially viable or effective. Others, like genetically modified organisms, or GMOs, are politically and socially controversial among environmentalists and many others, even though many agriculturalists believe GMOs are critical for dealing with the growing food demand in climatically challenged places like Africa.

Water management will be critical to achieving global food security because agriculture depends on irrigation for 40 percent of its production and consumes approximately 70 percent of global freshwater supplies. A lot of water is wasted: irrigation wastes about 60 percent of the water taken from freshwater sources. Efficient water management will be required to sustain a necessary increase in agricultural productivity. Even though desalination might be economically feasible for household and industrial water, such technologies are unlikely to produce irrigation water at a low enough cost to be feasible for agricultural use. As water scarcity increases, adopting technologies that increase water-use efficiency will be the only option farmers will have for confronting global water scarcity. The array of such technologies includes precision agricultural and genetically modified drought-tolerant and salt-tolerant crops as well as micro-irrigation systems and hydroponic greenhouse technologies.

Micro-irrigation technology shows promise in improving agricultural water management because it can deliver a highly water-efficient solution.

Currently applied mainly to high-value vegetable crops, micro-irrigation is also suitable for other crops. Using today's leading micro-irrigation technologies, the percentage of water actually delivered to a field is some 90–95 percent compared to 35–60 percent for furrow irrigation or 60–80 percent for sprinkler systems where much of the water evaporates. Such efficiency is costly, however—some $2,500 to $5,000 per hectare over a 10-to-15-year period.

Rain-fed agriculture is responsible for 58 percent of global cereal grain production, but little effort has been put into developing technologies to enhance its productivity. Most rain-fed regions, such as South Asia, are struggling already with poverty, malnutrition, water scarcity, severe land degradation, and poor physical and financial infrastructures. Proven inexpensive practices—such as zero-till and mulching, which ensure more water gets to plants rather than lost to evaporation—are not in widespread use. Agricultural leaders are considering harvesting water through managed underground storage, which would reduce the reliance on available surface water.

As important for water management as new technologies is the need for governments to adjust their water-pricing policies to spur water efficiency. However critical the technologies are, these difficult political decisions, such as water pricing, are even more essential. Farmers typically pay as little as a tenth of the price that industry and households pay for water; thus farmers have little incentive to save water.

Besides better water management, food security can be enhanced through the application of modern molecular plant breeding and transgenic technologies. Transgenic technologies enable the transfer of genes from one plant species to another to produce a plant with new or improved traits. Scientists have identified hundreds of genes that could improve crop plants, but only a few genetically modified crops have been commercialized. However promising for achieving food security in the next 15 to 20 years, this group of plant technologies faces some of the most intense regulatory and public pressures of any new technologies, which makes widespread adoption of any of these potential advances uncertain.

Precision agriculture—another emerging technology—holds promise for increasing crop yields by decreasing the use of seed, fertilizer, and water, which minimizes the negative environmental impacts of farming and improves the quality of crops. The development of cost-effective, versatile, and highly automated forms of precision agriculture suitable for a wide range of farm types and sizes could help provide worldwide food security even in the face of resource scarcities and environmental restrictions. Trends in precision agriculture point to increasing automation of farm vehicles and implements. Within the next 5 to 10 years, autonomous tractors will begin to take so many roles in large-scale farming that commercial farms will start resembling automated manufacturing facilities. In 10 to 15 years, technological innovation could reduce the size of today's autonomous farming vehicles and implements. Smaller farm vehicles would allow farmers to use them on small sections of a field and small land holdings, leading to higher-yield, higher-intensity cultivation. It's not clear whether such systems will ever be affordable for use on small plots in developing countries where the greatest productivity gains are required.

The shale revolution is not moving us beyond dependence on fossil fuels, and it looks increasingly unlikely to in the next couple of decades. The potential for more abundant and cheaper supplies of natural gas to replace coal by 2030 would have undeniable benefits for curbing carbon emissions. "But to transform the current energy system to a post-hydrocarbon-centered system would require the electrification of transport, qualitatively improved energy storage capabilities, and a smart grid powered by clean energy—that is, some combination of wind, solar, nuclear, hydro, geothermal, and/or other renewable sources. Ironically, a consequence of an increased reliance on shale could be the lack of a major push on moving toward a post-hydrocarbon world."[23]

None of the necessary building blocks to a post-hydrocarbon-centered system look promising without a major push from government support, including ample financing. Smart grids provide a useful example of the challenges. A smart grid is the digitization of utility electricity delivery systems, bringing them into the twenty-first century and using computer-based remote control and automation to provide real-time communication on supply and demand between the producers, the grid, and consumers. Smart grids are slowly beginning to take shape worldwide, but renovating the grid infrastructures is a long-term process. In the US case, the federal government has already invested $11 billion, but the utilities will need to invest $17–$24 billion annually over the next two decades. Such investment would have $2 trillion in benefits to utilities and consumers in increased efficiencies, but the problem is sustaining the effort on such a large-scale and long-range endeavor.[24]

**SO LET'S GET BACK TO THE EXAM QUESTION:** To what degree will emerging technologies be a help or a hindrance? And the proverbial answer is, it depends. Many of the new technologies need a helping hand before they can really have an impact. As mentioned, governments in many water-stressed areas need to rein in the free use of water by farmers, and this is oftentimes very politically unpalatable. Farmers are a powerful lobby in many countries, such as India. It will take real leadership to put water pricing in place. Similarly, government attempts to reduce fuel subsidies, which keep prices artificially low, have caused riots and demonstrations in many places where it has been tried, such as Indonesia and Nigeria, but eliminating such subsidies is desperately needed to incentivize more efficient use of energy supplies.

In the US case, shale may be a crutch that discourages investment in alternative fuels, particularly with the low cost of the cleaner natural gas. Moreover, I and others worry that government funding and support for basic research is diminishing. All the technologies in the smartphone, for example, were US government funded and developed.

So boosting government's role is a key, one that could be a hard sell for some countries such as the United States, many of whose citizens worry about big government and appear unaware of the critical role played by their government in laying the scientific groundwork for many of the gadgets that fill our daily lives.[25]

China is a different story. On the last trip, I had what seemed like endless discussions on what constitutes innovation. How does one become an innovative society? They are investing heavily in technology, worried that the next large-scale breakthrough technology will pass them by. They have done a lot of right things—such as sending their students to study abroad in first-rate universities in the United States and elsewhere. Research and development spending is up 170 percent over the last ten years.[26] Their history would suggest—having been inventors of many of the critical technologies of the premodern world—that they can become a world-class innovative society again. However, we know that inventions are the product of intense international cooperation; the restrictions that the Chinese government places on free access to the Internet, for example, can't act as anything but an obstacle to that long-term ambition.

Despite these problems, I see China, and others such as India and Brazil, progressing. In most of the *Global Trends* reports, we have talked about the growing stature of the developing world in innovation and scientific discovery, even cutting into US overall leadership. We also saw that their own critical needs to prevent water, food, and in some cases energy shortages would push them to commercialize next-generation resource technologies. The Chinese government's 5-year plan includes spending $1.7 trillion in new generation IT and environment technologies. The China Development Bank already invested $26 billion in emerging green economy in 2012.[27] Being first may allow private- and state-owned Chinese companies to establish strong competitive positions. The United States has a lead in most of these technologies but that may diminish. It also does not have the same incentives—for the most part it is resource-rich and does not have to worry about any shortages.

Synbio is perhaps the most dazzling new technology, having so many applications from bioenergy to health miracle cures and therapies. This is where there needs to be a strong government role, in conjunction with industry and the scientific community, to prevent its bad use or its falling into the wrong hands. Any damage it does could be irreparable. Any misuse could spark a backlash against technology and forestall further progress, the bulk of which has been and could be used for positive purposes.

So we have come full circle back to the enabling environment as key to whether technologies are put to good use or not. Industry and government are both important and need to work cooperatively. Technology does not matter unless it is commercialized. However, the track record of industry supporting basic research is increasingly disappointing, so governments have to step in and ensure science continues to advance. The story of technology is, therefore, a tale of these other forces—the surrounding ecosystem—and the constellation of forces that must be gotten right in order for us to reap the full benefit from all the wonderful and fascinating innovations.

# CHAPTER 7

# *A Return to World at War?*

2014 IS THE CENTENARY OF THE OUTBREAK OF THE FIRST WORLD WAR, OR THE GREAT
War as it was called at the time. It is hard not to see the parallels with
our own age.[1] There was rampant globalization fueled by faster modes of
transport, from railways to steamships, and a communications revolution around the telephone, telegraph, and wireless—what we later came to
know as radio. Electricity was transforming human existence, immeasur-
ably boosting productivity. Some scholars argue that the technology revolution then had a more profound impact than even our own on changing
the human condition. Why and how did the long peace of the nineteenth
and early twentieth centuries end, and could we see a replay of a world war
in our own times?

Without trying to be Pollyanna-ish, I don't see a replay on such a grand
scale. While there are the striking similarities, there are many differences.
Today's age is much more democratic than the far more imperialistic age
of pre–World War I Europe. There is good scholarly research showing that
democratic powers tend not to go to war with one another. But this is not the
only difference. Pre–World War I was an age of rampant nationalism, anti-
Semitism, racism, and strong social belief in the inevitability of Darwin's
survival of the fittest, all of which is no longer prevalent.

While the possibility of a worldwide conflagration is overrated, the threat of major war does exist in a number of regions, and there are even more real threats of civil war, continued terrorism, and insurgency. But we need to first put the current conflict threat in some context. There is a bit of good news to report about conflict overall, and we'll start there.

For almost a decade, few conflicts between states—what are called inter-state conflicts—and no major wars have erupted since 1939, constituting the longest era of major-power peace during the past five centuries. There are a number of possible reasons for this long peace. Few if any periods in the past have seen global power so lopsided as it has been since the end of the Cold War with US military capabilities so superior to any plausible combination of powers. US military superiority is likely to remain for the next decade or two. New powers like China and India are rising, but they benefit from the existing international order. An increasing number of countries—most prominently the Europeans—have consciously chosen to maintain military capabilities far below their inherent financial capabilities. I believe this reflects their assessment of the modern utility of using force to achieve political objectives. Norman Angell, the famous author of the pre–World War I best seller *The Great Illusion*, about the uselessness of war, was probably ahead of his time. I don't believe countries or peoples are increasingly pacifists, but many more now have made the calculation that war is counter-productive to their main aim—economic development.

But we need to be cautious. The thesis of this book is that times are changing fast and the same assumptions don't necessarily apply anymore. For the moment, the United States is far and away the most powerful military actor, the only power with global reach. But with the rise of other powers—particularly China, which is investing heavily in defense—the post–Cold War equilibrium is beginning to shift. It is not just a question of capability, but also of will. If the United States is unwilling or less able to serve as a global security provider, the world will be less stable. The international system becomes more fragmented and deterrence against going to war begins to weaken. I don't think this is happening everywhere. The Europeans—which collectively constitute the biggest economic power—won't be going to war with themselves or others. Because of their experience of massive suffering during the world wars, they don't believe in war. This is a key difference from pre–World War I, in which all the major European imperial powers (including the Ottoman Empire) saw an advantage in wars.

Without the Europeans as players, nowadays the threat of war is on a regional level. And the chances are growing that conflicts could spill over and become wider regional ones with far-reaching impacts. The Middle East is the most likely arena, but other volatile areas include South Asia and, to a lesser extent, East Asia.

Before looking at these, let's examine the current patterns of internal or intrastate conflict. These have been less common in the post–Cold War era, but we are seeing an uptick, most notably in Syria. Wherever civil and ethnic wars have emerged, they have tended to persist. The average intrastate conflict that began between 1970 and 1999 continued for about six years without a one-year break in battle-associated fatalities. Some—including the Angolan civil war, Northern Ireland's Troubles, Peru's war against the Shining Path, and the Afghan civil war—endured for decades. In contrast, conflicts between states that began between 1970 and 1999 lasted, on average, less than two years.

Scholars believe the marked expansion in the size and number of peace support operations (PSOs) dampened the persistence of some conflicts and prevented the reemergence of others. The proportion of youthful countries experiencing one or more violent intrastate conflicts declined from 25 percent in 1995 to 15 percent in 2005. Peacemaking and nation-building—despite growing Western ambivalence about such efforts—have helped to keep down casualties.

Since the 1970s, roughly 80 percent of all armed civil and ethnic conflicts (with 25 or more battle-related deaths per year) have originated in countries with youthful age structures—a population with a median age of 25 years or less. Looking forward, the risk of intrastate conflict will probably decline in those countries and regions with maturing age structures (median age above 25 years). However, because many countries will still have youthful populations, the risk will remain high during the next two decades, particularly in western, central, and eastern portions of sub-Saharan Africa; in parts of the Middle East and South Asia; and in several Asian-Pacific island hotspots, such as Timor Leste, Papua New Guinea, the Philippines, and Solomon Islands. As we've seen, many of these countries also suffer from other destabilizing factors, such as poorly managed economies, deteriorating environmental conditions, and increasingly weak governments.

There are other reasons to be cautious about the prospects for a marked decline in the number and intensity of intrastate conflicts. First, continued reductions in scope and number of conflicts is dependent on continued if not increased global support for costly PSOs, but this isn't likely to be forthcoming. Second, a gradual increase in intrastate conflict is occurring in countries with mature populations overall, but which contain one or more politically dissonant, youthful ethnic minorities. Strife involving ethnic Kurds in Turkey, Shia in Lebanon, and Pattani Muslims in southern Thailand are examples of intrastate conflicts persisting in states that display an overall intermediate age structure (median age from about 25 to 35 years). Some have happened after the country-level age structure turned mature (median age from 35 to 45 years). Examples include the Chechen conflict in southern Russia and the Northern Ireland Troubles. Looking forward, the potential in sub-Saharan Africa for civil conflict is likely to remain high even after some of the region's countries graduate into a more intermediate age structure due to the probable large number of ethnic and tribal minorities who will remain much more youthful than various countries' overall populations.

IT IS NO SURPRISE THEN THAT the Middle East and South Asia are regions where intrastate conflict could spill over and cause major conflicts. Population growth is still fairly high, although it will be tapering off by 2030 in most Middle East countries. Youthful countries in 2030 will include the Palestinian Territories (West Bank and Gaza) and Jordan and Yemen. While only Afghanistan will be youthful by 2030, the aging that will occur among the large and growing populations in nearby Pakistan and India will mask youthful ethnic and regional populations in those countries that could remain a security concern. Tribal populations will remain youthful in Pakistan's western provinces and territories. In Pakistan and Afghanistan, the childbearing rates are greater than five children per woman among the Pashtun. In India, where the southern states and large cities have attained low fertility, youthfulness—which can contribute to instability in the absence of employment outlets—will erode more slowly in the central northern states of Uttar Pradesh and Bihar.

Conflict often begets more conflict, which, besides the destruction and loss of life, is probably the worst thing about conflict. Scholars studying conflict place the risk of former conflicts reverting to conflict to be about 40 percent in the first decade after conflict termination.[2] Even after the conflict stops, economic development tends to be slow and undermines whatever support exists for democratic governance. The civil war in Syria is particularly depressing, partly because it began so hopefully with largely peaceful demonstrations that had majority support. Successful civil resistance movements—such as the one Gandhi led against the British Raj in India—have a fairly good track record in leading to democratic government. Unfortunately, not only did the Syrian uprising devolve into an armed conflict with the emergence of radical Sunni Islamist groups, but it also has drawn in outside actors, internationalizing what started as an internal conflict. Syria sits on the Sunni-Shia fault line that divides several nations in the Middle East, so the conflict has increasingly taken on a sectarian hue. The Bashar al-Assad regime has used a strategy of fear to rally support among the country's main minorities, including the Druze, Alawites, and growing portions of the Christian community. Assad strengthened the sectarian dimension by relying on paramilitary self-defense groups belonging mostly to his Alawite community. In reaction, increasingly empowered Salafist militants and al-Qaida-inspired or -affiliated jihadist groups have grown in number and importance within the opposition.

Finally, the Syrian conflict is becoming a proxy war for Saudi Arabia and Iran,[3] in some ways reminiscent of the Spanish Civil War in the 1930s in which external communist and fascist forces took sides in an internal Spanish fight and fought each other. In the new regional cold war, Saudi Arabia has taken the part of the anti-Assad opposition and called for regime change in order to deprive Tehran of its main Arab ally and cut Hizbollah's main supply lines, which run through Syria. Iran, fearing a much weakened position for itself, has taken an active role in supporting the Assad regime. Iran has enlisted Hizbollah to help achieve its aims. Increasingly, regional geopolitics best explains the evolving dynamics on the ground.

If this is not enough, the large refugee flows and the increasing presence of al-Qaida forces throughout the region were cause for alarm. In late 2013 over 2 million had fled Syria and over 4 million were displaced inside Syria. In Iraq, al-Qaida forces have become reenergized, aggravating Iraq's dangerous sectarian divisions. Lebanon faces a potential breakdown as sectarian tensions grow and it reels from under mounting pressure from the massive influx of Syrian refugees. Jordan also faces mounting economic challenges from the flows of refugees.

At the regional level, sectarianism in Syria is becoming a contributing factor to growing radicalization. Sara Assaf is a Lebanese woman who regularly tweets about the Syrian civil war. In November 2013, she tweeted about the impact of the downward spiral of events and growing radicalization of even moderates like her:

I am originally half Syrian and half Iraqi, but I am born and bred and proud to be Lebanese. I went to a French Lycée school. I graduated from an American college. I made a career for myself in advertising and media. I travel to London and Paris for my vacations. I wear Converse shoes during the days and Louboutin pumps during the nights—in short, all the clichés that come with being a Westernized woman of the 21st century....

Like many others, I tweeted the Syrian revolution every single day. I watched the massacres and the atrocities. The women raped and the children killed. The millions of homeless refugees. Every time Assad crossed yet another line, we foolishly believed that the international community was bound to react. But to no avail...

Today I grasp why Sunni terrorism is prospering so quickly to fight Shiite terrorism. The atrocious images stemming daily from Syria are simply fueling a sense of injustice stronger sometimes than any voice of reason. The West has in parallel failed to effectively support the moderate forces across this region. Extremism and radicalism are thus gaining momentum over tolerance and moderation. To the West I say: Expect a whole new breed of terrorists in the decades to come....[4]

Once the sectarian genie is out of the bottle, can it be put back in?[5] If Syria follows the pattern similar to other civil wars, it won't end soon, meaning that sectarianism will only increase. According to some scholars, it could last "over nine years," even longer than the average six-year duration for most civil wars.[6] And it's not as if the rebels have a good chance of winning. "Even with support from outside states, violent campaigns in such circumstances from 1900–2006 had less than a 30 percent chance of succeeding. During that time, fatalities, casualties, and displacements are likely to increase, leading to humanitarian catastrophe even worse than what has already transpired."[7]

Unfortunately, the faltering Middle East economy will not help the situation. The fertility rate is coming down, but the youth bulge will last until 2030. Only a small fraction of the global foreign direct investment went into the Middle East even before the conflict, and most investors are going to be wary of taking a chance now in view of all the violence. There has been traditionally little to attract investment apart from energy, tourism, and real estate. And since the 2011 Arab Spring, tourism has collapsed in countries like Egypt. Many Middle Eastern countries are far behind on technology, and the region is one of the least integrated in trade and finance.

The richer Gulf countries are in a better position to help—their sovereign wealth have built up sizeable assets in recent years and a growing share of petrodollar or energy wealth could be invested in local and regional markets, but it will come with strings. In a sense, Saudi Arabia and other Gulf countries are a part of the problem, fueling the feuding with Iran, which is exacerbating the sectarianism. Over time, Gulf states also face stiff economic challenges if energy supplies increase substantially from the exploitation of US shale gas and oil deposits, which could undercut high energy prices. As the costs of its social welfare outlays increase, the fiscal break-even price of oil for Saudi Arabia keeps rising to somewhere between $80 and $90 a barrel, according to the IMF,[8] suggesting spiraling budget expenditures that could outpace oil price rises. Without politically controversial hikes in the internal oil price, which would reduce rising domestic consumption, Saudi Arabia is on course to become a net oil importer in several decades.

Could we see the situation get even worse? Yes, and it looks increasingly likely. Even if a cease-fire is patched together in Syria, it would be a temporary fix absent major outside intervention to redirect energies toward economic development. And there seems little appetite for offering such large-scale help on the part of the United States and Europe. I fear this isn't a repeat of Bosnia in the 1990s. That initially shaky peace endured because of the enormous investments that were poured in, first with a large NATO peacekeeping force, but more importantly with a long-term political and economic commitment by the United States and especially the European Union. Croatia is now a member of NATO and the European Union, and other former Yugoslav states have expressed interest in joining.

It's hard to see the West today commit to such an extensive stabilization program for the Middle East despite the risks of not doing so. The region could be engulfed by conflict, one that comes close to resembling World War I but on a regional level. Sunni fear of Iran is linked to Tehran's apparent nuclear ambitions. Iran has agreed to freeze its nuclear program, and further negotiations are aimed at making it impossible for Iran to break its promise not to develop nuclear weapons without being detected. But I believe Iran wants to retain the ability to develop nuclear weapons in the future. Even the fact that Iran will have such a capability is destabilizing. We are at risk of seeing other countries in the region seek their own nuclear capability in reaction. Such a breakdown would have implications for the broader global nonproliferation regime and would totally undercut the goal of a nuclear zero world. It would also mean that the Sunni-Shia conflict we see today would be further fueled by a nuclear arms race. Such a nuclear arms race might never fully erupt in full-scale war, but even in the most optimistic of scenarios the race would add a much higher dose of uncertainty to developments in the Middle East.

Could it turn out differently? Am I missing a more optimistic scenario? Possibly, but it is a receding one, particularly if the talks on Iran's nuclear program result in an impasse. However, an easing or end to international sanctions after an international agreement tightly restricting Iran's development of nuclear weapons would stir strong public pressure inside for long-deferred economic modernization. Eventually, the regime would cave to public demands and the focus would shift to development. This is certainly where President Hassan Rouhani wants to take Iran, but it's not clear he can do so without being strongly opposed by the hard-liners. Under this scenario, Iran, like China and India, would focus on development, gradually resulting in a more pro-Western, democratic Iran. Unlike much of the rest of the Middle

East, Iran stands out with an urban middle class that is highly educated and just needs to be liberated from its current confines. In such an optimistic scenario, there would be the potential for a more stable region. If Iran reorients itself, with likely international support, toward economic development like the rest of the world, it is possible to see lowered Sunni-Shia tensions and a turning away from the current path to major regional war.

LIKE THE MIDDLE EAST, SOUTH ASIA will face a series of internal and external shocks during the next 15 to 20 years. Impacts from climate change, including water stress, in addition to low economic growth, rising food prices, and energy shortages will increase challenges to governments in Pakistan and Afghanistan. Afghanistan's and Pakistan's youth bulges are large—similar in size to those of many African countries—and, when combined with slow-growing economies, portend increased social instability. India is in a better position, benefiting from higher growth, but New Delhi will still be challenged to find jobs for its large youthful population. Young rural Indians aspiring to leave the life of the farm for better opportunities in cities face bleak prospects in the next few years, as the rate of national job creation is expected to slow sharply from its already sluggish current pace. A new independent research study forecasts that India's economy will create 25 percent fewer nonfarm jobs in the next seven years than in the last seven years, due to its sharp economic slowdown and increased automation in manufacturing.[9] The report underlines that with around half its population still under the age of 24, India needs to absorb 10 to 12 million new entrants to the labor market each year for at least the next decade and a half, if not longer.

Inequality, lack of infrastructure, and educational deficiencies are long-standing problems in India. India also faces an intransigent rural insurgency—the Naxalites—which remains a big internal security challenge. Rapid urbanization in India and Pakistan will transform their political landscapes from more traditional control by rural elites to one shaped by the increasing numbers of urban poor and middle class.

The neighborhood has always had a profound influence on internal developments in all the countries in the region, increasing the sense of insecurity and bolstering military outlays. Pakistan's large and fast-growing nuclear arsenal—proportionally the biggest nuclear buildup of any power in the world—in addition to its doctrine of "first use" is intended to deter and balance against India's conventional military advantages. Unfortunately it is potentially both destabilizing for the neighborhood and Pakistan itself. Pakistan's nuclear arsenal will be dispersed to ensure its survivability, but that also makes the dispersed devices more vulnerable to falling into the wrong hands, whether an outside militant group or a rogue element inside the Pakistani military. Pakistan's poor track record on controlling the proliferation of nuclear technologies is not very heartening. Rogue state nuclear weapons programs in North Korea, Libya, Iran, and Syria all benefited from Pakistani help.[10]

India worries about a second Mumbai-style terrorist attack from militants backed by Pakistan. A major incident with many casualties and Pakistani fingerprints would put a weakened Indian government under tremendous pressure to respond with force, with the attendant risk of nuclear miscalculation. A Pew Research survey in 2013–14 found that "Pakistan is seen as a greater danger to India than any of the other potential dangers included on the poll. Eight-in-ten Indians consider Pakistan a very serious threat to the county."[11] Afghanistan could become the focus of future Indian-Pakistani competition, particularly after the drawdown in US and NATO forces post-2014. Both countries want to deny giving the other a strategic advantage. For them, the world is still zero-sum, and any benefit one gets is seen immediately as a debit on the other side. Widespread distrust and the hedging strategies of all Afghanistan's neighbors—not just India and Pakistan—will make it difficult to develop a more cooperative relationship.

Increasingly China is driving India's threat perceptions, partly because of China's role in supporting Pakistan, but mostly because of China's increasing global and regional profile. Indian elites worry about the widening economic gap between China and India. Intensifying competition between India and China could lead to a great power conflict that would not be limited to the South Asian theater; it could draw in the United States and others.

For the *Global Trends 2030* work, I developed three scenarios[12] for the region and possibility of conflict, which still seem valid and a good way for framing future developments.

In a *Turn the Corner* scenario, sustained economic growth in Pakistan based on the gradual normalization of trade with a rising India would be a critical factor. An improved economic environment would give youths more economic outlets, lessening the attractiveness of militancy. Intraregional trade would be important in building political trust between India and Pakistan, slowly changing threat perceptions, and anchoring sectors with vested interests in continuing economic cooperation. A strong economic engine in India could lay down new foundations for prosperity and regional cooperation in South Asia. Over several decades, Pakistan would develop into a stable economy, no longer requiring outside assistance and International Monetary Fund tutelage. Suspicions of India would undoubtedly persist in military circles; even so, both nuclear-armed countries could find means to coexist in order to avoid threatening the growing economic ties.

Many experts see this scenario as unlikely, but we mustn't be too dismissive. We've seen some positive signs: with the May 2013 general election, there was the first civilian transfer of power following the successful completion of a five-year term by a democratically elected government. Despite the widespread violence during the campaign, voter turnout was 55 percent, the highest since the 1970s. This optimistic scenario is probably still a long shot, but it can't be ruled out. It would require sustained and more capable civilian government in Pakistan and improved governance, such as better tax and investment policies to spur new industries, jobs, and more resources for moderate education. A collapse in neighboring Afghanistan would probably set back any such civilian-led agenda, reinforcing security fears and retrenchment. On the other hand, Indian policies to open up trade and visa access with its neighbor could serve as a countervailing force, building up new Pakistani constituencies for reform.

In the *Islamistan* scenario, the influence of radical Islamists in Pakistan and the Taliban in Afghanistan would grow. Signs of growing influence of radical Islamists would include more broadly held extreme interpretations of sharia law, proliferation of jihad-oriented militant bases in settled areas, and greater control of local government by Islamists. As Pakistan became more Islamicized, the army would become more sympathetic to the Islamic cause. Consequently, the military would likely cede control of territory to Islamist insurgents and would be more willing to engage in negotiations with these Islamists.

In an extreme *Unraveling* scenario, all the destructive forces lurking in the region—such as weak government, large numbers of unemployed youths, and food and water crises—would come to the fore and result in the social and political fracturing of Pakistan and Afghanistan. India would be left trying to defend against the spillover of militancy, increased tensions in Kashmir, and potential radicalization of its Muslim populations. Despite large-scale assistance efforts, Afghanistan remains on the top of all the indices that measure risks for state failure. Even absent the bleakest scenario of the Taliban gaining control of some areas, militancy will be on the upswing as US and NATO troops withdraw and the economy will be worse off if the assistance tap slows down. It is well to remember that the Soviet-backed Mohammad Najibullah government in Afghanistan stayed in power for nearly three years after the Soviet exit, and the main trigger for Najibullah's fall was the Russian refusal to extend assistance after 1992.

**TURNING TO EAST ASIA,** surging economic growth, dramatic power shifts, nationalism, and aggressive military modernization—not just in China but in India and elsewhere—have amplified rather than diminished tensions and competition among the rising powers and with Japan. Owing to the unusual nature of the post–World War II settlement in Asia—and the persistence of conflicts on the Korean Peninsula and Taiwan Strait as a result of that settlement—historical grievances have festered and intensified in Asia. Fear of Chinese power, growing nationalism across the region, and possible questions about US staying power will fuel these tensions over the coming decades. Economic growth and interdependence have not diminished Asians' grievances, as seen in the difficult relations today between Japan-China, Japan-Koreas, China-Koreas, India-China, and Vietnam-China.

Regional trends probably will continue to pull countries in two directions: toward China economically but toward the United States and each other for security. Since 1995, Asian powers—including Japan, South Korea, Australia, and India—have gradually moved away from the United States and toward China as their top trading partner but have coupled growing economic interdependence with the continued "insurance" of close US security ties. This pattern will continue for the time being. However, should political liberalization in China—such as rule of law and more transparency on its military modernization program—then the region's security concerns would lessen, reducing the necessity for current hedging and reliance on the United States. Continued Chinese economic growth and Beijing's successful transition to an innovation-and-consumer-based economy could increase Beijing's magnetic pull on regional trade and investment, increasing China's status as the leading provider of Asian foreign direct investment. Alternatively, a serious or prolonged Chinese economic crisis would take the steam out of China's regional clout and reinforce latent fears about an unstable China.

As global economic power has shifted to Asia, the Indo-Pacific is emerging as the dominant international waterway of the twenty-first century, as the Mediterranean was in the ancient world and the Atlantic in the twentieth century. US naval hegemony over the world's key sea lanes, in this and other oceans, will fade as China's blue-water navy strengthens. This could beg the question of which power is best-positioned to construct maritime coalitions to police the commons and secure universal freedom of passage.

Four broad pathways for Asian order are possible during the coming decades:

1. A continuation of the present order that mixes rules-based cooperation and quiet competition between US and China with most of the other Asians in the middle. Continued US maritime preeminence and the US alliance system sustain a security order in which China's militarization, North Korea's nuclear mischief, and other potential security dilemmas in Asia are mitigated by the United States' current preponderance of power. Asian institutions continue to develop roots and economic integration continues to be oriented around a Pacific rather than an exclusively Asian axis. The biggest threat for conflict would be a minor military incident that escalates and gets out of hand, igniting underlying popular nationalistic fervor.

2. A balance-of-power order of unconstrained great power competition fueled by dynamic shifts in relative power and a reduced US role. A US retreat into isolationism or economic decline would increase perception of a weakening of the United States' commitment, such as its willingness to remain the security guarantor in East Asia. Such

a regional order would be "ripe for rivalry."[13] Some Asian powers might develop or seek to acquire nuclear weapons as the only means of compensating for less US security. This would be a worst-case scenario in which East Asia would be headed into potential regional conflict even on a greater scale than we see in the Middle East. East Asians have more of the needed economic and technological means for waging war on a deadlier scale than in the Middle East.

3. A consolidated regional order in which an East Asian community develops along the lines of Europe's democratic peace, with China's political liberalization a precondition for such a regional evolution. Such a pathway for regional order presumes that Asian regionalism will seek to preserve the autonomy of smaller Asian states. A pluralistic and peace-loving East Asian community would probably still require a role of the United States as the region's security guarantor. This is the least likely scenario at the moment with growing fears of Chinese power.

4. A Sinocentric order in which China sat at the summit of a hierarchical regional order presumes that Asian institution-building would have to change direction and develop along closed lines of Asian exclusivity, rather than through the open transpacific regionalism that has been the dominant impulse behind Asian community-building since the early 1990s. It's hard to see this scenario happening without China becoming much less threatening and building better bilateral ties to its neighbors.

Should India fail to rise or Japan to temper its relative decline, the Sinocentric order becomes more likely. Should the United States' core Asian partners possess less capability or willingness to balance the Chinese themselves, the United States may need to step up involvement as a counterbalance, risking a direct contest with China.

Besides a continuing US commitment to a strong role in the region, Chinese weakness is perhaps the biggest uncertainty. If Beijing gets caught in the middle-income trap and fails to transition to an advanced economy, it will remain a top-tier player in Asia, but the influence surrounding what has been a remarkable rise will dissipate. Under these circumstances, China may become a more aggressive power with the leadership trying to divert attention away from its domestic problems. A conflict with one of its neighbors or with the United States that China lost could also puncture its standing. On the other hand, a victory would increase the chances of a Sinocentric order.

WITH THE 2014 UKRAINE CRISIS, a return to conflict in Eastern Europe and Eurasia no longer seems remote. Most of the countries on Russia's periphery are relatively new, dating from the breakup of the Soviet empire, and contain significant Russia minorities. Because most empires in history have been polyglot and multiethnic, their breakups have tended to be marked by high levels of conflict. Inevitably, the new countries that sprout from empires contain mixed populations of ethnic or national groups that don't see eye-to-eye or have the same loyalties. The collapse of the German, Austro-Hungarian, Russian, and Ottoman empires after the First World War is reckoned by scholars to have laid the groundwork for the Second World War, in part because the countries carved out were weak and oftentimes fragmented and not able to stand up to Nazi and later Soviet aggression and domination. Even before the Ukraine crisis, there have been separatist enclaves in Georgia and Moldova that have sought protection from Russia in their fight for autonomy from the national governments. Within Russia, there are also a number of regions—such as Chechnya—where non-Russians outnumber Russians and conflict has been endemic. Overall, however, given the immense scale and the multinational character of the Soviet Union, it's a wonder there weren't more conflicts attending the breakup of the Soviet Union over the past couple decades.

The crisis in Ukraine is much more serious than the largely contained conflicts in Georgia and Moldova. Ukraine has all the ingredients for sparking civil war and broader conflict. Its public is almost evenly split in its loyalties between a Western or Russian orientation. Just as important has been the fact that Ukraine governments have been corrupt, with rulers interested more in self-enrichment than solving the country's substantial economic problems. It's no coincidence that the political crisis has coincided with an economic crisis. The economic crisis has opened the door to a growing role for dueling outside actors. Russian president Vladimir Putin needs Ukraine to establish his Eurasian Economic Union, while the Europeans backed by the Americans pushed an EU association agreement.

With the ouster of the Yanukovych government and Russia's escalation of tensions with the annexation of Crimea, the stage is potentially set for a slide into more widespread and violent conflict even though the Ukrainian military wisely did not try to fight Russians for control of Crimea. Other areas in mainland Ukraine have large numbers of pro-Russian supporters, especially around Donetsk, who have been encouraged by the Crimean annexation to stage protests. Those areas are more mixed, so demonstrations by either side have the potential to get quickly out of hand and turn violent.

Some Ukrainians and Western supporters have called for armed resistance against Russian aggression in Ukraine, which would likely expand the conflict. A 2011 study that examined 323 violent and nonviolent resistance campaigns from 1900 to 2006 found that the nonviolent campaigns succeeded 53 percent of the time, compared to a paltry 27 percent for armed struggles, even against similarly repressive opponents.[14] The research has also shown that armed resistance has historically delivered neither faster nor better results. It takes on average three years for a civil resistance campaign to run its course, in contrast to nine years for armed resistance. Additionally, any civil resistance needs to "attract widespread and diverse participation" to be successful.[15] Any successful movement by pro-West Ukrainian supporters against Russian actions therefore needs to be inclusive and nonviolent. A violent campaign that splits the country even further could be devastating and be the pretext for more Russian intervention.

As we've seen, once civil wars get started, they are hard to end, as violence feeds on violence. A civil war just on Europe's border would be hard to ignore. The United States and Europe have vowed against any military intervention, but, in the event of any growing violence, pressure would build for arming pro-West Ukrainians in addition to stationing troops in NATO countries like the Baltics and Poland, which directly border Russia. Soon the world could see the return of a cold war situation.

Russia, Ukraine, the United States, and Europe will need to find a face-saving diplomatic solution before violence breaks out and takes hold. But for any settlement to be long lasting, it will also have to deal with Ukraine's failing economy. Even though Russia has a lot at stake, Putin's vow to defend Russian minorities makes it difficult for him to back away from supporting pro-Russian forces without completely undercutting his political position. The Russian economy could take a terrible beating, particularly if sanctions increase and the West severs its economic ties. The damage may be already done if Europeans decide to diversify their energy sources, thus reducing their dependence on Russian imports. This could take years,[16] but an enduring crisis could be the spur.

There are larger global implications. Russian success in establishing a sphere of influence could end up being a tipping point toward the breakup of the world into regional blocs. It could encourage some in China's elite who want to make it the recognized leader in East Asia. A firm global effort—not just from the West—to counter Russian aggression is needed. I say global because it's striking that the opposition from emerging powers like China, India, and Brazil have been lukewarm to the Russian aggression. The US and Europe have to be careful that their actions don't alienate global support by appearing to be the only ones to set the standards for good behavior.[17]

BESIDES GROWING TENSIONS IN SEVERAL REGIONS, the other big factor increasing the chances of war is the wider availability of lethal and disruptive technologies. This gets us back to the first chapter on individual empowerment. We live in an age in which states no longer have the monopoly on being able to perpetrate killing or disruption on a large scale. The next 15 to 20 years will see a wider spectrum of more accessible instruments of war, especially precision-strike capabilities, cyberinstruments, and bioterror weaponry. The commercial availability of key components, such as imagery, and almost universal access to precision navigation GPS data is accelerating the diffusion of precision-strike capabilities to state and nonstate actors in the next decade or so. The proliferation of precision-guided weapons would allow critical infrastructures to be put at risk by many more potential adversaries.

This is a potential nightmare for the Middle East, particularly where there are multiple terrorist and insurgency groups. Imagine Hamas or Hizbollah with missiles that have a much better accuracy in hitting their targets. Even the United States with all its capabilities could be threatened. The proliferation of long-range precision weapons and antiship missile systems could pose problems to forward-deploying forces. It could discourage third parties from cooperating because of fears of becoming a victim of these precision weapons with greater lethal consequences. More accurate weapons could lead attackers to become overconfident in their military capabilities and therefore more apt to employ such systems. Precision may give attackers a false sense of their abilities to tailor attacks to create specific, narrow effects.

The threat of cyberweapons has been widely talked about. There is a lot of hyperbole about it completely changing the nature of warfare. Its threat is mostly in surprise and various levels of disruption. Potential cyberwarfare scenarios include coordinated cyberweapon attacks that sabotage multiple infrastructure assets simultaneously. One scenario would involve a case where power, the Internet, cash machines, broadcast media, traffic lights, financial systems, and air traffic software simultaneously fail for a period of weeks. The trends in cyberattacks so far suggest that although some computer systems are more secure than others, few if any systems can claim to be completely secure against a determined attack.[18]

For some attackers, cyberwarfare offers other advantages that have seldom been the case for most warfare: anonymity and low buy-in costs. These attributes favor the employment by disaffected groups and individuals who want to sow mayhem. So far the cyberweapons wielded by criminals and malicious individuals are unsophisticated in comparison to what state actors can deploy, but this is likely to change as criminal organizations become more adept and potentially sell their services to those state and nonstate actors with even more dangerous intentions.

The most famous cyberattack so far has been the Stuxnet worm that proved a setback, but only a temporary one, to the Iranian nuclear program. The Stuxnet worm had damaged the operation of approximately 1,000 centrifuges used in the enrichment of uranium fuel. By detecting the virus and removing the infected 1,000 tubes, experts believe the Iranians mitigated further damage. Some experts fear the most wide-reaching implication of the Stuxnet attack may be the potential for reverse engineering. The malware could be modified to attack any industrial control system—electrical power grids, oil refineries, nuclear power plants, or hazardous chemical plants.[19]

Terrorists for the moment are focused on causing mass casualties, but this could change as they understand the scope of the disruptions that can be caused by cyberwarfare or other emerging technologies like synthetic biology, discussed extensively in chapters 3 and 6.

As somebody who has had a career in intelligence, I am often asked about terrorism and where I see it going. Terrorism is an age-old tactic that will never disappear, but the current phase, with a centralized core al-Qaida running a far-flung network from hideouts in Afghanistan or Pakistan, was coming to an end even before Osama bin Laden's death in 2011. The killings of Muslims diminished the organization's broad appeal; the war in Afghanistan cost al-Qaida its initial base and forced it to move into the more difficult environment in the tribal areas of Pakistan; and US attacks killed many senior leaders and key operatives in addition to bin Laden. Al-Qaida affiliates in Syria, Iraq, Somalia, Libya, the Arabian Peninsula, and elsewhere who are more focused on local adversaries will continue to pose a threat. Shia groups such as Hizbollah see terrorism as a means of achieving their objectives. The current turmoil in Syria and Iraq is tailor-made for terrorist groups who want to establish de facto safe havens amid the upheavals. Unfortunately, the kinds of lethal and disruptive technologies widely and increasingly available to disgruntled individuals and small groups means that current and future groups will pose bigger threats in terms of the scale of disruption or destruction.

That said, many terrorist groups historically have ended up alienating many of their supporters. Most waves of terrorism last no more than 40 years. They usually overreach themselves by creating a flood tide of violence that often hurts their followers as much as the intended foes. Terrorist groups who form at the crest of each wave—as core al-Qaida did—usually dissolve before the entire wave does, which is where we might be. My worry is that growing turmoil in the region, sapping the hope triggered by the Arab Spring, will give it a second wind.

In 2012 when I wrote my last *Global Trends* forecast, I was cautiously optimistic that the reductions in the number and the casualties from conflict of all types would continue to be the trend line in the future. Conflict, including terrorism, was not going away, but a historic turning point was beginning to take hold. I am still optimistic about most regions. There is far less than a 50 percent chance that China will start a major war with one of its neighbors despite the increased possibilities for skirmishes and miscalculation. Too much is at stake, and I don't believe the regime—even one facing a more nationalistic public—wants to gamble with its future. However, the greater Middle East is of much higher concern, and the Syrian civil war lays the groundwork for a broader regional conflict, especially if there is also a nuclear arms race. With even the richer countries such as Saudi Arabia and the Gulf countries—facing more uncertain economic futures with growing oil and gas production elsewhere—the conditions may be ripe for a throw of the dice.

# CHAPTER 8

# *The Last Days of Pax Americana?*

THE D-WORD. IT STANDS FOR *DECLINE,* AND I WAS TOLD TO AVOID USING IT TO DESCRIBE THE United States in the *Global Trends* works. In the end, I could not avoid talking about relative decline. How could I avoid it? The last three versions all talked about an increasingly multipolar world characterized by rising powers. Since the 1950s, the United States has been gradually losing its share of world GDP. It stands at approximately 18 percent of world GDP measured in purchasing power parity. It went up slightly in the 1990s as US productivity and growth swelled with the IT revolution and budget cutting. After the Second World War, the United States held over 50 percent of world GDP, but the pie was much smaller. The fact that the US share is shrinking is a reflection of US success. The open trading system—which the United States erected upon the ashes of war-torn Europe and Asia—has benefited all.

Robert Kagan's famous article "The Myth of American Decline" appeared in the *New Republic* just as I was drafting the most recent *Global Trends* edition.[1] According to media reports, President Barack Obama read and was influenced by the Kagan article. At the State of the Union on January 26, 2013, President Obama stated, "Anyone who tells you that America is in decline or that our influence has waned, doesn't know what they're talking about."

The Kagan article has good points that I agree with. Just as Great Britain in its nineteenth-century heyday did not get its way everywhere and suffered defeats, so US failures in Iraq, Afghanistan, and elsewhere don't mean US power is completely draining away. Americans have periodically experienced a sense of decline and then managed to rebound. Will this be any different in the future? The antideclinist argues that the future is not going to be any different than the past. In Kagan's words, "The United States suffered deep and prolonged economic crises in the 1890s, the 1930s, and the 1970s. In each case, it rebounded in the following decade and actually ended up in a stronger position relative to other powers than before the crisis."

Japan's rise and fall is the classic case. I must have heard it a thousand times: Japan was thought to be on the verge of surpassing the United States in the 1980s and then it was hit with two decades of economic stagnation beginning in the 1990s. Japan's model of state-guided industrial policy no longer looked appealing. The waves of declinism are just that—peaks of frothiness on an otherwise endless horizon of ocean, or Pax Americana.

Somehow I don't think so: it is going to be different this time. I am quite comfortable with the formulation that the United States will be the "first among equals" of nations. But I don't think that equates to what most think of as Pax Americana. US leadership will have to reinvent itself to deal with a much-changed world.

There won't be any one domineering power—no Pax Sinica to replace the post–Second World War Pax Americana. I can easily see a strong and revived United States set among a constellation of other powers. Others can't imagine a multipolar world, believing that hegemons are needed to enforce international order. For them, a world without a hegemon automatically equates to disorder. However, if the United States tried to return to being a unipolar power, it would meet with strong resistance not only from newly emerging powers like China but also from its European partners, most of whom opposed the United States over Iraq in 2003. The kind of leadership required is new—something akin to herding cats. The number of players—nation-states and nonstate actors—has exploded. America is the only power that could attempt to manage such a multifaceted and multipolar landscape, but it is a far cry from domination or hegemony. Pax Americana—if it is to exist in the future—will have to be reinvented. From the point of view of the outsider, the ideal world is a Goldilocks world— one in which the United States is not too domineering, but one in which there is some manager who can herd the cats to avoid total chaos. It will be a hard act.

Perhaps counterintuitively, the scenario in which the United States is healthiest economically is the one where the rest of the world grows even more. For me this underlines the key point that the US economy and power will depend on how well others do. This is a far cry from a zero-sum world in which one power's strength depends on weakening others.

The game has changed, and this is a difficult point to get across. At times senior policy makers have pushed back hard on our analysis, saying the West can just absorb the emerging powers the same way Japan, South Korea, Singapore, Taiwan, and others who rose during the 1960s, 1970s, and 1980s were integrated and became part of the West. They did not ruffle many feathers nor change the basic structures of the US- and Western-dominated international order. Of course, in those past decades, it was a world largely split between the United States and the Soviet Union, and Washington was the clear-cut leader in the struggle against communism. It was a matter of two camps, and you were aligned with one or the other. The United States was the bulwark behind which the Free World could shelter. This bolstered US power.

I have found that younger audiences who are far from the Washington beltway get how much the global landscape is changing. Many are very pessimistic about the future. I remember discussing possible scenarios for the future with engineering students at Penn State in the fall of 2011 and being shocked at how gloomy they were about the world's prospects. They were especially down on Washington and the political system's ability to solve big problems. This was not a fluke. Other student audiences I've encountered also saw a bleak future. Pew Research Center found in a February 2012 survey that only about half of Americans believe their culture is superior to others, compared with six in ten in 2002. And the polling finds younger Americans less apt than their elders to hold American "exceptionalist" attitudes.[2]

I think the American person-on-the-street is on to something. However you cut it, the West will increasingly be in a minority and in a much more power-diffuse environment. The health of the global economy will be increasingly linked to how well the developing world does. Global wealth is shifting. In 2008, China overtook the United States as the world's largest saver. By 2020, emerging markets' share of financial assets is projected to double. Emerging markets will become a more important source of capital for the world economy.

The post–World War II era was characterized by the G7 countries— which were allies and partners—leading both economically and politically. US projection of power was dependent on and amplified by its strong alliances with Western partners, which were forged during an extensive struggle with fascism and then communism.

Looking ahead, regardless of the various realistic economic growth scenarios one can construct, the G7 overall will account for a decreasing share of total global military spending. The United States will remain the leading military power in 2030, but its ability to maintain near-current levels of defense spending is open to serious question. The trend for national defense spending as a share of the US economy has been downward for several decades. With an aging population and the prospect of higher interest rates in the future, the rising entitlement costs will consume an increasing proportion of the federal budget without major reform of the programs or substantially increased tax revenues. The G7's historic military superiority over others will diminish.

Nevertheless, because of shared values, Europe is one of the most critical factors for the United States. This is not a typical American point of view. So many in the US foreign policy elite discount Europe, criticizing it as old and tired, less able to be a good partner for the United States.[3] Starting out as a Europeanist in my professional career, I may have a better appreciation of what is at stake for us and them. Certainly Europe faces multiple challenges. Even before the recent euro crisis, the European Union was suffering an identity crisis, with opinion growing more negative since. Sixty percent of Europeans tend not to trust the European Union, according to a 2013 poll—a drastic increase compared to the 32 percent level of distrust reported in early 2007.

Almost half of all Europeans said that they were pessimistic about the future of what is now a 28-nation bloc, up from a quarter in late 2007.[4]

Nevertheless, I would make the case that Europe is very important for future US interests. A weak Europe will make it less likely that the United States' post–World War II idea for international liberal order can be maintained as the world becomes more and more multipolar. By contrast, a strong Europe that shares many of the traditional US values on multilateralism would bolster those chances.

It turns out that talking in European capitals about whether Europe is in decline is almost as controversial and sensitive a topic as America's discussion on its own future. I was at one meeting in Brussels where the discussions got heated and some denied that Europe was in any kind of decline at all—relative or absolute. Others—including many Europeans at the meeting—saw Europe playing less and less of a role in the world.

In all this doom and gloom, leaders in Washington were surprised when European leaders pressed for free trade negotiation in late 2012—the so-called Transatlantic Trade and Investment Partnership, or TTIP. In part Europeans were worried about a US tilt completely away from Europe. The Obama administration had announced a "pivot" to Asia in October 2011, which involved, besides a small military redeployment, a redoubling of effort on negotiating a Trans-Pacific Partnership (TPP) with twelve Pacific Rim countries, including the United States. With Japan's recent accession to the negotiations, it is estimated that future agreement would cover 40 percent of current world GDP and one-third of total world trade. With a US-European TTIP, together they would cover nearly half of world GDP and another third of global trade.

The two sets of negotiations with the United States in the middle show the United States' ability to be linchpin for both Europeans and many Asians fearful of China's rise. The fact that TPP involves broadly asymmetric market openings—significant concessions that involve more economic and political pain for Asian countries than for the United States—shows that Asians want to anchor the United States in Asia. Equally, TTIP, if it is eventually agreed, will probably involve European concessions, testifying to their commitment to the transatlantic partnership.

For transatlanticists on both sides of the pond, there is a feeling that TTIP presents a last chance for bolstering the ties as we enter into a whole new historic era of greater multipolarity and increased Asian clout. As Bruce Stokes,[5] a longtime transatlanticist and international economist, has written: "A decade from now both trade and investment ties with Asia may well outweigh those across the Atlantic. American and European companies will be ever more deeply imbedded in China, India and Southeast Asia. Their interests will lie in Asian technical norms and regulatory practices. . . . TTIP will ensure that Western values and regulatory principles—transparency, due process, accountability and the rule of law—prevail in the promulgation of the new rules of the road for the 21st century economy. It is the assertion and strengthening of these norms of democratic capitalism that could prove to be TTIP's most enduring legacy."[6]

All of this bodes well for US leadership in the world, if handled carefully. The dual negotiations could help anchor an open liberal trading system, particularly if TPP and TTIP lead to a new global trade negotiations, which are currently stalled. Alternatively, if this doesn't happen, they could then reinforce the growing trend toward more regionalism and fragmentation of the globalized system. In particular, if TPP and TTIP are used to try to isolate China—instead of incentivizing it to participate in an open system—then I think they will be failures and, more importantly, dangerous, throwing more fuel on the fire of rising tensions in Asia. Under most scenarios, China is slated to become the central player in world trade and the largest trading partner of most countries in the next couple of decades. China has negotiated or is in the process of negotiating free trade agreements with many its neighbors as a way of parrying US efforts with TPP. Without some reconciliation between the various US, European, and Chinese regional arrangements, US and European firms could end up being discriminated against in the Chinese market. Firms from Asian countries with free trade relations with China would have the advantage.[7] Fortunately, Chinese interest in joining TPP is on the increase. The leadership may see TPP as a way of pushing through the reform agenda of the economy.

The prospect of a fragmented global system is a real threat, and a growing one if US power slips too much. I've emphasized the changing international environment that makes it dangerous for the United States to try to operate as a unipolar power. Turning the tables, a United States that is too weak and turns inward is also a threat to stability and could lead to an equally dangerous outcome. This was a worry everywhere I briefed *Global Trends*, even in China and Russia. One senior Chinese official summed it up this way: "After the end of the Cold War, there was too much of a euphoric atmosphere and the United States went too far in the unipolar world. As a Chinese saying goes, when you go to the peak, you will go down."

Whether the United States comes down the peak gracefully or far too precipitously is important in others' eyes. The keystone of national power for the United States remains its economic strength and innovation. Much rides on where the United States would be economically in 15 to 20 years. For that, we looked at two potential scenarios for the US economy in *Global Trends 2030*. In the optimistic scenario, the United States would address its structural weaknesses, including falling education standards, skyrocketing health-care costs, and fiscal deficits and debt. Outside the United States, the euro zone would remain intact, eliminating one of the major threats to US recovery in the short to medium term. Continued prosperity in emerging market countries, where at least 1 billion people will be added to the world middle class by 2030, could play to US economic strengths. These newly empowered consumers will be avid for education, entertainment, and products and services driven by information technology—all goods the United States excels at producing. Moreover, as a global technological leader, the United States could be boosted by innovations in medicine, biotech, communications, transportation, or energy. Under an optimistic scenario, the US economy would grow steadily at about 2.7 percent a year on average, up from 2.5 percent during the last 20 years. US growth would reflect both solid labor force growth and technological advances. Average living standards would begin to rise again—almost 40 percent in this scenario—fostering social mobility even though the relative size of the US economy in the world would decline. Trade would still shift eastward; though its growth would slow significantly by 2030, China would be the largest trading partner of most countries.

There are a lot of buts and real concern about our ability to live up to the potential of this upbeat scenario. In early 2014, there is growing optimism fueled by the US energy boom, but the recovery has been long and unemployment still elevated. For me, the most troubling is the sagging educational achievement. From being on top at the end of the Second World War, American students placed at only 31 out of 65 countries in mathematics and 22 in science in a survey that includes developing countries. The US educational advantage has been cut in half in the past 30 years. Without large-scale improvements in primary and secondary education, future US workers—whereas past workers have benefited from the world's highest wages—will increasingly bring only mediocre skills to the workplace. This is very worrying because US workers with or without high-level skills are probably going to face increasing competition from low-wage workers overseas and the new technological innovations like robotics and IT automation that are killing even high-level jobs (see chapter 6). Without the best possible educational and vocational education, workers are entering the new competitive global workplace with one hand tied behind their backs.

A starkly different picture emerges—both for the US and the international system—should the US economy not fully rebound and growth in the United States slows significantly below the 2.7 percent average in the optimistic scenario. Weaker international trade as well as spillovers from likely US domestic crises would slow growth in other countries. Slower growth would hold down US living standards. The US middle class has already experienced stagnant income growth for the past couple decades. In this scenario, the middle class would be pulled down even further. Although the United States may not be in absolute decline in this scenario, most Americans and many observers would perceive America as falling down, making it harder for the United States to lead. In this scenario, there is no doubt in my mind that America would turn inward and isolationist.

The optimistic scenario of a reinvigorated US economy would increase the chances of the United States remaining engaged in the growing global and regional challenges. Using a completed TTIP and TPP, Washington could lead to a new global trade round, strengthening the rules to govern the international trading system. A stronger United States would be in a better position to deal with an unstable Middle East and prevent the slide of failing states elsewhere. The more outward United States could continue to act as security guarantor in Asia where the rise of multiple powers—particularly India and China—could spark increased rivalries. However, a reinvigorated United States would not necessarily be a panacea. Terrorism, WMD proliferation, regional conflicts, and other ongoing threats to the international order will be affected by the presence or absence of strong US leadership but also driven by their own dynamics.

The impact would be much more clear-cut in the negative case in which the United States recovery falters. In that scenario, a large and dangerous global power vacuum would be created, and very quickly. With a weak United States, the potential would increase for the European economy to slow. Progress on trade reform as well as financial and monetary system reform would probably suffer. A world of inward-looking trading blocs would be more likely.

In this negative scenario, the United States would be more likely to lose influence to regional hegemons—China and India in Asia, Iran in the Middle East, and Russia in Eurasia. As we've seen, tensions are already high in the Middle East—Sunni against Shia and Israel against Iran—increasing the prospects for open conflict. This would be a world reminiscent of the 1930s when Britain was losing its grip on its global leadership role.

A stronger United States will not be impregnable. Just as a CEO keeps his job by disentangling and preventing crises, the United States as first among equals will be expected to manage the international order to keep it intact. The accent here is on "managing" in the sense of rounding up others—as befits the increasingly multipolar context—to help with stemming destabilizing crises and anticipating untoward developments. Of course, events are unpredictable: one is reminded of the response of Harold Macmillan—British prime minister after the 1956 Suez crisis—to a journalist's question about what is most likely to blow governments off course: "Events, dear boy, events." Suez—which brought down the Anthony Eden government and brought Macmillan to power—was a perfect example of a history-shaping event.

As a global manager, the United States has a big problem with the number of regional situations that could go awry, particularly, too, as some scholars believe we may have reached a tipping point where the world is becoming more violent. Political scientists who have studied violent conflict believe there was less of it in the last 25 years than might have been expected. The shift to new governments, for example, after the breakup of the Soviet Union was mostly peaceful. However, with the lack of peaceful settlement in Syria or Crimea, we may be seeing a new pattern develop.[8] Just as the more peaceful disputes that were resolved had a certain momentum over the last couple of decades, if the lack of peaceful settlements becomes a trend, expectations will also decline about the ability of the United States to resolve disputes.

At the moment the bar is still pretty elevated, with most of the world having high expectations of the United States to solve the world's problems even if America's capacities may begin to slip. Should Asia replicate Europe's nineteenth- and early-twentieth-century past and become a region divided by power struggles and rivalries, the United States would be called upon by many—including potentially even a rising China—to be a balancer to ensure regional stability. All countries would want and need stability to ensure their continued internal development. Potential crises that could occur in the next couple of decades—such as Korean unification, Sino-Japanese confrontation in the East or South China Seas, or a China-Taiwan conflict—would lead to demands for sustained US engagement at a high level. Asia is a region with a large number of unresolved territorial and maritime disputes, especially in the East and South China Seas where dueling claims could easily escalate with growing interest in exploitation of valuable seabed resources.

Other obvious regions requiring some sort of supervision from the United States include the Middle East, Eurasia, and South Asia. More likely than not, there will be more serious military conflict in one or the other of these regions in the next decade or so. One can easily imagine widespread calls for strong US leadership to stave off an open Indian-Pakistani conflict, defuse a nuclear arms race in the Middle East, or reverse Russian or Chinese incursions in Central Asia. Middle East governments—particularly Gulf Arabs and Israel—worry about a United States less interested in their region because of growing US energy self-sufficiency. The United States won't be in a position—if it ever was—to intervene everywhere. It will have to figure out which situations present such vital interest that there is no option but to intervene to preserve global peace and security. Too little intervention could be as bad as too much.

Humanitarian crises—particularly those involving the need for US lift and intelligence capabilities—will also help ensure demand for a continued

US role. Environmental disasters are likely to become frequent and more severe; as a result, the US military assets will be in greater demand. Providing technological solutions for growing resource scarcities and in some cases spearheading diplomatic arrangements for better sharing of existing resources such as water could be prime areas for US management of the international order. US success or failure in managing these crises will directly affect the world community's perception of US power.

Historically, US dominance has been buttressed by the dollar's role as the global reserve currency, which De Gaulle called the United States' "exorbitant privilege." The end of the British Empire was propelled by the United Kingdom's bankruptcy as the Second World War came to a close. The future is probably not going to be as dramatic or catastrophic for the US dollar, but it can't be ruled out. Unless the United States and China get into a conflict and China takes a huge financial loss and dumps its over 1 trillion holdings of US Treasury bills, the more likely scenario is an increasingly multipolar arrangement with the dollar as one reserve currency but also flanked by the Chinese renminbi and the European euro.

Nevertheless, the fall of the dollar as the dominant global reserve currency and growth of a much more multipolar system would be one of the sharpest indications of the decline of the US global position. Professor Barry Eichengreen—the expert who has studied the question of the dollar's future most closely—believes "a change in the international monetary order is all but inevitable within a decade."[9] He believes Chinese banking authorities increasingly have their eyes on making the renminbi into a convertible and reserve currency. This involves more than lifting capital controls and building more liquid financial markets; it means a government that is more transparent and rules-bound. This means the Chinese would have to get serious about rule of law, which is a goal set by the Party's recent Third Plenum. Despite the necessity for far-reaching structural reforms on China's part, Eichengreen nevertheless believed even several years ago that China was committed: "It has an agreement with Brazil to facilitate use of the two countries' currencies in bilateral trade transactions. It has signed renminbi swap agreements with Argentina, Belarus, Hong Kong, Indonesia, South Korea, and Malaysia. It has expanded renminbi settlement agreements between Hong Kong and five mainland cities, and authorized HSBC Holdings to sell renminbi bonds in Hong Kong. The Chinese government issued in Hong Kong about $1 billion worth of its own renminbi-denominated bonds. All of these initiatives are aimed at reducing dependence on the dollar both at home and abroad by encouraging importers, exporters, and investors to make more use of China's currency."[10]

In October 2013, the European Central Bank and the Chinese central bank agreed on a currency swap mechanism, facilitating commercial exchanges between the eurozone and China. According to the Bank of International Settlements, the renminbi had become in late 2013 one of the top ten of the most exchanged currencies in the world, whereas in 2004 it was only in thirty-fifth place.[11]

Change to a global reserve currency can happen more quickly than is generally assumed. As late as 1914, the dollar played absolutely no international role. Instead, London was the world's banker even though the US economy was already twice the size of Britain's. The United States lacked the market infrastructure needed for the dollar to play an international role, which changed in 1914 with the creation of the Federal Reserve System. In setting a goal for Beijing and Shanghai to be global financial centers in 2020, the Chinese are trying to make the renminbi a global currency sooner rather than later.[12]

How quickly or slowly greater financial multipolarity happens will also be a function of US domestic actions. During the 2013 political storms about congressional decisions to raise the US debt ceiling, there was widespread concern that the US government was risking the dollar's status. Others have not quite lost confidence, and with the Chinese renminbi not being widely convertible and Europe's recovery lagging, there aren't a lot of other places for investors to put their money. Despite US banks being the cause of the 2008 Great Recession, US Treasury bonds and equities are seen as a safe haven. However, as options increase elsewhere, the United States may pay a higher cost for its political misbehavior.

In that vein, the nonpartisan US Congressional Budget Office projects that federal debt would reach 100 percent of US GDP in 2038 unless some measures are taken—either cutbacks in entitlements and health-care costs or increased revenue.[13] However, even before we get to 2038, without something to set the budget on a better trajectory, investors and buyers of

T-bills are likely to get anxious. Interest rates would rise, compounding the problem of reducing deficits and the debt. This is the nightmare scenario America needs to avoid. It is all the scarier as no one knows at what point investors lose their patience; at that point it might be impossible to put Humpty-Dumpty back together without major disruption to our way of life and position in the world.

There is one final scenario we should consider, and one that if we were sitting in the early twentieth century we would think of as the obvious outcome. Just as the contest between Britain, the superpower of its day, and a rising Germany helped trigger the First World War, so too are the United States and China destined to go to war. Many Chinese believe that however much America's designed liberal international order has made it possible for China to rise, the United States will pull the plug and not allow China to be an equal. Some political theorists worry that both the United States and China are passing through difficult inflection points that will increase bilateral tensions and lead to conflict. In their calculations, Chinese power is still increasing, but the rate is slowing. This is most evident in their slowing annual economic growth rate, still high at 7 to 8 percent by Western standards, but off its peak from the last couple of decades.

If the previous period of accelerating power led to confidence, decelerating increases may invert the trend, leading to fear. Rather than keeping its head down in pursuit of economic growth, China may become more assertive, seeking for its power to be recognized. Many observers have been puzzled by China's aggressiveness against its neighbors, reversing what had been the dominant trend preached by Deng Xiaoping in his famous 1990 statement: "We should keep a low profile and bide our time."[14]

The United States is also passing through an inflection point, having difficulty recovering from the recent recession in addition to experiencing setbacks overseas in Iraq and Afghanistan. Some commentators worry that the Obama administration's 2011 pivot to Asia will help set in motion an antagonistic, escalatory cycle of mounting tensions.

My own view is that we are nowhere near a point of no return. Since the pivot, the Obama administration has held a successful Sunnylands Summit with Chinese president Xi Jinping in June 2013, in which the two presidents agreed to the idea of building a "new type of great power relationship."[15]

Yale professor Paul Kennedy, foremost expert on great power rivalry in the pre–World War I era, wrote an article in the *New York Times* that contrasted today's international scene with 1914: "All of these Great Powers (today) are egoistic, more or less blinkered, with governments chiefly bent upon surviving a few more years. But none of them are troublemakers. . . . They all have a substantial interest in preserving the international status quo, since they do not know what negative consequences would follow a changed world order."[16] Putin comes closest to trying to change the status quo, but in May 2014 he appeared increasingly conscious of the economic consequences of a total break with the United States and Europe.

How much time does the United States have to reinvent itself as a different kind of global leader? The good news is that America has a second chance. There is no replacement out there. Europe wants a strong partnership and is not in any competition with the United States. Russia is struggling to maintain its influence in its own region, and though it would like to be treated as the coequal of the United States, it is falling behind in opening up. India and Brazil will be stronger regional powers, eventually casting a much larger shadow on the world stage, but are not comprehensive global powers. China is the only emerging power that could aspire to global stature with the United States and Europe, but as we have seen, it will be more focused on domestic developments.

The question for the United States is whether it wants to remain a global power, pursuing global interests in the belief that what will benefit the world the most is also good for long-term US interests—the way it bet on a recovering Europe and Asia in the 1950s. Or will it be content with being a great power—one still very powerful but less capable and less interested in molding a new international order? This is what the declinist debate doesn't really get at—what the power is for. If the purpose is to hold onto the status quo, it probably won't work. If it is to remold the international system to take into account the greater diffusion of power, then that could mean continued global leadership, albeit different from the role we have been used to in which we set all the rules of the road.

What would a reinvented US-led international system entail? A much more aggressive effort to remake the multilateral global institution. A first step would be to give the rising powers more say in the international system. The United States and Europe together have an effective veto power, for example, in the IMF, even though the economic power has shifted. China is a major bilateral assistance donor, reportedly extending more loan commitments than the entire World Bank, but China has little clout. Time after time I heard complaints during my talks about the lack of legitimacy of these international organizations in the eyes of many younger citizens of emerging states.

For the United States to be in a position to reinvent the international system, it would also need to reinvent itself. Domestic politics have always been an important factor shaping international outcomes. A divided United States would have a more difficult time of shaping a new role. A strong political consensus is a necessary condition for establishing the basis for greater US economic competitiveness. And equally, the revitalization of US economic strength is the irreplaceable foundation of any sustainable international strategy.[17]

What would happen if we don't try to reinvent ourselves and the current international system? Most likely greater fragmentation—a world of regional blocs—which would make it harder to deal with the global challenges. There are already signs it is going in that direction. Nearly two-thirds of European trade is within the European Union; NAFTA represents more than 40 percent of total US trade. East Asian intraregional trade is 53 percent; excluding Mexico, Latin American intraregional trade is roughly 35 percent and growing rapidly. As we saw, China will be the dominant trading partner for Asians. Investment flows between developing countries, also known as South-South relations, are also growing as a driver of international financial activity.

With shale gas and oil, the United States has the possibility of becoming almost energy self-sufficient, making the United States—unlike China—relatively independent in terms of critical resources. Public opinion shows increasing aversion to an activist role: according to a recent survey by the Chicago Council on Global Affairs, 38 percent of Americans want to stay out of world affairs, the highest share since 1947, and the figure rises to a majority among young Americans who came of age during the Iraq and Afghanistan wars.[18]

**THE PRESENT RECALLS PAST TRANSITION POINTS** when the path forward was not clear-cut and the world faced the possibility of different global futures. There are parallels between the current period and the European "long peace" after 1815 set in motion by the Congress of Vienna. Similarities include a period of rapid social, economic, technological, and political change and an international system that is largely multipolar. The Europe of 1815 consisted of a diverse set of autocracies like Russia, Prussia, Austrian and Ottoman Empires, and liberal states such as Britain and France. In such a world, Britain occupied a special role: it managed to play an outsize role despite its lack of overwhelming power capabilities—in 1830, Russia and France were roughly the same size as Britain in terms of GDP, and by 1913 the United States, Russia, and Germany all had larger economies. Its global financial and economic position and empire, role as offshore balancer in Europe, and protector of commercial sea lanes linking its overseas dominions and colonies gave Britain the preeminent global role in the international system during the nineteenth and into the twentieth centuries.

The current multipolar system is also very diverse, with an even larger number of players (think G20) across the whole world—not just Europe—and international economics and politics is much more globalized. In 1815, coming out of over 25 years of conflict, the great powers had conflicting views that they did not disguise, particularly at home. The Holy Alliance of Russia, Prussia, and Austria sought to fight against democracy, revolution, and secularism but ended up finding it hard to coordinate collective efforts; in any event, their efforts proved only effective temporarily as revolutions and separatist and nationalist movements continued across Europe throughout the length of the nineteenth and into the twentieth century. A long, general peace among the great powers prevailed, mostly because no one wanted to risk imposing its will on the others for fear of the larger consequences. Equilibrium was achieved in part because of the differences.

Britain's stabilizing role outlasted its demise as a first-rate economic power and, despite the rise of several competing states, it stayed preeminent in part because the others were reluctant to wrest leadership away from it until the First World War. For the United States, the challenges of trying to manage such a complex, diverse, and increasingly dynamic international system are so much more immense. Still, the United States has better tools, more past successes, and wider admiration for the strength and diversity of its society. Leadership in navigating the new shoals of a post-Western world will be the key to whether a new kind of Pax Americana is born and takes hold.

# PART III

# *Alternative Worlds*

WE'VE GROWN ACCUSTOMED TO A NARRATIVE THAT SAYS THAT THE WORLD, THOUGH PRONE to more crises, is still in manageable shape. The world we wake up to tomorrow will be somewhat different but recognizable. We're still on a continuum that stretches back at least to the eighteenth-century Enlightenment: we believe progress is the order of the day. Sure, the twentieth century gave us some nasty scares, when we thought all was lost. But the victories against imperialism in the First World War and fascism and communism in the Second World War and Cold War, while keeping us in suspense, showed that the forces of Good will always win out. Our faith in progress was vindicated. I still hope in my heart that this is the case, but I don't think we can be 100 percent sure anymore. Too many of the megatrends are dual-edged, harboring the seeds of destruction as much as progress. Even if there is global progress, it might not be the progress we are comfortable with—like progress that leads to a less dominant West. Despite the recent shocks and surprises, it's still hard to imagine anything different happening other than just incremental change.

Hopefully the stories in this section will end that complacency. Not all the imagined changes in this section are bad; some are good. But we should have learned from all the surprises and shocks over the past decade or two that the unthinkable happens more often than we think. What if nuclear war occurs? What if we wake up to a real revolt of the middle class? What if bioterrorism gets out of hand and a pandemic occurs? What if the United States and China establish a truly "new type of great power relationship" instead of talking about it, as the two presidents did at the 2013 Sunnylands summit?

# CHAPTER 9

# *The Enemy of My Enemy Is My Friend*

JAMIL KHOURY WOKE ONE NIGHT IN A COLD SWEAT, SUDDENLY REALIZING WHAT HE HAD done. He had always considered himself a peace-loving man. Having grown up in Lebanon, he had seen what war had done to his country, and he would not have wished its war-torn fate on anyone—even his enemies. But now it looked as if he would be responsible for a new outbreak of war and a possible nuclear war at that.

He could not get back to sleep. He thought of his family's honor and how what he had done would forever besmirch it.

The glow from the sun crept in through the shutters. In a panic, he decided to get the next flight to New York. He had to go and see his friend Lars. Maybe he could help.

He spent the time on the flight going over the past. In the beginning, all he had wanted was to become a medical doctor, which had also been his parents' ambition for him. His grandfather had been a highly respected doctor, and Jamil had wanted to emulate him in every sense. Jamil had gone to the famous Jesuit medical school in Beirut and afterward to Paris to do his residency at the Pitié-Salpêtrière hospital. He wanted to be a cardiac surgeon and was attracted to its tradition of excellence in cardiac treatments.

Lebanon was still recovering from its civil war and many of his relatives had fled the chaos. As his residency was winding up, Jamil began to think about his future. He really did not want to go home—in fact not to the Middle East at all. But he could not stay in France. He applied for several jobs at Paris hospitals but lost out. The competition for these positions was fierce, but he suspected discrimination although he was never able to prove it. He once brought his concerns to one of his favorite professors who dismissed his suspicions, arguing that "there were plenty of Arab doctors in France. There are just too many good candidates for the available slots."

Jamil was offended. He wasn't just another Arab; he was a Lebanese Christian Maronite. Hadn't France been their protector since the days of the Ottoman Empire? It was also a huge blow to his personal plans. Jamil had been going out secretly with a Moroccan Jew. Myra's very wealthy family lived part of the year in Morocco, the other part in Paris. Myra was petite and pretty. But more than her looks, it was her wit that attracted him. Even over the phone, he could see her eyes sparkle as she recounted the latest idiocy in her office—a very chic advertising firm. But they had to be careful. Her family strongly disapproved.

If he left Paris, he would lose her. They talked one evening after his job options were exhausted. She admitted that she didn't want to leave her job or Paris. She was apologetic but unswayable. "I won't go abroad. I won't start over. Anyway, I hate the Middle East."

He didn't argue. He knew what the challenges would be for her as a Jew and did not want to be responsible for separating her from her family. He did not want to leave either. But how would he practice his profession when there were no positions for him? They vowed to stay together, but both knew it was a lost cause.

His family had a long history in Saudi Arabia. His grandfather had known Jack Philby—the father of British spy Kim Philby—when Jack Philby headed the British Secret Service in Palestine and his grandfather was a surgeon in Jerusalem in the early 1920s. Some thought it strange that Philby used a French-speaking Maronite doctor when there were British or Jewish doctors available. But Philby was known to be anti-Jewish and also suspicious of his fellow Brits. Jamil suspected his grandfather had been a spy for French interests when the British and French were rivals in the Middle East, but his grandfather never admitted anything—even in his dying moments.

His grandfather followed Philby to Saudi Arabia and soon became one of Ibn Saud's physicians while Philby was his political advisor, effectively betraying British interests. By the time Jamil was born, his grandfather was very old and still living in Saudi Arabia. Unlike Philby, he never broke with the Saudi royal family and even after he retired remained on friendly terms with them.

After leaving Paris, Jamil used those family contacts to establish himself as a doctor in Riyadh. Most of his patients were in the expat community. In the beginning, he was dreadfully homesick for Paris, but after a while he began to enjoy the expat lifestyle. He was reasonably well off and the work was not too hard—nothing like the long hours he had worked in Paris.

He married a fellow Lebanese who came from a venerable Christian Maronite family, part of the Lebanese diaspora that had moved to America in the 1970s. He met Soraya when she visited some American friends in the expat community.

Soraya was very American despite the family's Lebanese roots. She spoke Arabic badly and hardly any French. But he was desperate to belong and Soraya was his ticket—or so he thought in the beginning. On the surface, he often appeared standoffish when he was just shy. She was popular with the kind of people he hoped to attract as patients.

She did not seem to have given much thought to why she was marrying him. The expat lifestyle in Riyadh resembled life in Florida. It was one big round of get-togethers and parties, punctuated by shopping trips to the Gulf or, when one had a chance, Paris or London. Maybe Soraya didn't have any better options in Florida? She certainly wasn't searching for her Middle East roots.

Two years later their daughter, Adeline, was born. He wanted a son, but Soraya told him that she had her hands full already and did not want to get pregnant again. He still hoped to change her mind. That was at the back of his mind when he planned a trip to Paris.

He decided to treat Soraya to a stay at the Ritz in Place Vendôme. Their first evening in Paris, he went down to the lobby to get some cigarettes. There, he was approached by a well-dressed man in his forties.

"How are you, Dr. Khoury? I'm sure we've seen each other in Riyadh or Jeddah?" The stranger spoke quietly and in English.

Jamil responded in French, "Monsieur, are you quite sure?" Jamil had become fluent conversing in English with his wife but still preferred French. He had been soaking in the atmosphere and was rather put out to be interrupted.

"Your grandfather served my grandfather, as I recollect," the stranger said with a smile.

Jamil was suddenly intrigued. He had been thinking a lot lately about his grandfather and the whole Philby connection. He muttered a barely audible, "Oui, peut-être."

The stranger said, "Your family proved their loyalty and we are grateful. We need your services again. Meet me tomorrow at midnight in the bar. Don't bring your wife." The stranger turned just as Jamil was about to reply.

Jamil did not give it much thought that night. He planned to accompany Soraya on her shopping rounds next day. They were getting on better. For once, she appeared focused on him. After dinner they were curled up on the bed when one of her American friends called. Soraya was still gossiping with Sally an hour or two later when Jamil remembered the stranger from the night before.

It was close to midnight when the stranger reappeared in the Ritz bar. As he entered, Jamil heard the maître d' address him as *Prince*. There were one or two other customers there but more than enough space to have a private conversation. The prince began by saying that he had had his eye on Jamil for some time.

"You're well known in the expat community, not only as a good doctor but as a bit of a *bon vivant*, as the French say. I saw you enjoying yourself at the US ambassador's July Fourth party."

"That was business. Many of my patients are Americans."

"You must like Americans?" the prince asked.

"I have to. My wife's family relocated to the States during the Lebanese civil war. What about you?" Jamil replied, trying to turn the tables.

"They are not very dependable anymore," the prince said. "You must know the history. Your grandfather was here at the start. Jack Philby was British but he was more like an American agent, sneaking in the American oil interests behind London's back. FDR gave his word that he would protect Saudi Arabia, and presidents down the line have been equally committed— at least through the Bushes."

At that point the prince eyed a pretty woman entering the bar. He turned back to Jamil and said very softly, "Would you do a favor for me? Don't answer me now and don't act as if we know each other well. I'll come to your office."

By the time the now traditionally dressed prince came to his office back in Riyadh, Jamil almost had forgotten the earlier encounter. The prince began by asking if the American ambassador was his patient.

"Yes, he has come here for special consultations; he has…well, he has a heart condition."

"Yes, we know that. I want you to get him to talk on political subjects."

"Spy on him?"

"If you like. Get him talking. I think we both share some concerns about America. They didn't help you much in Lebanon."

"We don't talk much substance. He's from Florida and my wife's relatives live there, so we chat about the lifestyle there, golf courses, et cetera."

The prince started for the door and, turning, said, "You have spying in the blood. Your grandfather wasn't just a doctor. He learned the trade with the best of them. I am sure you have it within your powers."

Jamil did not know what to say. He hadn't expected the comment about his grandfather and it wounded him. The prince knew more than he did about his family. But later that day, he remembered thinking, *How can I refuse? He's quite powerful.* In a sneaky way, he also welcomed it. The prince's comings and goings could be good for business.

As it happened, the American ambassador did have an appointment in the next couple of weeks. Later, Jamil realized, the prince must have known.

On the surface, Gerald Jackson seemed like most US ambassadors at big posts. They were appointed, not for any special affinity for the country they were sent to, but because they had donated a six-figure sum to one or the other US political party. Ambassador Jackson had in fact made a fortune in real estate development in Florida and was a longtime fundraiser for the Democratic Party. But Gerald was different. He came from a long line of missionaries who had toiled in the Middle East, mostly Lebanon. His father had sided with Secretary of State George Marshall when he argued against US backing for the creation of Israel in 1948. Jackson's grandfather and father had both sent letters to President Harry Truman warning that US support would forever alienate the Arabs. Gerald kept this under wraps, fearing such knowledge could undermine his position in the Democratic Party. His business interests in South Florida also dictated silence. But he strongly believed that US foreign policy had shortchanged the Arabs. Israel's side was taken too often over that of the Palestinians.

Gerald was also special in that he had turned down the ambassadorship to Tehran, the first ever since 1979. Many of his acquaintances couldn't fathom why he would want Riyadh instead. There was real excitement in America about the new ties with Iran. Iran had helped settle the Syrian civil war and was also helping to stabilize Afghanistan. The nuclear agreement whereby Iran opened the door to inspections of all its nuclear facilities was convincing Western powers that it was abiding by its promise not to enrich weapons-grade uranium. Iran was the United States' new partner, and both Riyadh and Tel Aviv felt the United States no longer cared so much about their interests. Their resentment was exacerbated by the hard economic times in those countries. US oil exports were bringing down the price of oil, causing austerity in Saudi Arabia. Iran had to withdraw a lot of its financial support for Hamas and Hizbollah to gain US recognition, but Israel believed Iran was still supporting them covertly. US officials no longer wanted to know. Gerald sensed that the Saudis felt betrayed, and he tried to make Washington see this, but it was becoming more difficult.

Gerald had spent some of his youth with his missionary parents in Lebanon before he was sent off to boarding school in the States, so he genuinely liked and understood Jamil. He found it easy to talk to him. But recently he had heard that Jamil was associating with the head of Saudi intelligence. News circulated quietly among the expat community, and the prince's visit to Jamil's medical office did not go unnoticed. Gerald was curious about what Jamil was up to.

The ambassador walked in late for his appointment and apologized. Jamil came out to greet him, asking how he had been feeling. Gerald ambled along beside him, answering Jamil's questions in his southern drawl. "It's hard to keep to a normal schedule, you know. My days are too packed."

Gerald decided to see if he could bait Jamil. "You get out and about in high Saudi society. Do you know Prince Faisal?"

"Yes," Jamil said nonchalantly. "I saw him at a reception a week or so ago. Why do you ask?"

"He's dangerous. They say he's close to the king."

"He was very friendly."

"Not to Americans as much."

"Are you sure? I thought everybody loved Americans."

Without thinking, Gerald launched into a detailed discussion of his latest political concerns. "Both parties are at it, particularly the youngsters who know nothing. They're asking why we should be protecting the sea lanes so China can have secure access to Mideast oil. They don't know any history. Half of them don't travel these days. I can't remember the last time I had a congressional delegation in town. It's as if they think they can turn their back on the Middle East. For this new generation, 9/11 is a distant memory, and with no real terrorist attacks on US soil since, they don't see any need for the United States to concern itself with far-off developments in foreign countries."

Jamil interjected, "But surely this is a blip? Aren't Americans proud of their role in the world? All the blood, sweat, and treasure you have spent here. Why walk away?"

"I had such hopes when I came here," Gerald said. "I've been trying to update our mutual defense agreement with the Gulf states, but it's an uphill battle. Washington doesn't seem to care." He paused. "I wonder if you'd talk to one of my colleagues about Prince Faisal? He's got some concerns like I do."

Jamil reluctantly agreed.

JAMIL TOOK AN INSTANT DISLIKE TO Bill Daniels when he walked in and found him sprawled on the examining table.

Jamil cleared his throat. "I thought I'd act as if I was really sick so no one would suspect," Bill said. He took out a slim spiral notebook. "I won't beat around the bush. I want you to tell me everything you know about the prince. And could I see his charts or whatever medical records you have on him."

Jamil suddenly stood very erect. "I can't compromise my patient's privacy." *The arrogance*, he thought.

Bill said quietly, "OK, let's start again. Whatever you can tell me would be most appreciated. We're concerned that the prince seems to be acting rather bizarrely. He is now refusing to see any US officials. We're wondering if there is a medical reason. We're told he's been angry at work. It's odd because we could have sworn we saw him in Paris a couple weeks ago with a known Israeli agent."

"Well, I don't know any Israelis," said Jamil defensively.

Bill said, "Really? I thought the ambassador said you were in Paris too."

"Just for pleasure."

"Well if you can tell us anything, we'd like to hear. You know you're popular with the American community. And somebody told me that your wife's folks are Americans."

Not long after that, Jamil was visited by the prince again and he related what the ambassador had said.

"You've been a great help. I guess espionage does run in the family," said the prince. "I have more tasks for you. You need to find an excuse to get away for a couple days. Go to the airport next Sunday at 10 o'clock. You'll be met at the Air France desk."

"Can I tell my wife?"

"No. Make up a story. Say you have to go and see a patient in Dubai or somewhere."

Jamil remembered thinking, *Is this really me?* But the distraction from his increasingly boring life was too tempting.

The guy who met him at the Air France desk was very gruff. "You're on the next flight to Paris. Book yourself into a small hotel, none of your fancy ones. Here's the cell. Remember to ring this number. No, I'm not giving you the slip of paper. Memorize it. Once you ring on the cell, throw it away. Pay in cash. No credit cards. There's to be no record of this trip."

Several hours later, Jamil was in a taxi on his way into Paris.

It was good to be back—and on his own. He stayed on the Left Bank in a very small hotel close to his old hospital. Eventually he rang the number. A voice gave him the name of a café he fortunately knew because the meeting had been set up to happen in 15 minutes.

Entering through the revolving doors, he must have looked lost.

A waiter asked, "Vous cherchez quelqu'un?" But before he could answer, a man with heavy dark features approached and motioned for him to follow.

After a few minutes it was clear they were headed into the Luxembourg Gardens. Finally, the man slowed down and turned. "Do you know who I am?"

Jamil replied, "I don't have the faintest idea."

"Good. I work for the Israeli Ministry of Defense. That's all you need to know. This is very dangerous, but the prince and I need a go-between. I have some messages for the prince you must take back. In the future when you are sent on trips, you'll get a call that tells you where to go. You will find something there that you take back."

"Why did you choose me?"

"You're not Israeli; you're not Saudi; you're not Iranian. And you're a doctor. You can go undetected where others can't."

The trips went on for a year or so. Jamil knew Soraya suspected something—probably an affair. He reassured her as best he could, but he could not seem to stop.

Toward the end of the year, Bill Daniels called again and asked him about the prince. "We're worried you're getting in over your head. Saudi politics is a lot more convoluted than you think."

"He's good for business. We met once in Paris and he struck up a conversation. Why is that so significant?"

The questioning went on for some time. Jamil finally told him he had a patient waiting.

"All right, but this isn't the end of it."

Bill didn't actually think Jamil was hiding much. Maybe he was having an affair in Paris. It was just so improbable that Jamil was a spy. He had told the ambassador that if he was working for the prince, the last thing the two would do is meet in Jamil's office. US intelligence knew all the spies run by the prince. There was no Lebanese—let alone a Lebanese Christian—on the prince's payroll. Bill had a lot of experience dealing with ambassadors who did not know much about intelligence, but most did not try to second-guess him. This was getting irritating, because Gerald Jackson wouldn't drop the subject.

Thinking back to this point in the story on the airplane, Jamil realized that it was only then that he began to get worried, but also more intrigued. The cloak and dagger was becoming an aphrodisiac.

A week later, he got a telephone call from the prince for the first time ever, telling him to fly to Paris the next day.

He started to shake. Why had the prince called on an open line? The Americans probably tapped it. He would be walking into a trap.

He sat up all night, watching old French movies. Soraya and Adeline had already gone to her parents for the Christmas holidays. At least they were safe.

He left the next day for Paris fearing he might not get back home. The cryptic message he got just as he was leaving Riyadh was to go to the Luxembourg Gardens again. It was cold but sunny, and the park was full of Parisians wrapped up in heavy coats, scarves, and mittens, sitting in the sun. He suddenly wished himself back to his student days.

As instructed, he waited, freezing in the shadows by the Fontaine Médicis. He saw no one that bore any resemblance to his earlier contacts. Anger began to well up inside him. And fear. Suppose this was a hoax? Maybe the Americans are watching.

He started pacing, when he heard a quiet voice just behind him.

"Calm down. Don't act so nervous. We'll be spotted." He turned and saw a diminutive but good-looking middle-aged woman with a silk scarf peeking out from underneath the collar of a mink-trimmed coat. She looked like just another upper-crust Parisian taking a shortcut across the Luxembourg.

He was speechless at first but then blurted out, "Do you have it?"

She spoke in French—"Oui"—as she tugged at his sleeve to make him lean down and kiss her on both cheeks. "Don't be too brusque," she continued in French. "Imagine we're former lovers bumping into each other after a very long absence." She motioned to some empty chairs in the sun. "Why are you so nervous? No one can hear us."

"How do I know that you're the person I am supposed to meet?"

"What a funny way to address an old love."

Jamil could feel his heart rate slow. Speaking French—which he rarely did anymore—made him relax.

She lit up a cigarette and offered one to him.

"Could you tell me…what this is all about?" Jamil finally got up the courage to ask.

"You mean you don't know?"

Jamil stiffened.

"I'm going to break the rules. I can see you really don't know, which I find charming. You remind me of my seven-year-old son—totally winning, but somewhat naïve. We're in the endgame. This gives your masters, the Saudis, all they need to make the final decision. We know they fear the Iranians more and more and are struggling without a lot of success to develop their own nuclear weapons. The Americans don't want the Saudis to go nuclear. The Saudis have little option now but to try and destroy the Iranian program. Helping the Saudis is a risk on our part. But we don't have many options. We can't be totally without friends in the world. And the enemy of my enemy is my friend. They'll know how and where to attack. We've been giving them the intelligence. It's a little like the Suez Crisis in '56 when Israel colluded with Britain and France to attack Egypt. That time, the US stepped in and stopped it. This time around we're hoping the Americans won't get a chance. I'm sure you think I'm some sort of hard-line militarist. I used to be a liberal, fighting for rights for the Palestinians. But a nuclear Iran dominating all of us is something else. Ganging up on Iran gives us a chance of building bridges to the Arabs."

As they parted, she slipped a small package into Jamil's pocket. He had almost forgotten about it.

Jamil was very nervous as he went through passport control and then security. During the flight back, he ordered several drinks. He was not a drinker, but he never felt more desperate. At home, he took a sedative and fell into a deep sleep. But he could not escape forever. He awoke in a cold sweat to see the sun rising.

It was clear to him that the Saudis and Israelis were colluding to attack Iran. How could he prove to others what was happening?

There would probably be a cryptic message on his answering machine letting him know where to leave the stuff. He thought about taking the thumb drive to the Americans, but he did not want to put his family in the States in any sort of jeopardy. He was afraid Bill Daniels would try to use them as leverage against him.

While he was thinking through his options, his cell rang. The voice on the other end said, "No time to waste. Meet me at the usual place in an hour."

He did what he was told. But he also got his assistant to book him a ticket to New York.

**IT WAS HARD NOT TO LIKE LARS ERIKSSON.** If Jamil epitomized the glass half empty, Lars was definitely the glass half full. In fact, early in his career, Lars saw the future as a cup brimming over. His parents were both development economists and took Lars along on their trips to Africa. Lars saw the pervasive deprivation firsthand but was struck by the gradual progress. His parents had been deep into the 1960s peace movement, protesting against the US war in Vietnam. And for the rest of their lives, they remained highly critical of everything American, a bias that Lars rebelled against as he grew to be a teenager. Coming of age in the '90s, Lars saw the United States save Europe's bacon in Bosnia. He wanted so much to live in the United States, believing it to be the coolest place in the world. America had produced globalization, which was doing everybody a world of good. Annika, his future wife, fell in love with his sunny disposition. They tried having children but finally opted for adoption. At that time Sweden was accepting refugees from war-torn Iraq. He and Annika immediately decided to give a home to a boy and girl who had lost their parents at the very start of the US invasion.

Lars was working for an NGO that sent teachers to Africa and was about to go himself when the foreign ministry contacted him. They needed people who knew the NGO world and could act as liaisons to them out in the field. Sweden had a program for developing Saudi Arabia's technical universities and Lars was the perfect choice for coordinating it. With his engineering background and NGO experience, he linked up Swedish professors with the Saudi universities and helped the Swedish professionals relocate. Lars enjoyed the work, but otherwise found the ministry and many of his colleagues stuffy and cynical.

With their two children in hand, Lars and Annika arrived in Riyadh when things appeared to be looking up for the region. The economic outlook had started to improve and *wham!*—the Arab Spring came and lifted up everyone's expectations, only to see those hopes dashed with the civil war in Syria and the return of authoritarian rule in Egypt. But there was still a school of thinkers, including Lars, who saw the new turmoil as a temporary regression. The middle classes were growing; the democracy seed had been planted. It was just a matter of time.

As a young second secretary in the Swedish embassy in Riyadh, Lars managed to find some kindred spirits. There were rumblings inside Saudi Arabia; the younger generation, especially women, yearned for greater freedom. Everyone had to be careful, but Lars and Annika got to know some like-minded young Saudi couples.

Lars met Jamil when his father-in-law had fallen ill with chest pains on a visit from Sweden. He credited Jamil's speedy action and diagnosis with saving his father-in-law's life, and they began to see each other socially. Annika and Soraya got to be fast friends, but Lars thought Jamil rather cold and distant, holding in a bundle of conflicted feelings. Lars once asked him his opinion of the Middle East, and Jamil had replied that it was ungovernable. Having no history of ruling itself, it needed an outside force to maintain the peace, whether it was the Ottomans, the British, or Americans. "But when they do try to help, we spurn them. Too much pride. Someday, the Americans will get fed up with us, the same way we are about ourselves."

Lars was repelled. How could Jamil say that about his own culture?

After several years in Riyadh, Lars was reassigned to the UN. He coordinated one of the teams that inspected Iran's nuclear facilities. It was such a change for him. In the Riyadh embassy and other embassies he had served, he had been well respected. There was a protocol if not an esprit de corps that the diplomats had shared even when they sparred with one another over policy. Now, he was treated like just another UN bureaucrat. The big powers ordered him around—telling him what his job *really* was. If he tried to suggest a new policy to them, he was told that he was interfering in the sovereignty of a member state.

At times he had to stand up to the member states by arguing there was no evidence of Iranian violations. At one point, he got into a shouting match with the Israeli ambassador, who accused him of ignoring the writing on the wall. At the same time, he was convinced that Iran was hiding something. And it had become more and more difficult to get the permissions for the team to inspect the more dubious sites. He had gone to the Americans and British but could not get them to press the Iranians. They had no wish to repeat the mistakes of Iraq.

The Israelis, Saudis, and others were extremely unhelpful. They wanted to use the inspections for their own spying purposes. He had caught several members of his team slipping sensitive intelligence back to their home governments. He knew that the Iranians suspected the team of underhanded spying and that probably explained part of their increasing hostility to the inspections.

**JAMIL LANDED IN A SNOWY NEW YORK.** The next day Lars greeted Jamil warmly at lunch. "How's Soraya? You must be joining her in Florida?"

"Yes, I hope to. But I need to talk to you."

"Is there something wrong? You're still together?"

"Yes, yes. It's not that," said Jamil. "It's something more serious." Jamil decided to just blurt it out. "I got mixed up in something dreadful. I've been spying for the Saudis. Actually the Saudis and the Israelis."

Lars practically dropped his drink. "You what?" And then he smiled, as if the idea of working for such strange bedfellows was rather amusing. "How did you manage both? That's quite an achievement."

Jamil didn't see the humor. "It started as a sort of lark. I was flattered that this Saudi prince engaged me."

He stopped to catch his breath. "The last few weeks have been hell. The last Israeli agent told me that they were colluding with the Saudis on an attack plan against the Iranians. She said it would resemble the Suez Crisis except with a new twist. Israel has a new partner—the Saudis. She hoped the United States would just allow scores to be settled. She also intimated that the Israelis knew the Saudis were struggling to develop nuclear weapons, but did not care."

Lars looked across the table. "You're quite sure what she said. Do you have any proof?"

"I don't have the thumb drive."

"We have our suspicions about what the Saudis are trying to do, maybe with Pakistan's help. But we can't prove anything. And there is no way we could get permission to do any inspections. I've been wondering about the Israelis. Several years back they were all over the Americans to attack and destroy the Iranian facilities. They seem to have given up. I hadn't put two and two together. I don't know how to proceed. The Saudis, Israelis, and even the United States will block anything in the way of inspections or investigations in either Saudi Arabia or Israel. If I had proof, it might be different."

After lunch, Lars headed back to his office on the thirty-eighth floor. He stared out of the window at the East River. He was glad most of the staff had left. He would not have to put on a brave face. He had no doubt that Jamil had stumbled on the truth.

**AS IT TURNED OUT, IT WAS TOO LATE** to stop events anyway. The Saudis attacked on Christmas Day. The Israelis—who originally hadn't planned to join in the attack—followed the next day with an air attack on various Iranian military and civilian installations that the Israelis suspected were being used to develop nuclear weapons. The Israelis learned that the Iranians knew about Tel Aviv's collusion and now realized there was nothing to lose by attacking. The attacks were devastating. Initial casualties ranged upward to 40,000 as a direct result of exposure to chemically toxic substances. This did not include the destruction from the radioactive fallout that contaminated an important supply of water, condemning millions of Iranians to an increased rate of bone cancer as well as a significant rise in birth defects for decades, if not centuries to come.[1]

The US Fifth Fleet was mobilized, and a US ultimatum was directed at Israel and Saudi Arabia to cease their attacks, which all sides disregarded. US leaders went into high gear putting together a coalition of nations to put additional pressure on the combatants, but the fighting still did not stop. The United States began withdrawing its naval forces to avoid getting entangled in any crossfire. US supporters of Israel condemned the administration's harsh rhetoric against Tel Aviv, but public support for intervention completely evaporated with Iran's decision to use nuclear weapons. The Saudis had counted on being protected against such attacks by its missile defense shield. However, Iran succeeded in overwhelming the system with a nuclear-armed missile—showing the Iranians actually had an advanced weapons program—plus several conventional ones got through. With the withdrawal of many US military forces, which had helped run the missile defense system, it was easier for the Iranians to penetrate. One of the missiles disabled Aramco's giant oil processing facility at Abqaiq, sending the price of a barrel of oil skyrocketing to over $400.

Israel's defense shield largely protected the country against incoming Iranian missiles, although Hizbollah and Hamas succeeded in perpetrating several devastating terrorist attacks in Haifa and Tel Aviv.

It took over a month to get a cease-fire in place. By that time, total victims on all sides were in the hundreds of thousands.

Over the next two years Lars saw his world crumble before his eyes. America virtually turned its back on the Middle East and started building a firewall against spillover. Russia and China turned out to be the saviors, and Moscow particularly stopped the fighting the old-fashioned way: Russia threatened to fire missiles at whoever did not abide by the cease-fire. Moscow always thought the United States did not know how to use its power. China backed Russia because it was dependent on Middle East oil and was increasingly worried about the impact of continued fighting on its economy.

But the US withdrawal did not stop there. For many Americans, the best thing was to shore up the defenses and become truly independent. Yes, trade could continue in NAFTA and even parts of Asia, but America washed its hands of the Muslim world. Transatlantic ties suffered because Americans worried about the potential terrorist threats from disaffected European Muslims. Lars had to fight to get visas for his Iraqi-born children.

Some Americans protested the lack of support for Israel, but public opinion blamed Israel for starting the war. The administration released documents showing that Washington had begged Israel to cease hostilities. The pictures of scores of Iranian civilians dying, along with the contamination of Iran's water supplies by the initial Israel and Saudi attacks, had soured public support for Israel. Many Israelis countered that the United States forced the offensive on Israel. Washington had ignored evidence that Iran had restarted its nuclear weapons program. A lot of Israel's talented workers were moving abroad, tempted by opportunities elsewhere but also to get away from unstable conditions. Workforce participation in Israel was way down. Efforts to integrate Israel's two fastest-growing communities, Arabs and ultra-Orthodox Jews, were failing, and the economy was in a slow decline. Israel faced a choice of either seeing the region slowly coming under Iranian influence or trying to force America's hand with the hope of getting Washington back in the game of managing the Middle East.

When Gerald Jackson heard the news of the initial attacks, he was beside himself. But Bill Daniels shrugged his shoulders. He thought Iran had it coming and could not see the larger ramifications of the conflict.

Gerald had been right. The Saudis had felt betrayed for some time. The coup de grâce was certainly the US decision to restore ties with Iran. Economically Saudi Arabia also wasn't doing too well. Many working-age Saudi men were not very interested in working. Before the war, the price of oil was on a downward trajectory with the increased supplies coming from America. Saudi Arabia was no longer the only producer that had spare capacity. The United States was now in that position. Before, the United States had to come to Saudi rulers before they did anything drastic to make sure the Saudis would use their spare oil capacity to calm markets. As sanctions against Iran tightened in 2012, Iranian oil exports were hit, but Saudi Arabia's increased production kept oil prices steady. The Saudis no longer had that power over the United States.

The Europeans were caught off guard by the US decision. Center Left parties initially favored trying to enforce a cease-fire but then switched and decided the only way to save the social welfare state at home was to remain neutral. If Europeans got engaged, there would be endless resources going to enforce a fragile peace without help from the United States. Right-wing parties made an even bigger U-turn and began siding with Russia's policies of fighting fire with fire. The Chinese were desperate to restart the flow of oil. With the United States drawing back from policing the sea lanes in the region, the Chinese navy began to send armed convoys to the Gulf to pick up the needed oil supplies. They brought in Chinese workers to take over and restart the Aramco facilities. The Chinese workers were given protective gear but years afterward started to develop radiation-related cancers. Other Asians who were also dependent on Middle East oil were very grateful to the Chinese. Only the Japanese felt threatened, as they feared a big boost in Chinese influence throughout Asia.

For Lars, the bitterest irony was the fact that no one anywhere was now a supporter of a nuclear zero world. Instead, nuclear arms proliferated. Japan wanted them in case of a surprise attack from China. Russia sought more to bolster its power; China and India felt they had to keep up.

Lars heard that Jamil volunteered to work in the radiation ward where they were treating the victims of Iran's retaliatory attack. Soraya told Annika that Jamil had insisted that she and Adeline stay in Florida.

The United States had frozen Saudi funds, so Soraya could not access the bank account Jamil and she had kept in the States. It was also impossible for Jamil to wire money to his wife's family because the Saudi government had put on capital controls.

Soraya said that Jamil's practice had been destroyed with the departure of the expat community. He was coming under suspicion. There had been a shakeup in the royal family and the prince had been purged. Most Lebanese were unwelcome now for fear they had Shia connections. Shia were considered the fifth column, and Jamil had heard some horror stories about how Shia in the Eastern Province were being treated.

Soraya had started working as a clerk in the Palm Beach branch of Hermès. Her father had lost a lot of money in the stock market crash and was having a hard time supporting them all. Some of the customers were rude to her when they found out she had lived in Saudi Arabia. Adeline had gotten into trouble donating money to a refugee relief fund. The FBI turned up and accused her and her family of supporting a terrorist group. Soraya finally convinced the FBI agent that it was just an innocent mistake. She told the agent that Adeline was missing her father, but she wasn't so sure that Adeline hadn't fallen into bad company. She found her increasingly texting in Arabic.

**A YEAR OR SO AFTER THEY HAD** seen each other in New York, Lars got a letter from Jamil, asking him if he remembered their earlier conversation about the Middle East. He had admired Lars's optimism, but even before the war felt Lars needed to face facts. Jamil had learned the hard way. His whole life had been spent trying to break the mold and it hadn't worked. As a young man, he had hoped to practice not in his own country but in Paris and marry someone not of his faith or background. He was initially happy in Saudi Arabia, seeing it as a second chance. Many of his expat patients respected him for who he was, not what tribe he came from nor religion he adhered to. But the expat community lived in a bubble. The failure of his marriage brought home to him the impossibility of bridging the cultural gap with his Americanized wife. Oddly enough, despite the devastation, he now felt liberated. It was clear where everybody stood. He enjoyed his work in the radiation ward. His patients really needed him. The only real regret was not seeing Adeline. She was safer in America, but he missed her. He hoped she would do a better job of reconciling the cultural divides within her and achieving inner peace.

Lars's anger grew as he read. These people! Why did they have to be so fatalistic? If only they could learn to live together. It took some time for him to calm down, but he resolved not to give in to pessimism. The world would get better again. He was sure of it.

CHAPTER 10

# *East Is East and West Is West*

I WANT TO PUT DOWN ALL THAT I REMEMBER ABOUT THOSE WEEKS BECAUSE I AM
practically the only witness. It's not like the Cuban Missile Crisis where
President Kennedy was surrounded by his advisors. Rich and his Chinese
counterpart had to do everything in secret so their advisors would not know.

I once asked Rich, "Why can't you talk about this to Jacobs?" He told
me, "If I talked to him, he would try to derail what is a historic opportunity
for America. Besides, I didn't appoint him. I just inherited him. He isn't *my*
advisor."

But I'm getting ahead of myself.

It all began with an e-mail sent to my private Gmail account. It said:

"Madam, we have never met. I am the Chinese President and an admirer
of your husband. Tell me how I can talk to him secretly. Don't tell anyone
about this message. Please reply to the attached link without your name."

I was sure it was a hoax and showed the e-mail to the security officer on
my staff. She thought that my Gmail account may have been compromised.
She promised to investigate further and said that in the meantime I should
just not respond.

That e-mail was the last thing on my mind when I talked to Rich that evening. The Indo-Pakistan crisis was exhausting him. There had already been a number of terrorist attacks in India that were attributed to Lashkar-e-Tayyiba, the Pakistan-based terrorist group. The Indians were accusing the Pakistani government of being behind the attacks. Rich was worried that the Indians were about to take some drastic action, which would end in an all-out conflict that could go nuclear if the two sides did not dampen tensions. The next day an old school friend sent me a message, saying that she needed to talk to me urgently. I had known Cindy since college, but we were never close until she, Richard, and myself ended up doing a master's course at Johns Hopkins' School of Advanced International Studies, or SAIS.

Cindy was the person who got Rich interested in politics. His parents wanted him to be a banker. But Rich was more interested in policy making. He thought SAIS would open the door to a job in the World Bank or IMF. Cindy got him an internship on the Hill in her father's office. A staunch Republican, but not Tea Party (as the conservative wing used to be called), Congressman Leiter was the ranking member of the House Foreign Affairs Committee. Cindy was far more liberal but still managed to stay in his good graces. She convinced her father he needed an up-and-coming, bright Latino on his staff. Cindy's father took Rich on and they actually bonded.

That's also how Rich came to be Republican. I remain a Democrat. In the early days of our marriage, we argued continually over politics. Rich always maintained the Republicans had a better record on foreign policy, despite Bush, Cheney, and the ill-fated mistakes in Iraq. For all their social enlightenment and activism on civil rights, Rich thought the Democrats were rather timid and without many fresh ideas in foreign policy. They just wanted the status quo or to stay out of foreign relations altogether, which was impossible for a great power like the United States. He admired Nixon and Kissinger for the opening to China, which was the subject of one of his courses at SAIS.

Cindy kept in close contact and gave us needed advice as Rich built his political career. Through her father and his cronies, she got a lot of notice for Rich. Rich actually succeeded Cindy's father in his Wyoming seat. We lived out there for a while to establish residency and to avoid being considered carpetbaggers. It wasn't the easiest transition. I'm not a Westerner by any stretch and Rich was also out of place. But I liked to do volunteer work, and Rich took a job in the state government luring in new businesses. We were fish out of water, but we fell in love with the West.

Once Rich was elected, I stayed in Wyoming. Our kids went to the local schools in Cheyenne. It wasn't until they were older that we moved the family to Washington. Holidays were still spent in Wyoming.

Cindy always carried a bit of a torch for Rich. She helped get him chosen for the Campbell presidential ticket, knowing the Republican leadership wanted a Hispanic to balance his WASP-ishness. Tony Campbell was also on the mature side—close to 60—when he ran. Rich was the picture of vim and vigor by comparison.

When Tony suddenly died, Cindy also helped out. By that time, she had married one of Washington's big time lobbyists, Ken Cooper. Most people thought Cindy was the brains behind Ken's operations. She certainly proved herself in the months after Rich became president. Rich wanted to get rid of a lot of his advisors. Cindy counseled against that. Rich was reluctant to take her advice. I had to convince him. And every time one of them screwed up, Rich threw it back in my face. But Cindy thought that if Rich disbanded Tony's circle of advisors, they would all end up working against him and mobilize others in the Republican Party that did not think Rich was "one of them." I agreed.

Cindy rarely called us on our private line, but she did later the day I got that odd e-mail. She told me that Bob Sinclaire needed to talk to me and the president. Bob had been Rich's mentor and Rich had him around occasionally along with other professors to ask their advice on foreign relations. Bob had supervised a Chinese student who was a year or two behind us; that student, Chen Lanxin, was now president of China and trying to contact Rich.

After putting together the pieces, I pulled Rich aside before an event we were hosting in the East Room.

"Rich, Bob Sinclaire is desperately trying to reach you. Cindy says it is important. She called this afternoon."

"He probably wants some kind of endorsement for his book."

"Cindy wouldn't have called if it wasn't important. I haven't told you, but I got an e-mail supposedly from the Chinese president wanting to set up a back channel."

"Why didn't you tell me?"

"I thought it was a hoax. In fact, I showed it to security and she thought it might be some kind of prank or worse."

Later that night, Rich called Sinclaire from the private quarters. Bob said he would come over right away and show Rich the original message he got from the Chinese president. It said: "I desperately need your help. My military is demanding a fight and wants me to align with Pakistan and encourage a war between Pakistan and India. I know you don't want war but your advisors and Congress won't want you to cooperate with China. We must act together. How can we talk?"

"Do you think it's genuine?" Rich asked.

"Yes, I've kept in contact," Bob replied. "He's very direct, as you can see. He's got a lot of pressures on him. When he first came to America, he didn't have a very good grasp of English. He was a little too worshipful of his professors. I supervised his thesis so he sees me as a father figure. He's confided in me a lot over the years. He greatly fears what's happening internally in China. It's interesting. He devoutly believes in the superiority of Chinese civilization. We've had endless discussions on how the West has stolen 'history.' He believes most historians have ignored the achievements and discoveries of other civilizations."

"What do you think?"

"I think that may be true for him and his generation. But younger Americans put much less store in the whole Western thing. I can remember when the West was equated with the Free World. Now there are so many places that are free and much more exciting than America. Kids don't think much about the distinctions between East and West."

"I know," Rich said, "the old categories no longer apply. We really don't see ourselves as that different."

"I wouldn't go that far. That may be the ideal. But the Chinese—at least Lanxin—believe the Chinese are still the underdogs. They want to be modern—have everything America has or what in their mind they conceive Americans have—and yet preserve Chinese civilization too. It's an impossible dream. He's worried they may blow it again. After all, he did a study of nineteenth-century China—the so-called century of humiliation. His thesis was quite important in changing his thinking."

"How so?"

"He started with the same old ideas—how the West exploited China, beginning with the Opium Wars and the concessionary treaties."

"Wasn't that the case?"

"Well, yes. While there was no excuse for the way the British, Americans, Germans, Russians, and Japanese treated the Chinese, he blamed the Chinese for being too wrapped up in themselves. They hadn't seen what was happening around them. Or when they did, it was too late. Rather than face up to modernization, they exploded against it like the Boxers in the late nineteenth century. Lanxin fears this could happen again. In one sense, you have to be on the cutting edge in order to keep the past alive and that precious Chinese civilization.

"Lanxin is complicated. His father was a Red Guard who went around the countryside smashing vestiges of traditional Chinese culture but ended up working in a museum preserving ancient Chinese bronzes. His family thought Lanxin married beneath him. He keeps his wife in the background but is deeply in love. What do you want me to tell him, Mr. President? Do you want to talk to him?"

"Absolutely! But I'll have to think about how to do it. Tell him I will get back to him."

Over the course of the next days, Bob Sinclaire was besieged with cryptic e-mails, which he was careful to hand deliver to my niece, Sylvia, who happened to be taking his course at SAIS. Sylvia could easily slip in and out of the residence. She was considered as part of the family.

It was at this point that I actually urged Rich to talk to Jacobs, the national security advisor. But my husband was adamant that he first wanted to explore what Lanxin had in mind. "Once I bring Jacobs and the others in, they will want to shut it down."

"Jacobs is your national security advisor. If you don't trust him, why are you still employing him?"

"Everybody thinks I don't know a thing about international relations. I need to keep the Party happy. Jacobs gives them confidence I am doing what

Campbell would have done. Jacobs distrusts China—big time. He thinks they want to be top dog. He would see this as a Chinese trap."

Richard was always correct with Jacobs. He always asked his opinion. But I knew my husband, and that outward politeness disguised disrespect. He was actually gruff but only with those he trusted. Rich lost whatever respect he had for Jacobs after he convinced Rich to receive the Dalai Lama just before we were to host the G30, including Lanxin. Rich felt he owed it to Lanxin to hear him out, if nothing else.

I was a bit more skeptical, but Rich told me, "There was something genuine about the messages. I just sense it. Besides, Sinclaire trusts him."

I wasn't convinced.

"Well, Lanxin is an old SAIS classmate," Rich joked, "even if we didn't know him at the time."

I rolled my eyes. "I know several of our old classmates who I wouldn't trust at all. And you wouldn't either."

Rich laughed. Once he got an idea into his head, he rarely swerved. "I need to find a way of talking to him. I'm counting on you to come up with an idea." He smiled. I could see he was under enormous pressure.

I know other first ladies have been strong and courageous. But I'm not sure they had to hatch the plot like the one I came up with. Months later, Rich would tease me and say that I had read too many spy novels. I said I was just keeping up with tradition and recounted the famous anecdote about Kissinger's scheduler having to keep three different diaries in order to hide his China trip from some of his closest colleagues and the secretary of state.

I told Rich I had it easy. I didn't have to find an excuse for Rich to go to China. The Chinese president was coming to New York for an emergency session of the UN's Security Council. Rich was going too. But Rich couldn't go anywhere without somebody accompanying him—or could he? Dr. Philips—Sy—was the president's personal doctor and a good family friend. Sy had been my mother's doctor, tending her to the last. Rich was so impressed, he brought him into the White House. I knew he could be trusted. Sy had accompanied the president on any number of trips for the express purpose of dealing with possible medical emergencies. Having him around wouldn't send up a flare.

Rich went straight from Air Force One to the UN Security Council. The Chinese president had arrived the day before and was already in the council chamber. I knew the session would drag on into the night and fortunately it did.

Around midnight, Rich excused himself, saying he was feeling tired and a bit unwell. He told the US ambassador that he was going back to the Waldorf where we were staying. When Rich got there, he asked one of his staff members to telephone Sy. He came up to the residence and went into our bedroom, presumably to examine Rich.

"Sy, there'll be trouble if this blows up. You'll be seen as an accomplice. I may not be able to protect you."

"I understand. I'm doing this for you and Marsha. Besides, few doctors get to do cloak-and-dagger stuff. I'll be able to tell my grandchildren. I mean years from now when it's all right to talk."

A few minutes later, he came out and said he wanted to take the president over to New York Presbyterian for some tests. He was worried that the president may be suffering from an irregular heartbeat. Rich's chief of staff got a little agitated.

"Doctor, couldn't they do the test in the hotel? If the media finds out, there would be so many questions and we had enough on our hands with the South Asia crisis."

"It'll be a lot easier in the hospital. I don't want to take chances. I have some old colleagues over at New York Presbyterian. I think we can keep it out of the news. It's late. It will be easy to get him in and out without being seen."

"One nurse with a Twitter account and we're lost. I'm holding you accountable. Is that clear? The president trusts you too much. He'll rue that one day."

We drove in a regular government SUV—less conspicuous than the big presidential limousine. There was one unmarked accompanying car. You can't imagine how unhappy the Secret Service was.

Meanwhile, I had arranged through Bob Sinclaire that Lanxin would leave the Security Council about 20 minutes after Rich. He was going uptown to where he was staying, but purposely stumbled as he was getting into his car and fell on the pavement. His staff rushed about around him.

One of them suggested he go to the hospital to get checked out. He feigned not to want to, but then gave in. New York Presbyterian was an obvious choice.

We were up in the VIP suite when Lanxin was being brought into the emergency ward and put in a special room. Sy went down to the emergency ward where the Chinese president was. He told the nurse to leave and then conferred with the hospital doctor treating the Chinese leader.

Sy told Lanxin, "We'll take you up to X-ray. Once there, dismiss your security detail. Tell them to stay outside."

As with most hospitals there were multiple ways in and out. Lanxin was taken up to the VIP suite, still on a gurney with his face just partially visible. When he saw me, he raised himself up with a broad grin on his face and shook my hand warmly. Then Rich stepped in the entryway. I could tell both were very moved about finally seeing each other. They went into a private room in the suite right away, closing the door. They knew they had no more than an hour before suspicions were raised.

Lanxin was the first to speak. "As I remember, Kissinger spent hours getting to know Zhou Enlai before they got down to business. We'll somehow have to compress that time and just decide to trust one another."

"Apologies for the decor," Rich said. "Nothing like the splendor of the Great Hall of the People."

"Don't worry. We can talk more freely than if we were there or in the White House. I have a feeling that you might be a bit of a rebel, like myself."

"A rebellious streak perhaps, but I've been extraordinarily lucky in politics. Things fall into my lap. Or that's the way it seems. I believe something may be falling into my lap now."

"Yes, I hope you'll consider it that way. But it comes with some strings."

"Doesn't everything in politics?"

Rich told me that most of the meeting was devoted to the mechanics of how to defuse the crisis between India and Pakistan. Lanxin came with a plan. He had the draft text of a Security Council resolution for a cease-fire and stand-down by the Indian military. Lanxin knew the US side might find this difficult to agree to since, after all, the Indians were the wronged party. But Lanxin needed some time to persuade the Pakistani military to storm and disarm the militant hideouts, and they wouldn't do this while the Indians were threatening war. Both Lanxin and Rich agreed that the dispute over Kashmir needed to be settled to stop the Pakistani military from arming the militants. Once Kashmir was settled, the Pakistani military would focus on the militant threat to internal security and move definitively against them. Lanxin held out a large assistance package to induce the Pakistani government and military to go along.

But Lanxin told Rich, "We don't have any credibility with the Indians, least of all the Indian military that 75 years after the 1962 war is still smarting from its defeat. Mr. President, you will need to do some heavy lifting if we are going to get to a cease-fire."

Rich told me later that his heart sank then. How was he going to convince Jacobs and the secretary of defense, let alone get the Indians on board? But he pledged to do his utmost.

"How about I introduce the resolution draft while you are sitting in the US chair and instead of tabling it, you immediately agree to it?" Lanxin said. "They can't stop you if you announce to the rest of the world that the US goes along. The Pentagon will just have to swallow hard. And the Indians will know that they won't get any US support."

Rich liked the idea. It would be the equivalent of poking Jacobs and all the others in their eyes, paying back for all the disguised contempt they held for him—the first Hispanic president in US history. And he also thought Sheila Maxwell—the secretary of state—would go along. She did not want to see a full-scale war break out in South Asia and ruin her attempts at advancing the ever-plodding Middle East peace process.

But Richard told me that the best part was the last ten minutes they had together. At that point both spoke briefly about their hopes for their respective countries.

Lanxin told him: "China can't seem to get out of the middle-income trap. The middle class is getting particularly frustrated and turning more and more to nationalistic, inappropriate behavior. This is not the Chinese dream I have for my country. I need your help to stop our mutual antagonisms. Every day the media reports another US incursion on supposed Chinese sovereignty. We are on a collision course if we don't watch out. I've been rereading my old history books on the outbreak of the First World War and there are too many parallels."

"And vice versa," Rich replied. "We're turning into a Saudi Arabia with all the benefits and the drawbacks. We think we can just rely on cheap shale energy and all our problems will be solved. Just like the Saudis, Americans are getting lazy."

"What you mean is that Americans assume China's rise has stalled and there is now nothing to worry about," Lanxin said.

"Well, yes, that's certainly the standard view these days. I myself don't think that's the case. You and your countrymen want success too much. You'll find a way. This is a momentary pause," Rich said.

"Is there a way we can work together on our problems?" Lanxin said. "Ever since my SAIS days, I've admired America, particularly its technology prowess. China was once a technology heavyweight. I know we have it in ourselves to do again. But we need your help."

Rich paused and said, "Let me think about it. If we get through this, we can't let our cooperation go to waste."

At that point, Sy and I barged into the room and said Lanxin must get back to X-ray. His handlers were beginning to suspect something.

The Security Council session went as Rich and Lanxin planned. Lanxin made his points and before Jacobs could object, Rich had accepted. The other Security Council members were stunned. Russia was irritated that the Chinese had stolen a march on them. They had hoped to be the peacemaker.

I got a seat in the chamber behind the US delegation and saw Richard and Lanxin exchange looks; Lanxin had difficulty holding back a grin.

After the session ended, Jacobs followed Rich out of the chamber. "With all due respect, Mr. President, why did you accept so quickly? As it stands, it puts most of the burden on us. We have to get the Indians to stand down. And for what? A Chinese promise to see what they can do with the Pakistanis."

"Jacobs, you have to trust me for once."

"Mr. President, I think the point is that you don't trust me. Did you know beforehand what the Chinese would do? I suspect you did."

"Jacobs, what's done is done. It will work out."

"Mr. President. That's really not the point. Do you want a national security advisor, or do you want to do foreign policy all on your own? I have tried to loyally serve you, but from the beginning you thought of me as some sort of fifth column. Yes, I was close to Tony. We also had differences, but we worked them out. For whatever reason—and I don't know why—you don't want to work with me like that. Mr. President, I'm tendering my resignation."

"I know you're upset. We've been under a lot of pressure. You've done a fine job getting the interagency process in line. If you left now, you could put the cease-fire in jeopardy. And none of us want that."

"I wouldn't do anything that would hurt the country. But I can't stay if you don't trust me. I can't. I guess I underestimated you from the get-go. Under all that charm and urbanity, you're quite the stubborn bastard, aren't you? And a rather sneaky one at that…" Jacobs had turned ashen.

Rich worried that Jacobs would create a scene and stopped him. "Jacobs, I know you're mad. I probably would be in your shoes. But I fear you'll say things that will make it impossible for either of us to work together."

"Yes, you're right. This has been difficult for me—an unexpected blow to the ego, you could say."

"I know it is a sacrifice for you to stay. And I know I'm a tough bastard to work for. You're not the first to complain, believe me. I got to where I am by playing my cards close to the vest. I liked the game of it. But it's not always a nice thing."

"Most presidents end up operating within a close clique that grows narrower the longer they are in office. You seem to have only yourself. It's not a good position."

Rich told me later he was surprised by Jacobs's frankness and his own. It was probably the first time that Rich owned up to his secretiveness. Ironically, he gained a newfound respect for Jacobs. Rich always assumed Jacobs had a chip on his shoulder. He now saw him as a public servant trying to do his job. It was just that they did not see eye-to-eye on China.

The secretary of defense was also mad, and Rich had to soothe him. Although puzzled, Sheila Maxwell was the only one who was content. On Capitol Hill, the Indian American community tried to use their clout to get resolutions passed censuring the administration. But, in the end, no one wanted the war. I don't even think the Indian prime minister was actually that upset, although there were riots and the gate and other buildings around the American embassy in New Delhi were set on fire.

Rich told me years later that his presidency almost came apart. He took a huge gamble by agreeing to the Chinese resolution without consulting his advisors. He only understood later how much he had hurt and upset them. He lucked out. He told me if he understood all the risks, he may not have taken gamble. But once in, it was hard to back out. Moreover, he trusted Lanxin. He made one of those snap judgments that proved a success.

He kept his promise to Lanxin: he was not going to let the newfound cooperation go to waste. For some time, he told me later, he had been worrying that shale energy was becoming a crutch. Yes, it had helped us get out of the Great Recession, but it let us put off needed changes. Richard worried about the United States' storied leadership in science and technology and the chances we were taking with it. Recent budget cuts had completely hollowed out government investment in basic research, and the private sector wasn't picking up the slack. With gas and even oil now so cheap, green technologies were withering on the vine.

China meanwhile had the money needed for investing in a green economy. "But first we must lower the suspicions here and in China. I'm working with Lanxin on that," he told me.

By this time, it was widely known that Rich and Lanxin had a good working relationship. His staff accepted it, but many did not like it in the Pentagon or on the Hill. Rich had to find some way to make it seem that China hadn't gotten the better of the deal. Rich also wasn't so smitten with the Chinese president that he was going to allow himself to be walked over.

Lanxin had our private telephone number and made it a point to call late in the evening. Rich would later tell the new national security advisor what had been said. What Rich and Lanxin dreamed up was a proposal in which both sides made concessions—China maybe more so. Lanxin promised to cut back on the cyberspying, which had gotten out of hand as China desperately tried to develop more high-tech industries. The US business community had become completely turned off, and Rich knew any rebuilding of bridges had to start with an understanding of the rules of the road. Government-on-government spying was fine, but China's cyberattacks on the private sector had to stop. Rich also promised to rein in NSA attacks against Chinese firms.

"We don't spy on you," was Lanxin's initial assertion, sounding a little hot under the collar.

"Oh, come off it. I have the evidence. Moreover, others do too. The Chamber of Commerce just put out another report on the billions and billions of dollars in intellectual property you've stolen."

"I don't know how they come up with such figures. If it's true, why aren't we farther along in becoming an innovation economy? The best companies are still US or Japanese or European. We don't yet have world-class corporations; not the way you do."

"You won't get it by stealing. You're putting off investors. And, you're making it harder for your companies to invest in the US." Now Rich found himself getting worked up. "You need to get a handle on the rest of the government. I probably know more about what your military is up to than you do." Rich was exaggerating, but he thought it best for once to put his cards out on the table. He was concerned about Lanxin's growing weakness. The Vietnamese—who tended to exaggerate—had told the CIA that a palace coup may be in the offing.

Lanxin had his troubles at home. But he wasn't going to let the US president get that close. Unlike Rich, he bluffed.

"I don't know what you mean. The US should mind its own business and not interfere in the domestic affairs of others."

Rich said later they both did not have much choice once they started talking. Any failure now and both would be blamed. Both put their hope in joint projects that could build trust and disarm the naysayers. The joint projects would be great for the US economy as it would get the United States back into the game of exporting green technology to the rest of the world. US scientists and universities would be thrilled.

Rich proposed working together on biotech. He knew China was keen to be the first to commercially develop the wide array of uses for biotech, particularly in the medical drugs field. Biotech was one of the most potentially harmful technologies, and developing standards and protocols together would help enforce them. He was worried about the Chinese cutting corners. It had fewer moral or ethical inhibitions. Joint efforts could help to elevate security standards; at least Americans would have a much better idea what was going on inside Chinese labs.

China had been recruiting biotech experts from all over the world. Rich did not want China to have all the glory, particularly as US scientists had made all the big scientific breakthroughs. He remembered from his classes at SAIS that Britain had lost out commercially on many of the scientific break-throughs it discovered in the nineteenth century. Instead it was Germany and the United States who commercially exploited the discoveries, and that was one reason for Britain's decline.

Lanxin quickly agreed. He thought he could sell joint efforts as a great victory, helping to mollify his critics. He so wanted China to be an innova-tive society and knew China still had a lot to learn from the United States.

"Some in Congress and the Pentagon really don't like the idea of good ties with China," Rich told me. "They are only going along because they see Lanxin is having so much trouble convincing his military and party. They probably figure it must actually be good for America given there is so much opposition in China."

He shook his head. "Politics is really a funny business. You try to do your best for the country, but unless you show how you wounded the other guy, no one believes you."

Lanxin liked to gamble. The higher he had risen in Party ranks, the more he got a thrill from making big and risky bets. He had one advantage. He was a so-called princeling, being a great-grandson of one of Mao's com-panions on the Long March. He was one of them, but he didn't like what had happened to the Party, how it had become corrupt; he equated it with what happened with the old dynasties when they were past their prime. If some-how it wasn't stopped, China would never become a really modern country.

Lanxin had a miserable time getting acceptance for the joint projects. The PLA protested bitterly. It had benefited from the growing nationalism that Lanxin's predecessors had used to soothe middle-class frustration with the economic slowdown. The PLA had capitalized on the growing nation-alism to grab an increasing portion of the budget to expand its forces. Government leaders always had problems knowing what the military was up to. There were times that they only learned of maneuvers at the last minute even though those displays of growing military power had serious implica-tions for China's relations with its neighbors. Rich was right, but Lanxin would never admit it.

Lanxin knew the hard-liners in the Party and the PLA would sneak around him and continue spying on the Americans despite the new understanding. But he had Rich's help. Rich funneled information to Lanxin on what his military intelligence was up to. Several times, Lanxin surprised his military with revelations about their doings that he was not supposed to know.

Still, Lanxin had his allies. Intellectuals in China were galvanized. The private sectors in both the United States and China tipped the balance. They could both see the opportunities better relations could provide. With Lanxin's help, it was becoming easier for American firms to do business in China. And Rich reined in the US national security apparatus from putting too many restrictions on Chinese investments in the United States.

Richard told me once, "Look what happened after the Second World War: Americans battled Nazi Germany but they became Germany's biggest ally after the war. Americans are so generous-hearted, they can't stay mad at anyone for very long. Of course, it helps that we're still top dog. It wouldn't have happened back in the Great Recession. Too much resentment. We can afford to be generous.

"China is in it for the long term. They know how to sacrifice. China was once a technology leader. We'll see that again in our lifetime."

Two years after Rich died in the boating accident, I attended a commemorative ceremony at Arlington National Cemetery. He wasn't religious, but he had a mystical attachment to the whole idea of the United States, and for him Arlington represented personal sacrifice in the service of the country.

The senator who was the main speaker did too much eulogizing for my taste. He cast Rich as following in the footsteps of other great presidents in offering a helping hand—in this case to China.

Rich would have appreciated the kind words, but he was skeptical about the world we were heading into. He spoke publicly a couple times about the fragility of the international system and hoped leaders would start rebuilding global institutions like the United Nations and IMF to better mirror the changed power structure.

The boating accident was so cruel, cutting short a retirement that was just becoming enjoyable. Lanxin was still in office when Rich left. He had promised not to say much about their collaboration to spare Lanxin any embarrassment.

It's still difficult for Lanxin. I visited him a year ago. Together we climbed the sacred Yellow Mountain with all that wonderful ancient calligraphy carved into the rock. We stayed at the State Guest House near the summit. I gazed out the next morning from the terrace on a view that was otherworldly. Those dramatic peaks looking down on us with all those billowy clouds drifting below—it was a scene right out of those ancient Chinese scrolls. You feel close to the gods. It was a time for reflection. I asked Lanxin how he saw the last few years.

With that same grin he had when we first met, Lanxin replied, "The gamble paid off, although I was on the edge of my seat the whole time. I had to fight tooth and nail to get agreement on the joint ventures. But Chinese are practical—too many engineers who want to get things built. There was no other easy way. They remembered their parents' stories about the damage done by Mao's effort to carve out a solely Chinese development path with the Great Leap Forward, which sent us flying backwards. We could not quickly become an innovative society without help."

The Party was also increasingly anxious about the growing middle-class distrust of the Party. The Party had tried to divert attention with some saber-rattling. There had been some nasty skirmishes with the Vietnamese and Japanese, and in one notable case China had to back down in response to an international outcry. That was actually how Lanxin came to power. His predecessor had been unceremoniously shoved aside after one too many embarrassing incidents with China's neighbors and universal condemnation.

"The Party isn't comfortable with too much innovation. I worry that we could see another Tiananmen Square, if the Party doesn't start easing up. In Shanghai, you must have seen those huge demonstrations when the Party reneged on its decision to allow the mayor to be freely elected and not have to report to the Party chief. The leadership in Beijing initially wanted to conduct an experiment but then grew scared when they saw the slate of candidates, some of them with no Party affiliation. The people poured out in the streets. It almost got violent. It set off fierce internal debates with liberals and hard-liners blaming each other for the blow to Party fortunes."

He chuckled then. "I still don't talk about what happened that night at the hospital. The Chinese believe Rich sought out me. I wonder what the historians will make of it."

We talked about our families. He was so delighted that his grandson decided to have three children. It was back to the future, he said. He looked forward to a China of extended families again. A professor of ancient Chinese literature, his grandson had forsaken the Party for Confucius.

Several months later I was going through more of Rich's things. It had been hard right after the accident to touch anything of his. An archivist from the National Archives was helping me. I found an old volume of Rudyard Kipling's poems, a present from one of Rich's relatives who had studied in England. It looked like he had been rereading it. For me, Kipling smacked too much of white man's burden, empire, and a lot of other things that were so repugnant. I couldn't imagine what could have drawn Rich to it.

It was an old Everyman's edition and the spine was cracked. It fell open on that famous line about "East Is East and West Is West." But I did not know what actually followed:

"Oh, East is East, and West is West, and never the twain shall meet,
Till Earth and Sky stand presently at God's great Judgment Seat;
But there is neither East nor West, Border, nor Breed, nor Birth,
When two strong men stand face to face,
tho' they come from the ends of the earth!"

Did Rich sense when he met Lanxin for the first time that they could be the "two strong men" who close the gap between East and West? I'd like to think he did.

# CHAPTER 11

# *With Friends Like This...*

·

ON AN IMPULSE, LISA WENT TO SEE CLARA AT HER OFFICE FIRST THING IN THE MORNING. Clara had once treated Lisa's son, Ben, and they had become friends.

"Lisa, what a surprise! Unfortunately I don't have much time, but come in..."

The office had bright yellow walls, clearly intended to cheer you up. They had the opposite effect on Lisa. Sometimes no amount of sugarcoating would make things better.

Once Clara closed the door, she asked, "What's wrong?"

"The FBI came to see me," Lisa said. "I think Ben's in trouble. They had some suspicions about an outbreak of a virus in India and they have traced it to him. They asked a lot of questions. I wasn't able to answer most of them. I haven't seen him for a while. I get e-mails, but there's nothing in them that would suggest he is in any trouble or did anything wrong." At this point, Lisa began to tear up.

"I'm so sorry."

"I said it was preposterous. Ben wouldn't hurt anyone. Besides, he isn't anywhere near India. He's a thousand or more miles away in Southeast Asia. But there were things they showed me which surprised the hell out of me."

"What does Chris think?"

"He's up in Alaska on a fishing trip with some of his buddies. I haven't telephoned. I'm afraid he'll explode, get on a plane and go out there. He always overreacts to anything concerning Ben."

"What about Damon?"

"He was shocked. He had visited Ben several times when he was in England and thought he had made such great friends. He couldn't understand."

"Call Chris."

"I'm sure he'll worry that this could skew his chances for getting a Nobel Prize. We've heard he's under consideration along with two of his colleagues for their work on 3D printing. Politics is not supposed to enter into it, but I'm sure he'll think his chances will go down if there is some sort of scandal."

Lisa drove to her office but had difficulty keeping her composure around her colleagues. She decided to call it a day and drove home early. She checked her voice mails. Nothing more from George Taylor, the FBI officer she had met with, or from Ben. Agent Taylor had been rather vague. Lisa had asked if she should try to get in touch with Ben immediately. "Just act normal," he said. "I'm counting on you not to alert him to our suspicions. We'll know if you do. We're following his tracks, but it's a difficult investigation. And we have to deal with a lot of foreign authorities we don't actually trust."

Lisa sat down on the couch. The bungalow was typical for some of the less well-to-do communities around Stanford. They could have afforded a better house, but Chris and she never had the time to go out and choose one. She had not always been so busy. In the first years of their marriage, she was a stay-at-home mom. She grew up in a family where both her parents worked, and she remembered coming home to an empty house. She was an only child and for a while found it difficult to make friends. She wanted to do things differently. Unlike many of her female friends, she wanted to start a family as soon as she got married. She and Chris met as undergraduates at Stanford. She was more eager for marriage and parenthood than he was, but he went along with her wishes.

They had both been star students at Stanford. Unlike many students, money was not a big issue for them. He got a fellowship and, like many engineering students, also had a start-up business with some of his buddies that went into the black after a few years. It was never going to be a huge success, but it generated some extra cash that came in handy when Lisa decided to put her PhD work on the back burner while they started a family.

Damon was an easy baby. Lisa was very happy as a mom, even though many of her female friends were rather dismissive and kept asking her when she would go back to her graduate work. She convinced Chris to have a second child and got pregnant a year after Damon's birth.

Ben was his mother's child. It was several years before he was diagnosed with Asperger's syndrome, but almost from the beginning she had a sense that he needed to be protected. Gone were the plans for a third child.

Damon, by contrast, got on well with other children; he was an all-rounder—good in both sports and his studies—which surprised Lisa and Chris, who had had tougher times socially as kids.

Ben started preschool before she resumed her work. Her academic career went better than expected—at least at the beginning. The head of the department had supported her decision to suspend her PhD while she and Chris started a family. And her mentor helped to reintegrate her quickly. She finished her PhD well ahead of the timetable she had set for herself. She found a teaching position and then a tenure-track job in the department. She was working in the bioengineering field, particularly developing drought-resistant crop strains. Lisa hadn't actually spent time abroad, but she worked closely with a Brazilian scientist who was on exchange from his university in São Paulo. Lisa became fired with the dream of using her scientific expertise to work on a green revolution for Africa.

About the time Ben started kindergarten, he was diagnosed with Asperger's, which threw Lisa for a loop. Would he ever be normal? Was it something she had done?

"The worst thing you can do is coddle him," the pediatrician told Lisa and Chris. "He is extremely bright, but he will probably have to struggle to fit in. On the other hand, there are a lot of kids diagnosed with Asperger's around here. You should probably try to find a support group. It can be helpful to know other parents dealing with the same issues."

Lisa thought she would be able to deal with the Asperger's on her own. As she got more and more caught up in Ben's treatment, her academic career began to suffer. "You're at a critical juncture," her mentor told her. "If you don't get another paper published soon, you will undercut your chances of getting tenure. That would not be good for you or Ben."

But she couldn't rouse herself. She realized later that she had been suffering from depression. A year or so later the inevitable happened: her committee voted to deny her tenure.

Chris felt the blow more than Lisa. In college, he thought of them as the dream couple—both had straight A's and appeared headed for brilliant academic careers. He got a tenure-track position even before finishing his PhD—practically unheard of—and almost instant acclaim afterward. His work on 3D and 4D printing opened up huge manufacturing opportunities. Chris told Lisa that she was throwing away all she had worked so hard for. The marriage began to break down.

About this time Lisa met Clara through the special school that Ben now attended, where she was a consultant. The same age and both physically active, they bonded right away. As Ben improved, the marriage also mended. Lisa decided to go back to work. She was interested in connecting emerging technologies to the day-to-day practical needs of those poor or suffering. Lisa had the necessary scientific and technological knowledge. But more importantly she had the empathy and organizational skills to get things done. The care she had poured into taking care of Ben was now channeled into a new, all-consuming passion—helping West Africans deal with growing water and food deprivations.

Lisa founded an NGO, but it was more than that. She devised an organizational structure in which several governments, universities, businesses, and NGOs actively participated. It became the kind of real public-private partnership that everybody always had talked about.

She and her colleagues started at the village level working with women who form a high proportion of the farmers in Africa. They wanted to teach them how to increase their yields and how to time the sale of their products in local markets so that they would get a better price, which in turn incentivized them to try to produce more. They also worked to push local governments to change their laws so women could own the land they tended.

But she knew she had to scale up too. She knew that US scientists at the traditional agricultural research center at Purdue University were working on high-yield seed varieties that could bring about a green revolution in

Africa. It had already happened in Asia and Latin America but was yet to occur in Africa despite the growing population's urgent need. Lisa wanted to make it a priority for US scientists. Too many scientific geniuses in Silicon Valley put their efforts in designing the next best app or computer game while others were dying from starvation. She grew boiling mad with the Valley's dreamy-eyed prophets expounding their new religion about a limitless world. No more scarcities. Technology was the answer. But it clearly wasn't unless you put it into practice.

Lisa also engaged intelligence agencies, not only in the United States but across the world; they had the satellite imagery and analytic tools to detect patterns of growing population distress. Their imagery could spot where the migrant flows were headed and where rain had not fallen that season or where it was increasingly growing scarce because of climate change. There was good commercial satellite imagery, but she had found out that several of the intelligence agencies were using more advanced analytics—looking at all the factors, comparing current data to past patterns and being able to forecast rising tensions or growing famine. By orchestrating pressure through Congress, the US intelligence agencies could be pushed to make this a priority and a public service. She worked with other parliaments, foreign-based NGOs, and even business groups to get the cooperation of the other intelligence agencies.

Initially she got a lot of push-back. But that only made the challenge more interesting. Lisa's obsessive side came out and she pushed hard, using her congressional and parliamentary backers to counter the government resistance. She eventually won.

For Lisa everything seemed to be falling in place, including Ben. He was now boarding at a special school, which had made things easier at home. Ben's obvious progress in making some friends helped assuage Lisa's guilt.

She remembered arguing with her mother: "He is so much better off. The teachers are all brilliant at their jobs and Ben is beginning to show a real flair for science and technology. Did you know that they think Mozart had Asperger's?"

One downside was that Damon and Ben did not get to know each other like other siblings. When Ben came home on weekends, Lisa and Chris tried to organize family outings. But popular Damon had his own friends and activities. Ben still found it difficult to fit in with people he did not know. Lisa often ended up taking Ben to science fairs or museums or classical concerts while Chris attended Damon's sporting events. Damon took up swimming in junior high school and soon was competing in statewide meets. Chris tried to attend as many as he could. Lisa only went if they were close by and did not interfere with her being with Ben on weekends.

For the last two years of high school, Lisa and Chris decided to take Ben out of his special school and put him in a highly rated public school. Intellectually, Ben could compete with the best of them, particularly in science and math. They weren't worried on that score. But they wanted to see how he would fare socially. Chris had told Lisa, "If we wait until he goes to college, it could be a total shock."

Lisa agreed. Ben was initially hesitant because he liked the teachers at his old school and had a fear of the unknown. He was a year younger than many of his classmates because he had skipped a grade at his special school. But he fared better than many of the counselors expected. Still, Lisa noticed he grew more withdrawn. She wanted to take him out and put him back in his old school. But Chris was against it. They argued with each other for the first time in some years.

The next morning, Damon told his mother, "Why don't you just let him be normal? You can't always be there for him!" and then stormed out of the house. Lisa was deeply hurt by his comments and she never forgot.

Ironically, no one had asked Ben's opinion. Ben changed the subject when Lisa finally did ask. He went on talking about the fascinating new planets being discovered. He had become obsessed with knowing whether there were humanlike aliens and spent hours talking about it. Finally, during the Christmas break, he mentioned that he wanted to stay.

Six months later, a decision had to be made about where Ben would go to university. Both Chris and Lisa were adamant that it would be Stanford. Damon did not have the grades and opted for out of state. He was going to University of Oregon. Ben could have gone to Stanford but surprised his parents one day by saying he wanted to go to Cambridge University.

"What would Cambridge offer that you can't get in our own backyard at Stanford?" Chris asked angrily.

"Stephen Hawking" was Ben's only response. He kept saying it over and over again, and he got louder and louder. He acted just like he used to as a child, when he could not stop repeating words.

Lisa sought to calm Ben, all the while glowering at her husband. "Stop badgering him."

In private, Chris was emphatic. "If he has problems fitting in, won't Cambridge be more difficult for him? We don't want him to fail."

Lisa did not want Ben to go to Cambridge either but was upset with Chris for his blunt talk with Ben. "You know Ben when he gets on one of these kicks. Don't pester him and he'll move on."

But weeks went by and Ben still talked about going to Cambridge. By the end of the semester, both Lisa and Chris were getting concerned that Ben would miss the deadline for all the schools they hoped he would apply to. They found out later that he had applied to Cambridge and early in the new year got an acceptance from one of the colleges—Darwin.

Chris was the first to spot a letter with a UK postage stamp in their mail. He asked Ben what it meant. Ben said they were asking about his housing preferences, specifically whether he wanted to live in College or in a hostel.

Chris had a hard time remaining calm and was on the verge of exploding when Lisa came home that night.

"You've gone behind my back! He got into Cambridge and accepted their offer. He's now deciding on his rooming."

Lisa was speechless. She had no idea. Ben never said a word, even though she had been badgering him about applying to American universities. She felt betrayed and terribly hurt.

Chris could see the pain. Ben had obviously fooled them both. "I guess we have to face up to the fact that he is grown up and beginning to make his own decisions."

It took Lisa some time to resign to the fact he was going away, and halfway around the world. She ran into Clara at a triathlon. "He has to be pushed out of the nest at some point," Clara said. "He can function just like the millions of others with the syndrome. Even if he fails, it won't be the end of the world."

Ben was raring to go. He had planned the escape for some time. He thought his parents believed he was too fragile. Yes, he still got flustered, but he felt stronger and was sure he could manage.

Darwin College is named after the Darwin family. Charles Darwin's second son, George Darwin, owned some of the property the college now occupies. Until a few years before Ben's matriculation, it had been a graduate-only college but now admitted a select few undergraduates who were interested in reading mathematics or natural sciences.

It hadn't been Ben's first choice. He had put down Queens because Stephen Hawking had been a member there. As it turned out, a close college to Queens is Darwin.

Ben wanted to follow in Hawking's footsteps and study astronomy and astrophysics but during his first year had to spend time on other scientific subjects, including biology and evolution. Perhaps it was the atmosphere of Darwin College—with its framed extracts from *The Origin of Species* or the many photos of Charles Darwin's extended family—but Ben soon found himself getting deeper and deeper into biology. He was fascinated by man's ability now to create life. By his second year, he decided to specialize in biology.

Ben still had a hard time making friends, but the social tensions were far less. There were so many intense oddballs at Cambridge, he stood out less than he did at home where being well-rounded was more the ideal. Darwin wasn't stuffy like some of the other colleges because it had so many foreign students. Many of them did not have a thorough command of English, which made it difficult for them to connect socially. For the first time in his life, Ben felt at home.

Quickly viewed as a genius, he got a "starred first" on his first year's Tripos examination. He went on to become ranked as the number one student in biological sciences in his final year as an undergraduate.

In the next several years Lisa routed a number of her trips through Heathrow and went up and saw Ben for the day. He was cordial but distant. At first she was traumatized, but what could she do? Chris and Clara helped her become resigned to having an absent-minded genius of a son. It was less painful to think about him in that way.

Four years after sending him off to Cambridge, Lisa returned home one afternoon to find a postcard with a picture of a Buddhist monastery on the front and just a brief note on the back: "Liking my stay here. Working in a lab. Have made some new friends. Ben."

At first, Lisa was annoyed. Why didn't the tutor mention Ben's trip? She thought she had an understanding with Francis that he should inform them of any major developments.

The next day, she called him.

"Yes, I guess I should have mentioned it. I've been swamped with exams. I apologize, but I wouldn't worry so much about Ben. He'll do fine. He's gone out there to work in a lab for the summer."

"But I do worry," Lisa said. "Asia's a long way off and so different from England."

"Yes, it's beastly hot out there." He shifted the focus of the conversation. "He'll be working in a new lab geared to investigating bird flu. You should be proud. This is the long vac so they don't need to get back before end of September."

"Do you know anything about this lab?"

"No, not much. It's a new start-up. One of the foreign students here, I think, went back to help establish it. They asked for Ben specifically. He'll get some good hands-on experience."

Ben thought he had struck gold. The lab was doing some highly experimental work, manipulating various strains of viruses to understand how they could mutate. Southeast Asia was ground zero for the production of dangerous viruses. Most scientists had long anticipated that the next major pandemic would come out of that region. Countries there had largely relied on international organizations like the World Health Organization to help detect them. They did not have the facilities or the scientists to cope on their own.

The lab was an effort to get ahead of the threat. By understanding how viruses mutate to become a danger to humans, they could also begin to develop antidotes. They could also start establishing their own pharmaceutical industry. But they needed help from foreign scientists to get them where they wanted to be. Ben was part of that effort.

He was making friends who shared his passion. Most of the interns were from Southeast Asia, including Indonesia, Cambodia, and Thailand. There were also a few from Pakistan and India. They had some university training, but not up to Ben's level.

In the last week of his internship, his supervisor came up to Ben.

"You have a real flair for this stuff. Have you worked in other labs?"

"Just at Cambridge."

"You're the best intern we've had from Cambridge. I'm hoping I might convince you to stay on?"

With a time difference of seven hours and Francis on holiday in France, it took several days before Ben and Francis spoke.

"I don't want this to slow down your doctorate," Francis said sternly.

"I can do both."

"The regulations state you don't have to be in Cambridge except for three terms. Most candidates in the sciences don't leave. You can stay for only a couple more months. Is that clear? By the way, have any international teams come through to inspect the lab recently? There's a new World Health Organization report about the proliferation of labs out there and their worries that that the technicians are not being vetted. I'll send you the link."

There was no dearth of new assistants. The lab rotated one batch after another, mostly drawn from the same countries in Asia. After a while, Ben's supervisor began assigning interns to him. Ben was supposed to continue his lab work, but now he was also responsible for teaching others his laboratory methods.

Ben was thrilled. He'd never been a mentor. At Cambridge, the graduate students were not expected to do much teaching. Increasingly aware as he grew older of what it meant to have Asperger's, he understood that this was a great opportunity to work on his social skills.

He made one friend in particular, Aiyaz. A hard worker, Aiyaz also wanted to learn how to test the various virus strains on whether they would be transmissible from human to human. This involved working with ferrets.

Many of the interns disliked seeing the animals die and avoided that part of the work. But Aiyaz was clearly fascinated. One of the interns complained to Ben's superior, Dr. Cong, that she thought Aiyaz was mistreating the animals, running too many tests on them. Cong talked to Ben, who said Aiyaz was the most brilliant of the interns. "He's trying to fit in as much study as possible before he goes back to India," Ben explained. "I think it is just jealousy on the others' part."

After a couple months, Aiyaz asked if two friends from his college could join the team. Ben looked at their resumes. He also had Skype interviews with them.

Ben told Dr. Cong that they seemed qualified. "Go ahead," said Cong. "You're the boss. The director has been so impressed by your work."

Aiyaz's friends came; they did not speak English very well so it was hard for the rest of the team to communicate with them. Aiyaz treated them as his assistants, which even Ben found odd.

A couple months rolled by and Ben got a rather stern e-mail from Francis back in Cambridge: "I thought you were coming back for Lent term. We had set aside a room in college. This is a huge inconvenience. I must say, Ben, I am rather disappointed. I thought you had a lot more common sense. If you don't come back, your College scholarship for next year will be in jeopardy. Several fellows raised the issue at the last fellowship meeting. They have a point. Why should we be supporting you while you work at a lab halfway round the world? It's not clear that you're doing much on your PhD. If you don't come back by Eastertime, we will have to ask that you drop out of your PhD course."

Ben did not want to make his champion angry, but he loved the work at the lab. He decided to drop out of Cambridge. He could get by on the pittance of a salary that they paid him. He lived with the other interns in an annex. They all cooked together, which added to the camaraderie that he was enjoying for the first time in his life. The dinner conversations, especially with Aiyaz, were good because they talked work.

It took some time for Lisa to get through to Ben on Skype after she heard of his decision. "Honey, I'm not sure you know what you're doing. You have got to finish your PhD! The lab is great, but no one stays in place for ever. Can you come home so we can discuss this?"

"Mom, you don't understand. I feel at home here."

Lisa knew she was not getting through. "Ben, I love you, darling. If you can't get home, maybe I or your dad can come visit."

"I don't know where you'd stay. I don't think you'll like the annex. I have to go. Dr. Cong wants to see me."

Dr. Cong did want to see him at that moment.

"Ben, Aiyaz and his friends were in the lab last night."

"They work late."

"I saw one of them downloading files using a thumb drive. I asked what he was doing. He said he needed to do some historic analysis and was looking at past trials. Some of this information is proprietary. You don't know who they are working with back in India. I'm sure some of the pharmaceutical firms in India would love to get their hands on our data."

"I don't think you have too much to worry about. They're very anticapitalist. One of them keeps spouting Maoist phrases. Dr. Cong, I think they are just very industrious. They've been a big help to me."

"OK. But they can't work unattended. That goes for Aiyaz as well. If they rip off some of our data, it will be my head and yours. You need to supervise them more closely."

Aiyaz saw Ben storming out of Dr. Cong's office and followed him.

"What's the matter?"

"I am supposed to supervise you and not let you work without me in the lab. I won't do it."

"Ben, you're upset. It's all right if you want to watch us more closely. We shouldn't ruffle Dr. Cong. He's very powerful. I don't want to go home. Not just yet."

Ben calmed down. He had never known anyone who was as considerate as Aiyaz. He had thought that once of his supervisor, Francis. But Francis no longer seemed to care about what Ben wanted. Aiyaz would sit down with him at the end of day and the two would go over the day's highlights in the labs. He could see Aiyaz was as passionate about the work as he was.

Months went by. Ben stayed late when Aiyaz and his friends wanted to work at night in the lab or on the computers. He was mostly in his little cubbyhole of an office so he could not see what Aiyaz or his friends were up to, but he was not worried.

Nine months after Aiyaz arrived, he went back to India. He was supposed to start a new course at a technical university and said he needed to spend some time with his family. Aiyaz's friends departed too. Ben missed his friend terribly, and Dr. Cong had grown ever more suspicious. He thought about leaving, but he loved his work. With bioengineering, man could play God. It was a huge responsibility.

At about this time, Lisa got her first visit from the FBI. Before her visitor could say anything, Lisa said, "Has something happened to Ben?" She had been increasingly worried about him; his mood seemed to have darkened in their last e-mail exchanges.

"I'm sorry to alarm you," Agent Taylor said. "And, yes, it is about your son. We don't have any evidence that Ben has done anything wrong. But I think he may have gotten mixed up with a dangerous group. Do you know much about his work?"

"I know he works in a new start-up lab that is looking to prevent pandemics by developing possible antidotes."

"Why did he go out there?"

"He's a PhD student—or was—at Cambridge in England. He did his work in biological sciences. I think a Cambridge graduate established the lab and recruited him. He's been there now almost a year and a half."

"Do you see him much?"

"No, I've been to Cambridge several times. Never out there."

"What about your husband or other members of the family?"

"Chris, my husband, hasn't, nor my other son, Damon."

"Does he talk about his work?"

"No, but he cares a great deal about it. I think he has found his niche." Lisa decided not to say anything about Ben's recent unhappiness.

"We got a tip-off from the Indian authorities that something criminal may be going on. Fake pharmaceuticals are big business out there. The Indians think your son is the mastermind." Taylor was overstating Ben's involvement to see how Lisa reacted.

"That's not possible," said Lisa defensively. "My son is no more a criminal than you. He lives on nothing and doesn't really care for anything except his work."

"Has he talked to you about his friends? Does the name Aiyaz ring a bell?"

"He said he was Aiyaz's instructor and Aiyaz was very industrious."

"Anyone else?"

"He mentioned he's made some friends, which is quite unusual for him. He's a bit of a loner." She paused. "My son has Asperger's. He's highly functional but he doesn't make friends easily."

"I can't emphasize how seriously we are taking this. So if you do try to warn your son, you could be charged with interfering with an investigation."

A few days later Taylor returned, looking more worried. "This will soon reach the media. A mysterious virus is spreading in one of the Indian states. The Indian government is treating it as a terrorist act. Highly contagious, the virus has been transmitted from human to human. It's not clear what the terrorists hope to gain. If they have supporters, they could be in harm's way. However, only some of those struck by the illness are succumbing. The WHO and CDC are on the case and have been working closely with Indian health authorities. They've been talking to the director of your son's lab, Dr. Cong."

Lisa was distraught, but Chris told her not to worry. "The FBI sees threats everywhere. They're so heavy handed. They want to close down every bio or 3D printing labs. They think we're going to send viruses to the terrorist groups."

A day later, he told Lisa that he talked to some lab people at Stanford.

"But he told us not to say anything."

"No, no. I just asked their opinion generally of the threat. I did not mention Ben or his lab. They think all the bioterrorism stuff is overrated. It's hard to control an attack. I wouldn't worry. And we know Ben. It's outrageous, honey, that they have come around and upset you so. I feel so bad about not being there."

Lisa actually liked Agent Taylor. He did not seem the pushy type, and she thought he was being very cautious.

A week later, he came back and talked to Lisa and Chris. "The Indians have arrested a ring of terrorists that includes Aiyaz and some of the other interns from your son's lab. The Indians have sent some officials to interview your son. I think he will probably be charged. Most likely he will be deported. We'll then have to see whether we want to charge him. That will be up to the federal prosecutors. My opinion is that he was probably unwitting but nevertheless a tool in the hands of the group. It's unfortunate. I think there's some scapegoating happening too. Dr. Cong said Ben did not take sufficient precautions.

"It's tragic, but it could be far worse. Total fatalities will probably end up in the hundreds. Fortunately the lab had worked on antidotes, which they offered to manufacture for free. I think they were aiming for a patent. There wasn't time. So they sent the DNA sequence for the antidote and it was bio-printed on site in India.

"Aiyaz, it turned out, was from a very wealthy family, but very angry. He infected himself and then purposely spent time at his family's country club. He knew the virus could spread to the servants so he had prepared an antidote. He portrayed himself a doctor to the club servants so they willingly took the vaccine. The virus was not too deadly; there wasn't enough time for it to jump to the next person before the first victim died. But enough did.

"When the story began to leak, a mob gathered outside the police station where he was detained and Aiyaz was lynched. I've seen the pictures—rather gruesome. Others in his group have gone underground."

Lisa started to shake. Chris got up and paced the room.

"What did Ben say when they interviewed him?"

"He refused to believe that Aiyaz could have done any of it. He repeated over and over, you've got the wrong person. Aiyaz is my friend. He went into a sort of catatonic shock. He hasn't talked much since. He's being detained by the authorities there. The American consular staff have gone in a couple times since. A US federal prosecutors' team is on its way out there."

"I've got to go," Lisa blurted out. "To make sure he's all right."

"I wouldn't advise it. He's only allowed official visitors. The prosecutor will be seeing him. Your son isn't in any immediate danger."

It did not take the media long to discover the full scope of the story. The Indian media focused on the American connection, portraying Ben as the mastermind and corruptor of young Indian students under his charge. Dr. Cong was the first to talk with the media. It was clear he just wanted to save his lab and deflect any charges of lax security standards onto somebody else. Ben was a convenient target.

Fortunately for Ben and his family, a young consular officer in the embassy understood what could happen if Ben wasn't deported quickly. Joe Myers was a recent arrival, but he had several tours under his belt.

As soon as Joe heard about Ben's detention, he started visiting him daily, encouraging him to send a message to his parents.

Ben rarely answered verbally. He just shook his head. On several occasions, however, he asked Joe for news of Aiyaz. At first, Joe wanted to spare him but knew Ben would find out eventually.

"He died."

"How?"

"You don't want to know the details."

"I see."

Ben's eyes began to well up. "Whatever they say, he was a true friend. He was so kind and good."

"He may have been kind to you. But he did an awful thing. Many people died."

"It wasn't him. He was just a tool. He said his family just exploited the poor. He was going to change that. He could not have killed people."

Joe dropped the topic.

Joe had heard that there was a debate raging in the Justice Department over the pros and cons of charging Ben. Those opposed worried that by prosecuting him in the States a lot would come out about the US government's lack of intelligence on the bioterrorist threat from Ben's lab. Ben's lawyers could tie up the court proceeding by showing how little the US government knew, and this would be embarrassing. There had been recent cuts to the government agencies that were responsible for tracking the biothreat. However politically embarrassing, Joe understood that charging Ben with a US offense would be the least bad outcome. Joe worried that the authorities there might decide to put on a show trial. If so, Ben would be incarcerated for months, waiting to appear in some very ugly court proceedings that the media would use to tarnish not only Ben and his family but also the US government.

In the end, Joe succeeded. The Justice Department charged Ben, and Joe worked behind the scenes to get Ben deported. But it did not end the nightmare for Ben or his family. Three months in prison had unhinged Ben.

He was detained upon reentry to the United States in San Francisco. His lawyers engaged several psychiatrists, including Clara, to examine him. He barely spoke. He hadn't been medicated for the depression he was suffering. All the psychiatrists recommended putting him into a mental institution so he could be better treated. Clara worried that he was suicidal. The lawyers used his mental state to get him released on bail so long as he was confined to a mental institution. Lisa and Chris paid for a private sanitarium. The judge approved. Ben was not deemed a flight risk given his mental state, but his passport was taken away and he had to wear an ankle bracelet that tracked his moves.

For the next few years, there was a court hearing every few months to determine if he was able to stand trial. Eventually the Justice Department dropped the charges. They were relieved not to have to mount a prosecution. Only the media and some in the public who hoped to use the trial to discuss the threats posed by bioengineering were disappointed.

A few years later, Lisa stopped for coffee in downtown Palo Alto after a long bike ride. She found a shaded spot on the café terrace.

Clara had seen her enter but wondered whether to say hi. She knew Lisa had been devastated by what had happened. Friends commented on how gray she had grown in the past year or two. Clara thought she might just want to be alone. But when Lisa noticed Clara, she smiled. Clara went over and sat down next to Lisa.

"How's it going?"

"I just started training and it's gruesome. I'm paying a price for having taken time off."

But Lisa knew what Clara was thinking. "These last few months, I've had time to think. I'll never get over it."

"How's Ben?"

"Not good. He's retreating more and more into his own world. We've had a couple of scares. They have him on a suicide watch again. He's being well taken care of."

Lisa paused to drink her latte. "At first, I kept asking why did it happen? Could I have prevented it? But I now look on it as a sort of Greek tragedy. We were doomed from the start. A son we desperately tried to help and may have sheltered too much. He finally found his legs. He got immersed in a science that was both breathtaking in what it could do and dangerous. He got little supervision at Cambridge. And he landed in a part of the world where hate still lives.

"Sadly, if anything, it's opened up a can of worms with the government. Have you been following the media stories about the extra scrutiny scientists are coming under? It's really astonishing. Some months after Ben came back, the FBI came back to see us. It wasn't Agent Taylor, and in fact this guy didn't seem to know Agent Taylor or to have met with him before he talked with us. He asked Chris for all his foreign contacts, saying they were investigating all possible leads on Ben's case. Chris, of course, told him that we didn't have much contact with Ben while he was at the lab.

"What was amazing, though, is that he then started rattling off names of many of the foreign scientists Chris deals with and then asked Chris to go through them one by one and give any personal information he knew about them. Chris asked him where he got the names. It got very heated with Chris finally telling him he would not talk without a lawyer.

"The next day one of his colleagues came into Chris's office and closed the door. He told Chris that he had been visited by the FBI—not the same agent but someone else—who asked to know all about his foreign contacts. Chris and Barney went to see the university lawyers who told them not to do or say anything until they looked in it. After several weeks, the lawyers came back and told them they'd have to comply. In fact, the FBI will be interviewing practically the whole department. The foreign scientists in the department got a terrible grilling."

"I thought I saw somewhere that some scientists' e-mails are being intercepted?" Clara said.

"Yes, the *New York Times* was reporting that after the attacks, the intelligence community feared other ones, and for the past couple of years, they have been collecting whole slews of correspondence by scientists across the world. The *Times* said the US government was in fact cooperating with various countries, including China of all places, on the interception and storage of e-mails. Apparently the FBI went to China to learn from them how to monitor the Internet for disaffected individuals. We think this new cooperation is behind what happened to Chris's student, Chu Hua.

"Chu Hua had been studying here with Chris on 3D printing. He said she was one of his brightest ever. A few months back, we were informed that she would have to go back to China and apply there for a new visa for the States. We couldn't fathom what was going on.

"Long story short, she went back, and the US consulate refused to grant her a visa. Chris raised a storm. Some of her relatives are dissidents, apparently. Chinese authorities contend they have ties to some sort of internal terrorist group. Chu Hua denies that and US authorities have no proof. But they've told the university they don't want to take any chances. Chu Hua is following up with an appeal. Chris is hopeful she'll be allowed to come back, but you can imagine all the time and effort this has involved. Chris has little time for any research these days."

Lisa stared down at the ground, "Who would have thought it would end like this? Not just a family tragedy, but one that is derailing all scientific inquiry. The trend for the last several decades has been for more joint endeavors across borders. Now the FBI wants to put limitations on that and the universities seem to be going along. They don't want to lose their federal funding—what little of that there is. What cowards! I don't know how we're going to live with this, now that it's out of the box."

# CHAPTER 12

# *Making the System Work*

THERE ARE MOMENTS WHEN EVERYTHING SUDDENLY CHANGES, AS IF THE SCALES FINALLY fall from your eyes. I'm thinking back to a couple of decades ago when I first heard Carlota Castillo speak. I had been involved in developing Google Glass—you know, the wearable computer-eyeglass that promised to once again revolutionize your access to instant information and feedback. We were just at the apogee of Silicon Valley's influence. A couple of years later, the whole tech industry was under a cloud. But when I heard Carlota that day, Google and the other tech giants were still riding high.

Several of us from Google had gone up to San Francisco for the meeting. Carlota was with one of the big management consultancies we used, and her firm had a conference room with spectacular views over a 180-degree arc spanning everything from the Golden Gate to the Bay Bridge on the Oakland side. Carlota and her team were helping us figure out ways to maximize the commercial benefits of Google Glass.

Originally from Chile, Carlota had one of those powerhouse personalities. She was wasting herself in this management consultancy that wanted everything honed so fine and did not want to ruffle anybody's feathers. Though diminutive in stature, she was fiery and strangely charismatic. I listened in fascination that late afternoon as the sun set on the bay—if not on all my tech illusions.

Carlota had the idea that we would use Google Glass to show Americans how much others sweated and labored so we could maintain our lifestyle. She had everybody put on Google glass prototypes and focus on a bowl of fruit to which she had attached fair trade tags. While consumers were deciding which bunch of bananas they wanted to buy, they could give a voice command and up would pop the working conditions out in the banana groves.

I can remember her saying ever more emphatically, "There is a view of the banana groves. You see well-dressed workers. There's a picture of the school where their children go. With a few voice commands, we can go deeper. We can ask what wages the field workers are getting. You get the point. We no longer just have a label that gives us confidence that the product is fair trade."

She did not stop there. She had visited some place in West Africa and seen small children haul up gold from the mines. The conditions were awful. There were over 200,000 children—most of them younger than 15—working themselves into an early grave. Carlota's idea was that young couples, picking out their wedding rings, would be assaulted with these appalling scenes on their Google Glass and steer clear of any rings made from the gold mined by children.

What was striking was her guts in making this presentation to us. I could see her boss getting more and more uncomfortable as she became ever more emotional. When one of my colleagues asked about the technical feasibility of what she was proposing, she shot back, "You're the guys with the algorithms. Can't you figure something out?"

At that point the scales fell. We were all so high and mighty in Silicon Valley. We alone were going to save the world. The customers just needed to give us their personal data and we would do the rest. The rest turned out to make us all very rich and eliminate scores of jobs through the automation we fostered. I went home that night to my penthouse apartment on Nob Hill, thinking she had a point. What was this all for? Is Google Glass just another luxury good?

Carlota turned out to be an interesting character we hadn't heard the end of. I knew her boss, Jake, pretty well in those days. He was in fact one of her biggest admirers, but he had to let her go after the presentation. Actually, I think it was by mutual agreement. She clearly had a higher calling.

After Carlota left the consultancy, she started a movement to demand more social responsibility from the tech companies. It was a time in the city where the resentments were rising fast against the tech companies. I was part of the problem. I had no intention of living in the Valley when San Francisco lay just a BART or bus ride away. Who could blame us? But the problem was that even at that time I was making high six figures well on the way to a seven-figure salary with stock options. With all that cash in our pockets, we in the tech industry pumped up property prices, making the old neighborhoods unaffordable to their current inhabitants. Then the inevitable happened: protesters smashed a window on a Google commuter bus taking employees from the city out to the Valley. There were also the shocking revelations about the companies providing the National Security Agency with the private communications of our customers.

Well, Carlota had a nose for where the wind was blowing. To be fair, she was no Luddite and believed in the promise of technology to deliver a better life for all. But she also knew her history. The benefits were often uneven. The ones who needed the help the most were often the last to see a benefit. Inequality was getting entrenched, and technology was part of the problem.

The Valley had amassed too many of the profits. It wasn't just the poor who weren't seeing a benefit, but the middle class was suffering. A lot of well-paying jobs had been eliminated. All of us at Google or Facebook lived in a bubble. Everything was handed to us on a silver platter, making us think we were the cat's meow.

The tech companies charged me with getting to know Carlota and then negotiating with her. She told me that "all revolutions are middle-class revolutions." It starts with small things. A fruit seller not being able to get a government license and immolating himself is one example. Many are contagious—think of 1789, 1848, or 1918. Or the waves of liberation movements that were led by educated middle-class lawyers—the Gandhis and Nehrus. She stressed that we have to make the system work for the middle class and poor.

She was such a tough bargainer. The problem for me was that I was really on her side. She convinced me that the tech companies had been living off others, preaching the gospel of sharing but refusing to share back. We were the new bankers. In fact, the *Economist* at the time predicted that tech executives would "join bankers and oilmen in public demonology."[1]

Carlota knew how to wield the guilt card. She led a campaign called "poor neighbors," arguing in scores of lectures, media interviews, and journal articles that the tech companies were amassing great wealth by putting many Americans out of work. That was to be expected in a technology revolution. But Carlota calculated that together they were hoarding cash—almost $500 billion—and not putting it to work.[2] She harped on the theme that they used Americans' personal data to make their fortunes but did not put anything back in the community. Why weren't they training the next generation? Or helping those whom they made redundant find and train for new employment? Unlike Ford at the turn of the twentieth century, they did not employ a lot of people. He put a lot of horses, stables, and those who drove the horse-drawn vehicles out of business, but he also turned around and employed these people for good wages so they could buy his cars. The new technologists did not spread the wealth. And they even tried to dodge taxes. Taxes that many communities were in desperate need of.

Carlota started a boycott against some of the product lines. Surprisingly, college students in the San Francisco area who were supposed to be the most addicted to their gadgets were the first to boycott and picket Apple and other stores.

Carlota got some unsolicited help as well. My company and some others suffered cyberattacks. There were some accusations that she had organized the attacks. I don't think so. I always thought it was an inside job. Her arguments were very persuasive, and I think there were some tech workers who used the opportunity to vent their frustration with management through a couple of well-timed and very embarrassing cyberattacks. The Snowdens of this world don't just work for the government, if you know what I mean. Anyway, the attacks and charges and countercharges only fueled greater controversy about the role of the companies. In the court of public opinion, she won her case.

I got the job of negotiating with her because about the time the cyberattacks occurred, I went to the CEO and told him he was going to lose big if he and other heads of big tech companies didn't make some concessions. It took some weeks of wrangling with him and the board. They just couldn't under-stand what the furor was all about. I remember the CEO saying he had just given several hundred thousand dollars to help school systems in deprived areas so they could improve their science and technology education. And that was just the tip of the iceberg. Hundreds of millions had gone to chari-table causes over the years. Moreover, a lot of their programs on the Web were free, such as maps where you could find the nearest clinics offering flu shots. The customers had benefited enormously from what the company had done. Why were they so ungrateful?

In the end, it was fear more than anything that drove the companies to make a deal. They worried that her campaign was beginning to get backing from some politicians who talked about making the tech industry "public utilities," which would give local authorities the ability to closely regulate them. We voluntarily agreed to contribute 5 percent of our revenues—which worked out to be $40 billion or so a year—to a fund that a nonprofit disbursed to needy school districts and retraining centers for the long-term unemployed. Carlota pressed to have the agreement put into law—the only thing she and her team eventually backed down on.

I have to hand it to her. No one else could have done what she did. Maybe it was because she had not grown up in the States that she was so effective. People looked up to her because they knew she had come up the hard way. She had a ruthless streak that served her well.

We remained friends after she left the city. She started a campaign to change the schools in Central America. A lot of teachers there drew their sala-ries but did not show up to school to teach every day. They would sometimes send others in their place, less qualified to teach the classes. It meant educa-tional standards were poor and the kids had a hard time succeeding. A lot of the parents wanted a better life for their children and realized it was only through education that they could move up the ladder. Carlota gave the kids miniature cameras to record the teachers' absences. A couple of the pupils who did this were kidnapped and their ears cut off and sent back to intimidate the parents. Carlota managed to get the police on the kidnappers' tracks to find the children. They were released. With all the publicity, central governments were forced to correct the problem and the schools noticeably improved. But some of the parents blamed Carlota for putting their children in danger.

After that she went back home to Chile and ran for mayor of a large city. Her opponent was an old-time party boss. Carlota wanted to root out corruption and make the city—ironically enough—into the technology hub in Chile. A former manufacturing center, it was losing out to Asian competition, but it had a good university. Carlota got back in touch with me to see whether Google or one of the big tech companies would want to set up a research lab there. But before I could respond, she went missing. This was a week or so before the election, which many thought she would win. She was never found, and now most people think she was kidnapped by a crime syndicate there and executed.

But Carlota's spirit still lives. The university in the city where she was running for mayor was renamed in her honor. The tech companies together endowed an institute at Stanford that is dedicated to examining the impact of technology on the global middle class.

A couple of years after her disappearance when everyone had lost hope of finding her, she was given the Amartya Sen Award, and there was a ceremony to honor her. Jake, her old boss, accepted it on her behalf. In his speech, he summed up what most of us learned from Carlota: like Amartya Sen, "Carlota stressed human development. When China pulled itself out of poverty, many had hoped that its development model would be something for others to emulate, but there's as much or more inequality there as in the West. Where's the economic model to make the system work for human development? Do we all have to send our sons and daughters to Yale, where Carlota studied, so they can make it? Are they all supposed to major in science and technology so they can earn a decent wage afterwards? What about the hundreds of thousands who don't go to Yale? Can they aspire to a decent middle class life for themselves and their families?

"Carlota saw that the system, whether in China, the US, or Latin America, wasn't up to the task of human development. Sure, we have seen real strides in reducing poverty. But big pockets of poverty still exist, which she saw on her trips to West Africa. Until everybody has a chance of realizing their full potential, we have failed. The individual has a responsibility for working hard. If he doesn't, he should not expect a handout from charity or the state. She learned this from her father. But many people are working hard and still cannot get ahead. This included many in the middle class who started off with many more advantages but still cannot make it. Technology is a double-edged sword. She believed a new popular movement was needed to take on the entrenched interests. It's my belief that she lost her life because those interests saw her and her work as a threat."

**AT THE TIME I THOUGHT THE COMMITMENT** we made to donate a part of our profits would be enough. And initially that seemed to calm the opposition and gave hope that we would see greater mobility. Many people put great store in the shale revolution to restore America's manufacturing might. And it worked for a while, until the rest of the world caught up and the energy price differentials weren't as great anymore and the United States did not hold a big advantage. I guess what was more startling for me was the progress others had been making in the new technologies, such as the green or alternative fuels. The United States, by contrast, was falling behind. For most of America, it was cheaper to convert to natural gas and not worry about climate change.

The auto companies led a revolt against the stringent CAFE* standards stipulating mileage per gallon for vehicles, which the Obama administration had put in place. The next administration extended the time for the automakers to comply. With such an abundance of shale oil at home, the global price of oil had stayed low and Americans were still buying big cars.

Other countries—particularly China—were getting ahead in green technology and other areas. I can remember back during the sequestration in the Obama period that there were graphs showing the dwindling amounts of federal revenues going to research and development. At the time, there was a big debate. Again the tech companies and others took the position that businesses could handle all the R&D, even though we in the tech industry didn't have the type of basic research labs like the old Bell Labs. We weren't pushing back the frontiers of science. Our research had to be fit for commercializing within a three-to-five-year window at the very most. Often management wanted an even quicker turnaround time. The universities had

---

* The Corporate Average Fuel Economy (CAFE) are regulations aimed at improving the fuel efficiency of cars and light trucks sold in the United States.

relied on federal support, and when this was no longer flowing, the pure research there also dried up.

We therefore found ourselves in the worst of all possible worlds. We were caught up in the automation revolution, which had gained momentum. IT, artificial intelligence, and big data keep making more and more job sectors redundant, eliminating middle-income jobs. Businesses could increase their profitability by eliminating more people. There was a tiny group of winners at the top and a vastly larger group struggling below. In 2012, the top 1 percent of Americans earned 22 percent of combined incomes, more than double their share in the 1980s. In the next decade or so, that share increased to over 25 percent. We had hoped the investment by the tech companies in schools and universities would help, but it clearly wasn't enough. More worrisome, US education levels were still middling: American kids continued to trail Asians in the league tables.

Another issue was also coming back to the fore—aging. During the Obama years, there was a lot of talk about cutting back on entitlements—Social Security, Medicare, welfare, etc. Health costs were spiraling out of control. The Republicans and Democrats fought viciously with each other. Republicans wanted to cut to the bone. Democrats did not want to give an inch; they were worried about cutbacks hurting the most vulnerable, including the shrinking middle class. Obamacare became a new battleground. Republicans contended we could not afford it; Democrats countered that it was a matter of social justice. The parties were so divided and so intent on not compromising that eventually any effort at restructuring entitlements and putting them on a solid financial footing—either through increased taxes or cuts in benefits—was shelved. The parties decided to let another generation solve the problem.

Since then the demographic picture hasn't looked as great as we once hoped. In the 1990s and the first decade of the twenty-first century, we had managed to keep up our birthrate, and that helped us maintain our position as a first-rate economic power. Of course, the dirty little secret was that it wasn't native-born Americans who were keeping up the birthrate; rather, it was largely due to the large intake of immigrants who had more children than most Americans. But, after the 2008 financial crisis, the birthrate of immigrants here began to fall.

At the other end of life cycle, we were also living longer. This was happening everywhere. That meant that there would be fewer in the workforce to support those in retirement if the retirement age stayed the same. But those in retirement would need to be supported longer. And retirees did not want to lose out to the rate of inflation. They wanted their Social Security checks to keep up with rising costs.

In the 2020s it was getting harder and harder to square the circle as the baby boomers were retiring in droves. And some businesses were hurting because those retirees had a lot of skills that the less-educated younger generation had not acquired. The younger generation was also hard hit. There were a lot of studies that showed that they had far less real income and wealth than their parents at the same point in their careers. Millennials who had been optimistic about their ability to do better than their parents even in the throes of the Great Recession were now losing hope.

Several years back I had to do a report on the US middle class for the tech industry, and I was amazed how much it had shrunk. I wasn't calculating by drops in real income or the widening gap with the super-rich. I was much more interested in Americans' own estimation of where they stood. Back in 2008 just as the financial crisis hit, the proportion of Americans who considered themselves middle class had stood at 53 percent. In 2014, it had shrunk to 44 percent. Even then there was a sense of Americans sinking, with 40 percent of people defining themselves as lower class. A decade on from that the picture has gotten only bleaker—particularly for the young. Now over 60 percent see themselves as lower class with no possibility of bettering themselves. I was astonished.

As I think I mentioned, at that time I had moved over from Google to head the industry body the tech companies had put together during the negotiations with Carlota. Besides handling the negotiations, the body then was reconstituted as the Big Eight Good Neighbors Trust, or "Begnot" as it came to be known in the media. You remember that the big oil companies used to be called the seven sisters. Well, we wanted to be gender neutral. We were fishing about for a name and then Carlota said, "Why don't you turn around the slogan I used and call yourselves 'good neighbors'?" All of the eight big US tech companies wanted to be involved, so we wanted to feature that in the title. I think it was the *Financial Times* that came up with the "Beg-not," which the members did not like, but it stuck.

The first director had floundered. From her perch in Central America, Carlota was beginning to make rumblings about the tech companies not living up to their promises. The CEOs of the big eight knew I had forged a good working relationship with her.

I think we did a good job. But our best was not good enough. Silicon Valley always prided itself on not depending on the government. In fact, we all had to pull together if we were going to lick the growing inequalities and underemployment problem. And for that we needed good government. And not just a federal government where the parties were civil to each other. We needed government to tackle real issues. The politicians needed to come together and make some hard decisions, ones that their core constituencies wouldn't necessarily like even if everyone benefited down the road.

I didn't think the political system was up to it, and I didn't know how it would ever be reformed in order to be able to make the needed long-term measures. The famous economist Milton Friedman once wrote that you should prepare your arguments ahead of time and then, when a crisis strikes, you could go into high gear and be there to offer solutions.[3] America was being rocked by several long-term trends coming together: aging, lack of basic R&D investment for innovation, second-rate primary and secondary education, an increasingly pessimistic underclass, and entitlement programs that were gobbling up most of the federal budget. You could not turn any of these around quickly. If you waited too long, it could be toast, in my estimation, for the United States. The emerging countries were surging ahead even if they had terrible problems that increased security demands on the United States.

I was pretty blue for a while.

But then I met the woman who put us back on track. Unlike Carlota, who stood out from the moment you met her, Melanie Johnson would have been the last to catch your attention in a room full of people. From the Deep South, she spoke very softly with a strong southern accent. Everything about her screamed—if that's the word—gentility, as in white parasols and mint juleps on the veranda. However, she actually came from a poor background. Her family had been first settlers in Alabama, but since the Civil

War had struggled to stay afloat. They scrimped and saved to send her to the University of Virginia where she eventually earned a law degree. She entered a small law firm back in Alabama and would probably have stayed there. But she fell in love and married an up-and-coming state politician who eventually won a seat in the House of Representatives. Unlike most couples, they both moved to Washington. Melanie and Jack hadn't started a family, and Melanie wanted to try her luck in establishing a career in the capital. Colleagues from UVA introduced her to some of the law firms in town and she accepted a job offer. She never made partner because she took time off to have their children—two boys. The law firm was laying off associates because they could get faster and cheaper results from robots doing case law review, so after a few years of working part time she was out of a job. The marriage began to break down, and after getting a divorce, she moved back to Alabama with the children. Jack came back a couple of weekends a month to see them, but increasingly it was just Melanie and the boys. She worked at a small law practice and had a hard time making ends meet. Jack was not rich, and as a congressman had to support two residences—one in Washington, the other in his constituency—and also pay child-care support. He remarried a woman with a couple of kids, and they lived in Washington.

I think Melanie's southern white upbringing was an important component in her later leadership. Melanie's family knew what it was like to struggle. When it came to her eventual political career, it was clear that it wasn't just her own up-and-down life story but also her family's checkered fortunes that helped her understand and connect. She did not give into adversity and that also counted. No one wanted a leader who bemoaned our sorry state. Whatever her mood, she was always supremely well dressed with every hair in place. I don't think we men have quite that same fortitude. It probably could only have been a woman, with not just the empathy but also the guts, who could have tackled our problems.

Several years after moving back to Alabama, Melanie got the political bug. She was upset with the school system. Her two boys had started in private school when they returned, but the cost was getting prohibitive. She decided to put them in public schools and was appalled at the quality of the teaching. She ran for the school board and won. All the parents worried that if their kids did not get a good education, they could not get into the better universities. Once she was on the school board, she realized that funding was a big issue. She knew other parents couldn't and wouldn't vote in a tax hike. Eventually she reached out to the Trust, and that's how I got to know her. We helped support the system even though it wasn't exactly in the most deprived area. But standards were sinking even in what had been formerly middle-to-upper-income communities.

Melanie was a joy to work with. She read up on all the studies on how to improve STEM education and had a lot of ideas of her own. I still would not have guessed that I was dealing with the first woman president of the United States. Her rise after that was meteoric. She decided to skip running for a statehouse position and instead contested a US House seat. The constituency lines had been redrawn so she was not running against her husband. In fact, like him, she was Republican. The incumbent retired and had known her through Jack and actually supported her candidacy. He helped her raise the funds. It was a safe Republican seat, so once she won the Republican Party primary, the expenses were not as great for getting elected as it was for most other new candidates.

Over the next four terms, Melanie rose up through the ranks. She wasn't very partisan, but she was popular with her Republican colleagues and the voters who saw her as going for practical solutions. She told everyone she wanted to get things done. I continued to see her because she worked on education issues. She also got turned on to the need to support pure research. This wasn't such a popular stance with her party, who thought the private sector knew how to "pick winners." She tried to explain that what she had in mind was different. She wanted the federal government to get back to funding DARPA and the National Institutes of Health at the old levels. She managed to convince people by playing the national card. She went on a tour of China, Brazil, and India, and everywhere she went she tweeted out pictures of new commercial successes there that had been achieved by government research efforts. She hoped to reach voters and sway them. The media picked up on her tweets, portraying her as a party maverick, which she was not happy about. She got the increased funding, though. Popular opinion was being swayed—why weren't we trying to keep our technological lead? She convinced her political colleagues it wasn't going to take huge amounts of money by comparison to the entitlement outlays.

At that point, I also got a taste of her hardball tactics. In the midst of her campaign, she went after the Trust—why weren't we doing more? She had her staff prepare graphs showing the big eight's funding of pure research had been going down. I pointed out to her that they had manipulated some of the numbers. She dismissed it, saying, "It's all in a good cause." "Yes," I said, "but the tactics should also be good." She just smiled.

She was already planning to try to get on the presidential ticket. She didn't have the financial backing but knew one of the Republican candidates who would do well to have a woman vice president. She had the profile then and popularity. Her candidate friend actually won but did not pick her. He lost the election, which to her was just desserts for his poor judgment in not choosing her.

Four years later she mounted a more serious effort. At that point, she was seen throughout the country as a viable candidate. She ran for president, but halfway through the primaries it was clear she was going to get beaten by one of the more hard-line conservative governors. With the presidential defeat four years earlier, many of the party faithful wanted to go back to core values. Though not disliked by the party faithful, Melanie had the reputation as a centrist. She thought she might have a chance of being picked as the running mate, but he made it clear several months before the convention that she was likely to be again passed over.

I was in Washington and met her just after she had been confidentially told she would not be picked. She was in the doldrums, perhaps the saddest I had ever seen her. Little did I know how quickly her fortunes would change.

I don't think we've had a really serious third party candidate since Ross Perot, and maybe Ron Paul. Most pundits would have said it could never be done. I would have agreed, but there were special circumstances. The Democratic president was highly unpopular even with his core constituency. He had been forced to scale back some of the entitlements. The economy was in another bad patch, a killer for any incumbent president. It wasn't anything like the Great Recession, but unemployment had shot higher from its already elevated level. For the Republicans, this should have been a golden opportunity. Instead the Republican core constituency took the party to the right. In the primary campaign, the Republican candidate talked about slashing the budget, including scrapping Social Security for everybody under 35.

This created an opening for a third party candidate, which is where I came in. I'm a pretty good fund-raiser. I've been handling the Trust's money, which means I know a lot of rich people—rich people who like me were getting more and more worried about the drift in American politics and wanted to change that. I was Melanie's paymaster.

How did she succeed? Obviously I was able to marshal the necessary financing, which is a must in American political campaigns. And then there was the weakness of her opponents. But it wasn't just about being in the right place at the right time. Melanie had new ideas. The public understood that some pretty dramatic changes were needed and the old left/right ideological battles were not getting us anywhere. Her story connected with others—a single mother who understood the everyday battles parents faced. Who else in high political office had served on the local school board and had to deal with improving education for their children? Her running mate, Minh, was the Democratic governor of Maryland, son of Vietnamese immigrants and originally a doctor. The two appealed to the growing segment of Americans who were trying to cling to their middle-class status.

Melanie was not out to create a third party. Her strategy was to leverage popular support from both parties and try to govern from the middle. I did not see how this was going to succeed. But Melanie and Minh got lucky. Her deft handling of a crisis in the Middle East early in her administration helped anchor her in everybody's judgment as presidential.

Melanie will perhaps always be best known for the civilian service corps she established soon after taking office. She offered young people the chance to get a couple of years of free university tuition if in return they devoted two years after graduation to working in any number of public service goods from hospitals and schools to NGOs and local government. This became a popular way for many middle-class families to afford sending their sons and daughters to university. Equally, Melanie used it as a leverage to force the universities to stabilize tuition costs. Universities were blacklisted from the program if they did not make their education more affordable. For those in the program, the federal government only paid a set fee and universities, if they expected to get research funds, had to agree to the tuition fees the government was prepared to pay. Several states also jumped in with additional service corps programs aimed at helping middle-class families afford college costs. To stay in the programs, students had to maintain a B average.

At the same time, Melanie got Congress to allocate more money to universities for basic research. She also demanded the Trust do more. She told me the tech industry wasn't going to get a pass just because we had bankrolled her.

The challenge for Melanie in all of this was where to find the money to pay for these innovative programs. She had to make some tough choices and in the end tilted in the direction of providing better skills for the young by exacting sacrifices from seniors, especially the wealthier ones. If the young were expected to spend a minimum of a couple years in low-paying jobs, then seniors also must sacrifice for the long-term benefit of the country. She demanded that wealthier seniors pay more of the costs of their Medicare. She got Congress to agree to a means test for Social Security recipients. No one would have thought this would have been possible years before. Melanie touched about every third rail there was in politics and still got a coalition of centrist Democrats and Republicans to go along. But the economic crisis the United States faced at her election—unlike the Great Recession—proved an opportunity to get agreement between the parties. A decade of high youth unemployment and sinking working age participation in the economy left America with few options.

This was a historic moment for the United States, but it had even bigger ramifications.

Other countries faced similar if not worse dilemmas. Some tried to wall themselves to avoid making any big changes, but they also faced an inevitable decline. For Melanie and Minh, it was vital that the United States avoid such a fate. On her tour of the emerging powers, she had been stung by accusations that democracy wasn't up to the big challenges. Everyone pointed to the logjam in Washington as evidence. She agreed that the US political system needed to be overhauled but strongly rejected the notion that democracy had had its day.

Minh was a huge help in all of this. For Melanie the initial attraction was that he personified the American Dream when others thought it had died.

His parents were political refugees who fled on one of the last US flights out of Saigon before the communists took over. Minh was born several years after their arrival in America. His parents had a restaurant on the outskirts of Washington where Minh worked through his college years. He went to medical school and became an orthopedist with the idea of joining a private practice. With his patients being middle-aged or elderly, he became interested in the aging process, not just physically but also mentally. This led him to think about how the education system needed to change. Lifetime learning was needed now more than ever, when people lived longer and both wanted and had to continue to work.

He saw daily in his medical practice that physical well-being is connected to maintaining mental agility. But with all the fast-paced innovations, a college education was out of date practically at graduation. Most firms no longer trained their people. Small ones did not have the means. The large ones assumed most employees would not stay longer than five years. Increasingly getting new skills necessary for moving up was now the responsibility solely of the employees, but this was difficult due to the expense or just finding the time.

Minh convinced the University of Maryland to conduct an experiment. Employees of some of the top firms in the state would have the option of contributing 1 percent of their income to be matched several times over by their employers. The money would support a program of lifetime learning. Employees could get time off to go back periodically to upgrade their skills. They could also prepare themselves for switching careers. After all, with better quality of life, you were now expected to work well past 65. Firms would have a workforce that kept up with the fast pace of technological change.

Universities would need to change, however. They could no longer be just the bastions of the young at the start of their careers. Participants in courses were increasingly of all ages. Professors' lectures were online, but Minh thought classroom discussions and laboratory experience was still critical. Minh also strongly backed the liberal arts. He was a scientist at heart but heard increasingly from firms that their employees lacked creativity and imagination. Minh thought there might have been too much of an emphasis on STEM education. Innovation was not just a matter of compiling lots of data. It was also learning how to reconceptualize old ideas—things that robots could not do. Minh's education task force—when he became vice president—dwelt as much on reviving the liberal arts—literature, art, music, and design—as improving STEM curriculum.

Melanie had to be persuaded. She had so many friends who were liberal arts graduates and struggled to make a living. Minh said it was not a matter of either/or. Being able to increasingly bridge the gap would be an important leadership quality in all walks of life, not just business.

Minh stood as an example of the important contribution made by immigrants. But fewer had come since the Great Recession. The United States had made immigration less attractive and more difficult; immigrants were going elsewhere. Some European countries that needed skilled workers started siphoning them away from America by offering them big incentives to settle, including fast-track citizenship. China was also making tempting offers, particularly to scientists. Fewer international students were coming to the United States.

Halfway into her first term once the economy had picked up, Melanie offered a courageous immigration bill. She told the country, "America has to stay young." She wanted to extend visas to PhDs who wanted to stay after they finished their degrees. She gave extra funding to universities to take in international students, especially in the sciences, and help them to stay afterward.

Melanie told me, "What distinguishes the US is its cultural diversity." Other countries had a distinct, often religious or ethnically based, culture, developed over ages. The United States was a mélange, and that would be its continuing strength. No one could top that.

She decided to take a historic step. I was in the Cabinet room when it happened, sitting with her other advisors along the wall. Melanie and Minh faced each other, surrounded by all the Cabinet members. She was briefing them on the State of the Union speech she was giving in the next week.

"You know how much Minh and I believe the US needs to return to its roots and be an immigrant country. Immigrants are what built this country, and our economic well-being and standing in the world depends on our remaining so. Immigrants need to know that they are welcome here."

"Madam President, with all due respect, we did pass an immigration measure, which has increased the intake of the highly skilled. I don't think it's fair for the Republican half of your Cabinet to have to go back to the well and drum up support for another measure," interjected the attorney general, a Republican.

"Madam President, speaking for the other half of the Cabinet, even Democrats are likely to get push-back," added the labor secretary. "The economy's much better, but there's still a lot of worry about jobs."

"I realize all this, ladies and gentlemen, and I'm not asking for another immigration bill. I want to change the Constitution. The lawyers here will recall that Section 1 of Article II of the United States Constitution states that no person except a natural born citizen is eligible for president. The framers supposedly wanted to protect the nation from foreign influence. I want to demonstrate that nothing stops any US citizen, wherever he or she was born, from becoming president."

There was a hush and some raised eyebrows. But Melanie got her way that day and, over time, in Congress. She is now urging the states to accede to the constitutional amendment making all US residents eligible.

From what Jack Jr. tells me, there's more to come. Melanie relied heavily on him since the time of the divorce. Now he works on long-range policy. His main interest is how to institutionalize the changes that have happened. He and Melanie worry that once she's out of office, US politics will revert back to the usual party-against-party fights. At Melanie's direction, he is working on other constitutional amendments that would cut back on the amount of money that can be spent in election campaigns, as well as making it impossible for state legislatures to gerrymander electoral districts. With these measures, politics can return to being about practical results. Melanie does not want to eliminate the two-party system, but rather strengthen the centrists in both of them. "She's just waiting for the right moment," Jack Jr. said in his strong southern drawl. The country may be getting more than they bargained for.

I'm not sure what we should call the new system. Somebody ventured that Melanie updated FDR's New Deal, and we should call the new system the New Deal 2.0. Melanie is still a Republican at heart. I doubt if she would approve. Melanie did more than tweak the modern social welfare system. She didn't try to dismantle Social Security or Medicare. But the system was running itself into the ground, benefiting many who did not need it. The growth of entitlement expenditures was making it impossible for government to fund anything else, like ensuring all youngsters had a good education or even a strong defense.

Just as important, she understood that times had changed. The tech revolution was qualitatively different from anything we'd seen. The gap with other countries was closing and we faced a lot of new competitors, a much different environment than when FDR introduced the New Deal. In starting to overhaul the political system, she took on the Constitution, you might say. Like many lawyers, she revered historic precedents and did not want to change for change's sake. But fundamental conditions had changed, and we needed to make radical changes if we were to preserve our basic values. Few other politicians would have taken the risk, but she wanted to make the system work again.

# Are We Prepared for the Future?

AS YOU MIGHT HAVE GUESSED, I DON'T BELIEVE WE ARE FULLY PREPARED FOR THE FUTURE. I fear America recently missed an opportunity to lay the basis for a more assured economic future. Crises are opportunities, and at the height of the Great Recession, we seemed poised to tackle the entitlement issues and long-term debt. The bipartisan Simpson-Bowles proposal laid out a long-term plan for reining in future budgetary deficits, ensuring future generations would not be bankrupted by funding Social Security for their elders while at the same time not cutting back substantially on benefits. By taking action now, the pain would be less all around for everyone in the future. This is a prime example of good planning, but political paralysis struck, and both political parties have to bear responsibility.

Ironically the longed-for recovery seems finally to be happening, but it has eased pressures on lawmakers to take the tough decisions on America's long-term future. The budget deficit is coming down to more manageable levels even though the debt could still grow dangerously high over the long run. In other words, the can was kicked down the road. Worse, if we wait too long, the markets may impose more draconian measures to rein in deficits and cut the debt.

All of this is perfectly predictable due to a shrinking workforce and an aging population. We're not in as bad shape as other advanced industrial economies, but Social Security and the higher health-care costs are not sustainable over the next 20 to 30 years without cutbacks or added revenues to support the programs.

Other issues come to mind where we can prepare for the future. Our infrastructure is crumbling and needs massive repairs. Historically low interest rates make reconstruction affordable if we have a plan for putting our economic house in order. Such infrastructure investment is more than ever needed, too, in view of the more extreme and destructive storms we are seeing along our coastlines. Hurricane Sandy was a foretaste. We don't know exactly where climate change impacts will be the worst, but we have enough historic data to know that the risk is growing for everyone. The United States will likely be spared the worst, but our coastlines are vulnerable to storm surges and, over a longer time frame, serious sea level rise. Forest fires that rage yearlong point to the likelihood of long-term drought for portions of the Southwest. Just as we insure our homes for fires that we hope won't happen, it's in our long-term interest to prepare for potential disaster.

Science and innovation are our future. Left or right on the political spectrum, the Internet, social media, and more recently shale energy are held up as symbols of US greatness—something other countries have a hard time duplicating. But government funding for basic research has been cut over the past couple decades. The sums are not large and if restored would not add significantly to the deficit or debt. Research has shown the private sector won't step in to fund basic research. Whatever the genius of Steve Jobs in designing the iPhone, it was US government–funded agencies like DARPA and the National Science Foundation that took the risk of developing the underlying path-breaking technologies.

Immigration reform is key too. The debate has focused largely on how immigrants take away jobs or put a burden on our social welfare programs. For the most part this is not true. The benefits of immigration largely outweigh the costs. A growing population is an important economic asset and provides the underlying basis for great power status.

Because the immigration debate has become so toxic, any legislative measures on it have been endlessly deferred. Important provisions that are probably not controversial get sacrificed. For years, universities have wanted their foreign PhD students in science, engineering, and technology to be able to stay after they graduate. Many newly minted graduates want to remain and set up new businesses that the United States needs. The numbers are small—hundreds or low thousands at most if you count their families. Lee Kuan Yew, Singapore's legendary leader and visionary, once quipped that the United States would remain strong so long as the world's best and the brightest wanted to go and live there. We still have that gravitational pull, but we will have to work harder to remain the top destination. Putting up self-defeating obstacles—particularly when they involve little cost—is no way to prepare for the future.

Problems of domestic inequality are much harder to solve. While inequality between nations has lessened, internally it's a different story, not just in the United States but elsewhere, including in the developing world. Although necessary for solving the big global challenges like resource scarcities, technology is displacing workers and, in some cases, eliminating whole categories of jobs. There is evidence that the threshold for taxing the rich could be raised without undermining incentives for the rich to save and invest. But it would entail political and economic risks, and it is unclear the degree to which it would eliminate inequality. Without significant efforts across a wide front—from better primary and secondary education to more targeted tax incentives for job creation and increased taxes on the wealthy— inequality could grow worse.

As mentioned, I have noticed in my visits to US universities a growing pessimism about the future, but recently the evidence has become more than anecdotal. In December 2013, 54 percent of those surveyed expect American life to go downhill, while only 23 percent think it will improve, according to a survey from the AP-NORC Center for Public Affairs Research.[1]

In interviews, most of those surveyed were content with their own lives but worried about what was to come. Technology was, interestingly, one of the topics mentioned as contributing to the downward trend. "Changes will come, and some of them are scary," says Kelly Miller, 22, a freshly minted University of Minnesota sports management grad. The news report said that she is looking forward to some wonderful things, like 3D printers creating organs for transplant patients. But Miller envisions Americans in 2050 blindly relying on robots and technology for everything from cooking dinner to managing their money. "It's taking away our free choice and human thought," she says. "And there's potential for government to control and regulate what this artificial intelligence thinks."[2]

The potential loss of a sense of self-determination with the development of artificial intelligence is disturbing. Without agreement on how artificial intelligence is used, robots and other devices could be literally making life-and-death decisions without much human involvement. For a number of years, some scientists have worried about "killer robots" relying on nothing but algorithms to decide which human targets to liquidate on the battle-field.[3] How do we make sure that our lives are not dictated by algorithms and that we keep a say in important decisions? We haven't started the debate on where to stop smart devices from making independent decisions based on preloaded algorithms.

Scientists believe parents will have the ability in the not too distant future to select the embryo with the most desirable combination of genes they would like to see in their offspring and then use in-vitro fertilization to produce them.[4] This opens up huge ethical questions. Should we have that right? And also profound social issues and even geopolitical ones: What if only the rich can afford the procedure? What happens when such a right is banned in one place but is offered elsewhere? These are difficult problems even for the most knowledgeable experts. What is worrisome about the deteriorating levels in STEM education is that the public will have even less technical background with which to approach and decide these issues.

The growing pessimism and caution reflected in the recent polling is a worry in itself. America's hunker-down mentality could not have come at a worse time. This new world has vestiges of the bad old one where geopolitical rivalries led to major conflicts. This book has described situations in East Asia, South Asia, Eurasia, and the Middle East that recall the lead-up to the First World War and may require outside intervention. We may be pleasantly surprised by the willingness of others to help but need to prepare in case they don't. Other countries are equally absorbed at home and many are opposed, in principle, to intervention in others' domestic affairs even for humanitarian reasons.

Luckily, the past few years haven't been a total rerun of the 1930s, when America walled itself off from the rest of the world. While now growing, there still hasn't been the public opposition one would have expected—given our high unemployment—to Trans-Pacific Partnership (TPP) and Transatlantic Trade and Investment Partnership (TTIP), the two far-reaching, US-proposed free trade agreements that many Asians and Europeans want.

Where there has been large-scale opposition by the American public is to any US military role in stopping the civil war in Syria and reversing Russia's aggression against Ukraine. This is a source of concern if it sets a long-term precedent. Military intervention in Syria or Ukraine might not be feasible for a number of reasons, but military intervention is a necessary tool that should not be discarded. Military intervention may be needed to stop regional conflicts from growing and putting the global welfare in jeopardy.

In this new multipolar setting, however, the United States will have to tread carefully if intervention becomes necessary. World opinion is still leery of US military operations overseas. For many, there have been too many examples of US military activity that either made things worse (Iraq) or did not accomplish the stated mission (a stable and democratic Afghanistan). Public attitudes across the world and also in the United States have grown hostile to any power throwing around its weight. Many people will see in any US military operation an attempt by the United States to serve its own interests and not others.

Recalibrating the international system so that everybody takes responsibility for global peace and prosperity will be difficult. It was tried after the First World War with the creation of the League of Nations; US absenteeism was one of the reasons for the failure of the League and the drift to war in the 1930s. For many emerging states, the current international order smacks too much of being geared to protecting Western interests. Getting buy-in from the emerging powers will be difficult, particularly as they aren't eager for any of the responsibilities.

On the other hand, with the global economic activity shifting Eastward, the United States and its traditional Western partners don't have the clout and legitimacy to run it alone. US administrations under George W. Bush and Barack Obama have made a stab at developing strategic partnerships with the emerging powers, but I doubt if it has converted them yet to embrace Western international institutions.

China and Russia are probably the biggest question marks. China's assertiveness in the South and East China Seas reflects its belief in its right to regional dominance. On the other hand, Chinese statements about de-Americanizing the global financial system appear to me overblown. For the moment, at least, China needs what America produces—the technology know-how and innovation that it is hungry for.

Russia may be more difficult to handle. Many Russians—not just President Putin—believe Moscow made many sacrifices in peacefully dismantling the Soviet empire and ending the Cold War that went underappreciated in the West and by its Eurasian neighbors. For many Russians, it's now payback time. You're less constrained when you believe the status quo is not legitimate. Breaking with the West will entail huge economic costs for Russia, only increasing the long-term challenges facing them. However, we in the West have to be careful not to count out Russia, which we've done too many times before in history. We'll have to find ways to keep channels of communication open during this fraught period. A new cold war is not in the West's interest; it will only further splinter what is already an increasingly fragile international system. Russia's biggest asset is its human capital, and once the regime puts greater emphasis on the development of this important source of power, we could see a Russia that is no longer in decline.

For many years, I have believed the Chinese, Russian, and other new powers are destined to rewrite some but not all of the rules governing the international system. Why shouldn't they have that ambition? All new powers have it, and we need to be prepared for it. This will be a difficult process, but it does not have to end in conflict. All sides will need to be prepared to compromise, but we have an advantage over most now. Most of the emerging powers are far too occupied with the challenges at home. By trying to reform international institutions, we can help make sure the international system remains rules-based and does not revert to the historical norm of balance-of-power politics that led to so many conflicts in past centuries. But I fear the window is rapidly closing on rejuvenating those institutions and, in view of the growing assertiveness of both China and Russia, we could be headed earlier than I or others thought into a multipolar world without multilateralism, increasing the potential for conflict down the road.

How prepared are other countries for the future? The 2008 financial crisis hit the hardest elsewhere, such as Europe. It's too early to tell, but having shaken the very foundations of the European Union, the financial crisis may have done European countries a favor by forcing them to face up to their structural weaknesses. Just like Sweden or Canada, which endured financial crises in the early 1990s, those countries that follow through with the often painful structural reforms will come out much stronger. The upward climb will be steep. I worry especially about the declines in education and support for science and technology in many European states, making them less competitive in the global economy.

After a couple of decades of stagnation, we've seen Japanese prime minister Shinzo Abe attempt to move the needle and chart out to a different future from slow decline. Japan faces some of the harshest demographic challenges, but the small country still constitutes the third-largest economy and one that is technologically advanced and the home of many world-class corporations. Its future economic picture may not be as bleak as sometimes portrayed even if high levels of growth are out of its reach.

The biggest challenge for the Japanese may be in accommodating themselves to a rapidly changing neighborhood and West. Next door is China, on the verge of becoming the world's biggest global economic power with a huge pull throughout the region. As mentioned, China is likely to become more assertive, following a pattern set by most rising powers. Japanese leaders may have a misplaced assumption that the United States will automatically take Japan's side in any confrontation with China when it is more likely that the United States will seek a way to reconcile its interests with those of China and avoid conflict. Navigating both a rapidly changing neighborhood and a new global order will present major challenges that Japan has been slow to tackle.

China is the best example of a large country that has done large-scale strategic planning and achieved major goals over the course of its three-and-a-half-decade rise. It's hard not to be jealous. I've heard American CEOs of major global firms wax eloquent about China's ability to undertake strategic planning. China has had some advantages: a party that has a monopoly of power and a public highly desirous of reversing two centuries of decline and colonial exploitation. Such a powerful and shared narrative helps the government get buy-in on long-term strategic plans. It will be harder going forward. There are more competing interests to be assuaged. The goal of developing an innovative society is more difficult, and it's not clear that it can be done without moving toward democracy. Even the Chinese admit this. From what we know of the erratic and difficult nature of democratization, trying to strategically plan a smooth pathway to democracy seems a bit of an oxymoron, and yet many Chinese insist democracy must be China's destiny. No one knows how to achieve it without weakening the other pillars of the Chinese state and society.

Think tanks and government agencies in many other developing states, such as sub-Saharan Africa, are some of most accomplished practitioners of strategic thinking and scenario planning, but they face daunting challenges. They face a perfect storm of climate change, population explosion, resource scarcities, and governance deficits. I've tried to make the case that helping is not just a matter of moral necessity but also a matter of security for all of us. It's an opportunity for technology to show how it can solve some of the biggest global challenges.

**FOR ANY COUNTRY, THERE IS NO** cut-and-dried recipe for doing strategic planning. Most government planning is short term, even though we know that not tackling early on the long-term challenges only makes the process more painful. Until recently, we Americans didn't seem to need to do much strategic planning. It was a less competitive global environment. The challenges were perhaps less complex. We face the difficult task of altering our "business as usual" operations during a period of high flux. But there is growing fear that democracies and the frequent rotation of leaderships don't lend themselves to long-term planning and execution.

A first step would bring together the analysis on future trends with the decision-making process instead of allowing crises to drive the decision-making process toward immediate solutions despite the longer-term implications. A former US deputy national security advisor, Leon Fuerth, has developed a proposal for integrating foresight within the high-level decision-making process. In the US case, it would put a foresight cell inside the White

House to work on trends and possible scenarios across both the domestic and international arenas. The cell would work on anticipating upcoming challenges and opportunities as well as undertake a structured analysis on the long-range consequences of any decisions. It would make it harder for decision makers to ignore the unintended consequences of their actions. Such a redesign of government decision making may help ensure further crises are not triggered by the attempt to cure the current one. The close coordination of forecasting with strategic planning and decision making could be a template for others in the private sector who face the same problem of planning for a future of increasing uncertainty and volatility.[5]

How long can we afford to wait? Not too long is my answer. The United States has perhaps the most at stake if the international system doesn't work. But the old Pax Americana is fading and a new multipolar world arising. We can try our luck and hope for the best, but that seems an irresponsible way to face the future. Change can be either good or bad. The effort here is to help steer the inevitable change we face into an opportunity and a good.

# *Notes*

## INTRODUCTION: DON'T KILL THE MESSENGER

1. Laura Rozen, "The Fatalist: The Man Reshaping How US Intelligence Views the Future," *Foreign Policy* no. 172 (May–June 2009), http://www.questia.com /library/1G1-199864806/the-fatalist-the-man-reshaping-how-u-s-intelligence.
2. The full quotation is from a speech that President Eisenhower gave to the National Defense Executive Reserve Conference in Washington, DC, on November 14, 1957. "I tell this story to illustrate the truth of the statement I heard long ago in the Army: Plans are worthless, but planning is everything. There is a very great distinction because when you are planning for an emergency you must start with this one thing: the very definition of 'emergency' is that it is unexpected, therefore it is not going to happen the way you are planning." Public Papers of the Presidents of the United States, Dwight D. Eisenhower, 1957, National Archives and Records Service, Government Printing Office, p. 818: ISBN 0160588510, 9780160588518.
3. William Gibson is reported to have first said this in an interview on *Fresh Air*, NPR, August 31, 1993.

## CHAPTER 1: THE POWER OF ONE

1. Raymond F. Betts, "The French Revolution," *Europe in Retrospect: A Brief History of the Past Two Hundred Years* (Lexington, MA: DC Heath & Co, 1979), Chapter 2, also available at http://www.britannia.com/history/euro/1/2_1.html.
2. Dominic Wilson and Raluca Dragusanu, "The Expanding World Middle Class and Falling Global Inequality," Goldman Sachs, Global Economic Paper No. 170, July 7, 2008, available at https://360.gs.com.
3. "Global Trends 2030: Citizens in an Interconnected and Polycentric World," European Strategy and Policy Analysis System (ESPAS), April 2012, available at http://www.iss.europa.eu/publications/detail/article/espas-report-global-trends -2030-citizens-in-an-interconnected-and-polycentric-world/.
4. "2030: The 'Perfect Storm' Scenario," Population Institute, available at https:// www.populationinstitute.org/external/files/reports/The_Perfect_Storm _Scenario_for_2030.pdf.

5. Homi Kharas and Geoffrey Gertz, "The New Global Middle Class: A Cross-Over from West to East," Wolfensohn Center for Development, Brookings Institution, 2010, available at http://www.brookings.edu/~/media/research/files/papers/2010/3 /china%20middle%20class%20kharas/03_china_middle_class_kharas.pdf.

6. "Asia 2050: Realizing the Asian Century," Asian Development Bank, 2011, available at http://www.adb.org/publications/asia-2050-realizing-asian-century.

7. Kharas and Gertz, "The New Global Middle Class."

8. Ibid.

9. Wilson and Dragusanu, "Expanding World Middle Class."

10. Forecast provided by Professor Barry Hughes, University of Denver, using his International Futures Model.

11. Ibid.

12. Ibid.

13. Ibid.

14. Ibid.

15. Ibid.

16. Jakkie Cilliers, Barry Hughes, and Jonathan Moyer, *African Futures 2050* (Pretoria, South Africa: Institute for Security Studies, 2011), pp. 20–25.

17. Forecast provided by Professor Barry Hughes's International Futures Model.

18. "Number of Deaths due to HIV/AIDS," World Health Organization, 2012, available at http://www.who.int/gho/hiv/epidemic_status/deaths_text/en/.

19. Mario Pezzini, "An Emerging Middle Class," *OECD Observer*, 2012, available at http://www.oecdobserver.org/news/fullstory.php/aid/3681/An_emerging _middle_class.html.

20. Ibid.

21. For more on recent finds, see Eduard Gismatullin, "Tullow Finds More Kenyan Oil to Boost East Africa Exports," *Bloomberg News*, January 15, 2014, available at http://www.bloomberg.com/news/2014-01-15/tullow-finds-more-kenyan-oil -boosting-east-africa-export-plans.html.

22. Branko Milanovic, "Global Income Inequality by the Numbers: In History and Now," Policy Research Working Paper 6259, World Bank, November 2013, available at http://www-wds.worldbank.org/external/default/WDSContentServer/IW3P/IB /2012/11/06/000158349_20121106085546/Rendered/PDF/wps6259.pdf.

23. "Asia 2050," p. 23.

24. Janet R. Dickson, Barry B. Hughes, and Mohammod T. Irfan, *Advancing Global Education: Patterns of Potential Human Progress* (New Delhi: Oxford University Press India, 2010), p. 24.

25. Ibid., p. 49.

26. Data using the International Futures model provided to author by Professor Barry Hughes, University of Denver.

27. Dickson, Hughes, and Irfan, *Advancing Global Education*, pp. 28–29.

28. "Asian Universities," *Economist*, April 23, 2013, available at http://www .economist.com/blogs/graphicdetail/2013/04/focus-4.

29. Caroline S. Wagner and Loet Leydesdorff, "Implications for US Science Policy of the Growth of Global Science," unpublished paper, November 2013, Microsoft Word file.

30. "French Employment 2020: Five Priorities for Action," McKinsey Global Institute, March 2012, pp. 1–3, available at http://www.mckinsey.com/insights /employment_and_growth/french_employment_2020.

31. "Changing the Fortunes of America's Workforce: A Human Capital Challenge," McKinsey Global Institute, June 2009, available at MGI_Changing_the_fortunes_of_Americas_workforce_full_report.pdf.

32. Ibid.

33. Amit A. Pandya, *Muslim Indians: Struggle for Inclusion* (Washington, DC: Stimson Center, April 19, 2010), pp. 42–49, available at http://www.stimson.org/images/uploads/research-pdfs/Muslim_Indians-Complete.pdf.

34. Rahul Choudaha and Li Chang, "Trends in International Student Mobility," World Education Services, February 2012, available at http://www.uis.unesco.org/Library/Documents/research-trends-international-student-mobility-education-2012-en.pdf.

35. William Wan, "In China, Parents Bribe to Get Students into Top Schools, Despite Campaign against Corruption," *Washington Post*, October 7, 2013, available at http://www.washingtonpost.com/world/in-china-parents-bribe-to-get-students-into-top-schools-despite-campaign-against-corruption/2013/10/07/fa8d9d32-2a61-11e3-8ade-a1f23cda135e_print.html.

36. Evan Osnos, "Will the Middle Class Shake China?" *New Yorker*, March 8, 2013, available at http://www.newyorker.com/online/blogs/comment/2013/03/will-the-middle-class-shake-china.html.

37. Donald N. Jensen, "In Search of Russia's Middle Class," Institution of Modern Russia, May 29, 2013, available at http://russialist.org/in-search-of-russias-middle-class/; Josh Wilson, "Russia's Elusive Middle Class," School of Russian and Asian Studies, October 22, 2004, available at http://www.sras.org/russian_middle_class.

38. See work by Richard Cincotta on this point in his article "Socioeconomic Studies," in *Seismic Shift: Understanding Change in the Middle East*, E. Laipson, ed. (Washington, DC: Stimson Center, 2011), pp. 29–36, available at http://www.stimson.org/images/uploads/research-pdfs/Full_Pub_-_Seismic_Shift.pdf.

39. The US$15,000 level is calculated at purchasing power parity (PPP) rates. PPPs are the rates of currency conversion that equalize the purchasing power of different currencies by eliminating the differences in price levels between countries. In their simplest form, PPPs are simply price relatives that show the ratio of the prices in national currencies of the same good or service in different countries. For more on the concept of PPPs, see OECD, *Purchasing Power Parities—Frequently Asked Questions*, available at http://www.oecd.org/std/purchasingpowerparities-frequentlyaskedquestionsfaqs.htm.

40. See Li Jian and Niu Xiaohan's study on "The New Middle Class in Peking: A Case Study," *China Perspectives*, January–February 2003, available at chinaperspectives-228-45-the-new-middle-class-in-peking-a-case-study.pdf.

41. Osnos, "Will the Middle Class Shake China?"

42. Ibid.

43. Ibid.

44. For more information on the methodology, see US Department of Labor website information on the CPI, available at http://www.bls.gov/cpi/cpifaq.htm#Question_9.

45. Quotations from personal conversation in late October 2013, during a visit to MIT. Similar views were expressed by Professor Alex Pentland in his article "How Big Data Can Transform Society for the Better," *Scientific American* 309,

Issue 4 (September 17, 2013), available at http://www.scientificamerican.com /article/how-big-data-can-transform-society-for-the-better/.

46. Alex Pentland, "Big Data: Balancing the Risks and Rewards of Data Driven Public Policy," *Annual Global IT Report*, World Economic Forum (forthcoming).

47. Keith Bradsher, "China Blocks Web Access to *Times* after Article," *New York Times*, October 25, 2012, available at http://www.nytimes.com/2012/10/26 /world/asia/china-blocks-web-access-to-new-york-times.html.

48. Michael S. Chase and James C. Mulvenon, "You've Got Dissent! Chinese Dissident Use of the Internet and Beijing's Counter-Strategies," RAND, 2002, available at http://www.rand.org/pubs/monograph_reports/MR1543.html. Cited material from pp. 40–43 in first chapter, which can be accessed directly at http://www.rand.org/content/dam/rand/pubs/monograph_reports/MR1543 /MR1543.ch1.pdf.

49. Rebecca MacKinnon, "Google Confronts the Great Firewall," New America Foundation, May 31, 2012, available at http://newamerica.net/publications /articles/2012/google_confronts_the_great_firewall_69819.

50. Chase and Mulvenon, "You've Got Dissent!"

51. "Google's Eric Schmidt: Internet Could Make Censorship Impossible," interview with Scott Pelley, CBS News, February 24, 2014, available at http://www .cbsnews.com/news/googles-eric-schmidt-internet-could-make-censorship -impossible/.

52. Eric E. Schmidt and Jared Cohen, "The Future of Internet Freedom," *New York Times*, March 11, 2013, available at http://www.nytimes.com/2014/03/12 /opinion/the-future-of-internet-freedom.html.

53. Ibid.

54. "The World's Muslims: Religion, Politics and Society," Pew Research, April 30, 2013, available at http://www.pewforum.org/2013/04/30/the-worlds-muslims -religion-politics-society-overview/.

55. "Nationalism and Russia's Global Image," Pew Research, May 23, 2012, available at http://www.pewglobal.org/2012/05/23/chapter-5-nationalism-and-russias-global -image/.

56. European Strategy and Policy Analysis System (ESPAS), "Report on Global Trends 2030," Institute for Security Studies, European Union, April 27, 2012, http: //www.iss.europa.eu/publications/detail/article/espas-report-global-trends-2030 -citizens-in-an-interconnected-and-polycentric-world/; Pew Research Center, "The Global Middle Class: Views on Democracy, Religion, Values, and Life Satisfaction in Emerging Nations," February 12, 2009, http://www.pewglobal .org/2009/02/12/the-global-middle-class.

57. "Rethinking Personal Data: Strengthening Trust," World Economic Forum, May 2012, available at http://www3.weforum.org/docs/WEF_IT _RethinkingPersonalData_Report_2012.pdf.

58. Dr. Jacques Bughin and Dr. James Manyika, "Internet Matters: Essays in Digital Transformation," McKinsey Global Institute, March 2012, available at MGI _Internet_matters_essays_in_digital_transformation.pdf.

59. Roman Friedrich, Bahjat El-Darwiche, Milind Singh, and Alex Koster, "Digitization for Economic Growth and Job Creation: Regional and Industry Perspectives," Booz & Co., 2013, available at BoozCo_Digitization-for-Economic -Growth-and-Job-Creation.pdf.

## CHAPTER 2: A SPLINTERED WORLD

1.  Data provided by University of Denver Professor Barry Hughes' International Futures model, available on the web at http://www.ifs.du.edu/ifs/. See also *Global Trends 2030*, p. 17, for explanation of the global power indexes used here and later in chapter 2, available at http://www.dni.gov/index.php/about/organization /national-intelligence-council-global-trends.

2.  There are various estimates. The Centre for Economics and Business Research forecast in its late 2013 report that China's GDP measured at market exchange rates: "CEBR's World Economic League Table Report for 2013," December 26, 2013, available at http://www.cebr.com/reports/world-economic-league-table -report/. Many economic analysts predict that on a purchasing power parity (PPP) basis China will soon overtake the United States as the world's largest economy. The Economist Intelligence Unit, for example, projects this could occur by 2019 and that by 2030, China's economy could be 18.6 percent larger than that of the United States. Wayne M. Morrison, "China's Economic Rise: History, Trends, Challenges, and Implications for the United States," Congressional Research Service, December 17, 2013, available at http://www.fas.org/sgp/crs/row /RL33534.pdf. For more discussion on China's rise, see chapter 5.

3.  Hughes International Futures model.

4.  Ibid.

5.  Dr. Richard Cincotta, demographer-in-residence at the Stimson Center in Washington, DC, provided the demographic data used in this chapter. He uses UN and US Census data as the basis for his projections. For more on Cincotta's pathbreaking work, see http://www.stimson.org/experts/richard-cincotta/.

6.  Martin Wolf, "Why Abenomics Will Disappoint," *Financial Times*, December 17, 2013, available at http://www.ft.com/intl/cms/s/0/cf682d66-642c-11e3-98e2 -00144feabdc0.html#axzz2xB1rm9Q8.

7.  "CEBR's World Economic League Table Report for 2013," Centre for Economics and Business Research, December 26, 2013, available at http://www.cebr.com /reports/world-economic-league-table-report/.

8.  Ibid.; Kevin Voigt, "World Top Economies in 2050," CNN Business360, http:// business.blogs.cnn.com/2012/01/12/worlds-top-economies-in-2050-will-be/. The Voigt report uses rankings developed by HSBC, the global bank. Sara Schaefer Munoz, "Latin Growth Tune Plays in Two Speeds," *Wall Street Journal*, November 30, 2012, available at http://online.wsj.com/news/articles/SB1000142 4127887324020804578151311678565042.

9.  Brian Bremner, "Russia's 21st Century Malaise in Five Grim Charts," *BusinessWeek*, November 19, 2013, available at http://www.businessweek.com /printer/articles/168260-russias-21st-century-malaise-in-five-grim-charts.

10. Anders Aslund, "Why Growth in Emerging Economies Is Likely to Fall," Working Paper 13–10, Peterson Institute for International Economics, November 2013, available at http://www.piie.com/publications/wp/wp13-10.pdf.

11. Ken Kremer, "China Considers Manned Moon Landing following Breakthrough Chang'e-3 Mission Success," *Universe Today*, January 15, 2014, available at http://www .universetoday.com/107716/china-considers-manned-moon-landing-following -breakthrough-change-3-mission-success/.

12. Megan Gannon, "1st Satellite Built by High School Students Blasts in Space," Fox News, November 19, 2013, available at http://www.foxnews.com/science /2013/11/19/phonesat-high-school-students-tuesday/.

13. Ibid.

14. Ibid. Also see Joshua Buck, "NASA Helps Launch Student-Built Satellites as Part of CubeSat Launch Initiative," NASA Press Release 13–343, November 20, 2013, available at http://www.nasa.gov/press/2013/november/nasa-helps-launch -student-built-satellites-as-part-of-cubesat-launch-initiative/.

15. The original four BRICs identified by Goldman Sachs are Brazil, Russia, India, and China. South Africa has recently joined the political grouping that was founded subsequent to the financial designation. South Africa is also one of the emerging 22 countries highlighted here as increasingly important actors in regional and global arenas.

16. R. P. Cincotta and E. Leahy, "Population Age Structure and the Risk of Civil Conflict: A Metric." *Environment Change & Security Project Report* 12 (2006/2007): pp. 55–58. Also available at http://www.wilsoncenter.org/topics/pubs /PopAgeStructures&CivilConflict12.pdf

17. Richard Cincotta, "Whither the Demographic Arc of Instability," Stimson Center, November 24, 2010, available at http://www.stimson.org/spotlight /whither-the-demographic-arc-of-instability-/.

18. Although Afghanistan will remain youthful under either scenario, there is some controversy over how fast Afghani fertility will fall in the future. "The UN believes Afghanistan's population (around 28 million today) will pass the 50 million mark by 2030, whereas the Census Bureau foresees a 2030 popula-tion under 43 million." See Richard Cincotta, "Afghanistan's Sky-High Birthrate Seems to Be Declining—and That's a Very Good Thing," *Foreign Policy*, November 16, 2009. Also available on Stimson Center website, http://www.stimson.org /spotlight/afghanistans-sky-high-birthrate-seems-to-be-declining-and-thats-a -very-good-thing/.

19. Richard Cincotta, "Minority Youth Bulges and the Future of Intrastate Conflict," Stimson Center, November 10, 2011, available at http://www.stimson .org/spotlight/minority-youth-bulges-and-the-future-of-intrastate-conflict-/.

20. Data provided by University of Denver Professor Barry Hughes using his International Futures model.

21. Richard Dobbs, Jaana Remes, James Manyika, Charles Roxburgh, Sven Smit, and Fabian Schaer, "Urban World: Cities and the Rise of the Consuming Class," McKinsey Global Institute, June 2012, available at http://www.mckinsey.com/insights /urbanization/urban_world_cities_and_the_rise_of_the_consuming_class.

22. "Envisioning 2030: US Strategy for the Coming Technology Revolution, A Report by the Strategic Foresight Initiative," Atlantic Council, December 2013, p. 12, available at http://www.atlanticcouncil.org/images/publications /Envisioning_2030_US_Strategy_for_the_Coming_Tech_Revolution_web.pdf. I am indebted to Peter Engelke and Banning Garrett, my colleagues at the Atlantic Council, for their work on urbanization.

23. "Harnessing the Dual Global Trends of Urbanization and the Demographic Youth Bulge," Un-Habitat Issue Paper, May 14, 2012, available at http://www .un.org/en/ecosoc/julyhls/pdf13/hls_issue_note_un_habitat.pdf.

24. Robert A. Manning, "Envisioning 2030: US Strategy for a Post-Western World," Atlantic Council publication, December 10, 2012, pp. 26–28, available at http:// www.atlanticcouncil.org/publications/reports/envisioning-2030-us-strategy-for-a -postwestern-world.

25. Mark Raymond and Gordon Smith, "Reimagining the Internet: The Need for a High-Level Strategic Vision for Internet Governance," Internet Governance Papers, paper no. 1, Centre for International Governance Innovation, July 2013, http://www.cigionline.org/publications/2013/7/reimagining-internet-need-high-level-strategic-vision-internet-governance.

## CHAPTER 3: PLAYING GOD

1. Ray Kurzweil, *The Singularity Is Near: When Humans Transcend Biology* (New York: Penguin Books, 2005), 205.

2. "Brain Implant Allows Paralysed Woman to Control a Robot with Her Thoughts," *Guardian*, May 16, 2012, available at http://www.theguardian.com/science/2012/may/16/brain-implant-paralysed-woman-robot-thoughts.

3. Chad Kister, "Brain Implants and the Brain-Computer Interface Is a Real Technology: An Interview with Jeff Stibel, Chairman of Braingate," March 31, 2013, posted on http://www.brainimplant.info/stibel.htm.

4. David Axe, "Combat Exoskeleton Marches toward Afghanistan Deployment," *Wired*, May 23, 2012, available at http://www.wired.com/dangerroom/2012/05/combat-exoskeleton-afghanistan/.

5. Shawn Brimley, Ben FitzGerald, and Kelley Sayler, "Game Changers: Disruptive Technology and U.S. Defense Strategy," Center for a New American Security, September 2013, available at http://www.cnas.org/sites/default/files/publications-pdf/CNAS_Gamechangers_BrimleyFitzGeraldSayler.pdf.

6. See www.rethinkrobotics.com; Kyle Alspach, "MIT Project Aims to Put Baxter Robot in a Magic Show," *Boston Business Journal*, October 9, 2013; "From Silk Orb Built by Man and Worms to a Robot Magician's Assistant: 5 Cool Things at MIT," OM Giga, October 11, 2013, http://markets.financialcontent.com/stocks/news/read/25351326/From_a_silk_orb_built_by_man_and_worms_to_a_robot_magician's_assistant.

7. "Surgical Robots: The Kindness of Strangers," *Economist*, January 18, 2012 available at http://www.economist.com/blogs/babbage/2012/01/surgical-robots.

8. Brimley, FitzGerald, and Sayler, "Game Changers."

9. There are numerous studies on the implications of the pensioner bulge. See for example, "The Battle of the Baby Bulge," *Economist*, November 18, 2013, available at http://www.economist.com/news/21589074-boomers-need-think-harder-about-their-retirement-income-says-larry-fink-chairman-and-chief. Also see Paul Taylor, *The Next America* (New York: Pew Research Center), 2014.

10. Tom Miles, "Global Life Expectancy: Life Spans Continue to Lengthen around the World, WHO Says," Reuters, May 14, 2013, available at http://www.reuters.com/article/2013/05/15/us-lifeexpectancy-idUSBRE94E16620130515.

11. For a discussion of the cost curve on DNA sequencing falling faster than Moore's Law, see Aaron Saenz, "Costs of DNA Sequencing Falling Fast—Look at These Graphs!" *SingularityHUB*, available at http://singularityhub.com/2011/03/05/costs-of-dna-sequencing-falling-fast-look-at-these-graphs/.

12. "Disruptive Technologies: Advances That Will Transform Life, Business and the Global Economy," McKinsey Global Institute, May 2013, available at http://www.mckinsey.com/insights/business_technology/disruptive_technologies.

13. Dr. Ian Gilham, "Theranostics: An Emerging Tool in Drug Discovery and Commercialisation," *Drug Discovery World*, Fall 2002, available at http://www.ddw-online.com/personalised-medicine/p148484-theranostics-an-emerging-tool-in-drug-discovery-and-commercialisation-fall-02.html.

14. Ronald Van Heertum, "Theranostics: The Right Therapy for the Right Patient at the Right Time," *Bioclinica*, July 24, 2013, available at http://www.bioclinica.com/blog/theranostics-right-therapy-for-right-patient-at-right-time.

15. T. C., "Computer-Aided Medicine: Doctor Watson," Babbage: Science and Technology blog, *Economist*, October 13, 2013, http://www.economist.com/blogs/babbage/2013/02/computer-aided-medicine.

16. Michael Specter, "The Gene Factory," *New Yorker*, January 6, 2014, available at http://www.newyorker.com/reporting/2014/01/06/140106fa_fact_specter.

17. Tiffany Trade, "Supercomputer Models Human Brain Activity," HPC Wire, available at http://www.hpcwire.com/2014/01/15/supercomputer-models-human-brain-activity/.

18. "Artificial Intelligence," *Wikipedia*, http://en.wikipedia.org/wiki/Artificial_intelligence.

19. Banning Garrett, "A World Run on Algorithms?," *FutureScape*, publication of the Atlantic Council's Strategic Foresight Initiative, July 2013, available at http://www.atlanticcouncil.org/images/publications/a_world_run_on_algorithms.pdf.

20. Viktor Mayer-Schonberger and Kenneth Cukier, *Big Data: A Revolution That Will Transform How We Live, Work, and Think* (New York: Eamon Dolan/Houghton Mifflin Harcourt, 2013), 191.

21. Ian Morris, *War! What Is It Good For?: Conflict and the Progress of Civilization from Primates to Robots* (New York: Farrar, Straus and Giroux, 2014). Morris loaned the manuscript copy in which this incident was related.

22. David Burg, "The Internet of Things Raises New Security Questions," PricewaterhouseCoopers (PWC) blog, September 30, 2013, http://usblogs.pwd.com/emerging-technology/the-internet-of-things-raises-new-security-questions.

23. Peter Haynes and Thomas A. Campbell, "Hacking the Internet of Everything," *Scientific American*, August 1, 2013, http://www.scientificamerican.com/article.cfm?id=hacking-internet-of-everything.

24. Ibid.

25. Ibid.

## CHAPTER 4: AN ERA OF SCARCITY OR ABUNDANCE?

1. There is increasing study of changing climate trends in the Sahel and West Africa and the likely impacts on stability. See "Changes in Climate Trends Impacting Livelihoods and Food Security in the Sahel and West Africa," United Nations Environment Programme, December 5, 2011, available at http://www.unep.org/NewsCentre/default.aspx?DocumentID=2661&ArticleID=8971; Michael Werz and Laura Conley, "Climate Change, Migration, and Conflict in Northwest Africa," Center for American Progress, April 18, 2012, available at http://www.americanprogress.org/issues/security/report/2012/04/18/11439/climate-change-migration-and-conflict-in-northwest-africa/; and Anthony Nyong, "Climate-Related Conflicts in West Africa," in "Report from Africa: Population,

Health, Environment, and Conflict," Wilson Center, available at http://www
.wilsoncenter.org/sites/default/files/Nyong12.pdf.

2.  The transcript of Dr. Fingar's June 25, 2008 testimony in front of House
    Permanent Select Committee on Intelligence and House Select Committee on
    Energy Independence and Global Warning is available at http://www.dni.gov
    /files/documents/Newsroom/Testimonies/20080625_testimony.pdf.

3.  See, for example, Statement for the Record of the Worldwide Threat Assessment
    of the US Intelligence Community given by Director of National Intelligence to
    the Senate Select Committee on Intelligence on March 12, 2013, pp. 9–10, avail-
    able at http://www.dni.gov/files/documents/Intelligence%20Reports/2013%20
    ATA%20SFR%20for%20SSCI%2012%20Mar%202013.pdf.

4.  Richard Dobbs, Jeremy Openheim, Fraser Thompson, Sigurd Marsels,
    Scott Nyquist, and Sunel Sanghvi, "Resource Revolution: Tracking Global
    Commodity Markets," McKinsey Global Institute, September 2013, available
    at      http://www.mckinsey.com/insights/energy_resources_materials/resource
    _revolution_tracking_global_commodity_markets.

5.  Bernice Lee, Felix Preston, Jaakko Kooroshy, Rob Bailey, and Glada Lahn,
    "Resources Futures," Chatham House Report, December 2012, pp. 62–63,
    available at http://www.chathamhouse.org/sites/default/files/public/Research
    /Energy,%20Environment%20and%20Development/1212r_resourcesfutures
    .pdf. The report indicates the number of countries vulnerable to high wheat
    prices might be larger and include the whole Middle East and Africa. In ear-
    lier exchanges with Bernice Lee, principal author, the four countries named here
    were highlighted.

6.  Ibid.

7.  See the Fund for Peace's website for current rankings and information on their
    project, available at http://ffp.statesindex.org/.

8.  The work on measuring impact on resource scarcities on security is ongoing.
    To get a flavor of the scope of the project, see Howard Passell, Len Malezyski,
    Marrissa Reno, and Daniel Villa, "Human Ecology, Resilience, and Security in
    2030," Sandia National Laboratories, November 2012, available at http://prod
    .sandia.gov/techlib/access-control.cgi/2012/1210320.pdf.

9.  Floyd Norris, "Population Growth Forecast from the UN May Be Too High,"
    *New York Times*, September 20, 2013, available at http://www.nytimes
    .com/2013/09/21/business/uns-forecast-of-population-growth-may-be-too-high
    .html?_r=0.

10. Dominic Wilson and Raluca Dragusanu, "The Expanding Middle: The Exploding
    World Middle Class and Falling Global Inequality," Goldman Sachs: Global
    Economics Paper No. 170, July 7, 2008, available at https://360.gs.com.

11. "India's Urban Awakening: Building Inclusive Cities, Sustaining Economic
    Growth," McKinsey Global Institute, April 2010, available at http://www
    .mckinsey.com/insights/urbanization/urban_awakening_in_india.

12. "Senegal Seeks French, Chinese Help as Water Crisis Hits Capital," Reuters,
    September 27, 2013, available at http://www.trust.org/item/20130927124904-rtluf.

13. Amy Myers Jafee and Edward L. Morse, "Liquefied Natural Profits," *Foreign
    Affairs*, September 16, 2013, available at http://www.foreignaffairs.com
    /articles/139932/amy-myers-jaffe-and-edward-l-morse/liquefied-natural-profits.

14. World Energy Outlook 2013, International Energy Agency, http://www
    .worldenergyoutlook.org/.

15. Lee, Preston, Koorosky, Bailey, and Lahn, "Resource Futures," pp. 62–78, 106–110.
16. Ibid., pp. 91–113.

## CHAPTER 5: A REVOLUTIONARY CHINA?

1. Angus Maddison, *Chinese Economic Performance in the Long Run*, 2nd ed. rev. and updated, 960–2030 AD (Paris: OECD, 2008).
2. Wayne M. Morrison, "China's Economic Rise: History, Trends, Challenges, and Implications for the United States," Congressional Research Service, December 17, 2013, available at http://www.fas.org/sgp/crs/row/RL33534.pdf.
3. Quoted in ibid.
4. Ibid.
5. Hans Timmer, Mansoor Dailami, Jacqueline Irving, Robert Hauswald, and Paul Masson, *Global Development Horizons 2011: Multipolarity, The New Global Economy* (Washington, DC: The World Bank, 2011).
6. Ibid.
7. Leslie Hook and Pilita Clark, "China Eyes Cap on Carbon Emissions by 2016," *Financial Times*, May 27, 2013, http://www.ft.com/intl/cms/s/0/61cd4ec6-c6b1 -11e2-a861-00144feab7de.html#axzz2qrLHuFJ3.
8. Data provided by University of Denver Professor Barry Hughes, who created the International Futures model. $15,000 is measured in purchasing power parity.
9. Ivalo Izvorski, "The Middle Income Trap, Again?," blog, East Asia & Pacific on the Rise, WorldBank.org, February 9, 2011, available at http://blogs.worldbank .org/eastasiapacific/the-middle-income-trap-again.
10. Alejandro Foxley and Fernando Sossdorf, "Making the Transition from Middle-Income to Advanced Economies," Carnegie Papers, Carnegie Endowment for International Peace, Washington, DC, September 2011, available at http:// carnegieendowment.org/files/making_the_transition.pdf.
11. Ankit Panda, "Was China's Third Plenum a Bust?," *The Diplomat*, November 14, 2013, available at http://thediplomat.com/2013/11/was-chinas-third-plenum-a -bust/; Cheng Li, "Xi's Reform Agenda: Promises and Risks," John L. Thornton China Center, Brookings Institution, March 6, 2014, available at http://webfeeds .brookings.edu/brookingsrss/centers/china?format=xml.
12. Weibo is the Chinese word for "microblog." Weibo uses a format similar to Twitter; Sina Weibo is the most-visited social chat site in China.
13. "Report: China Microblog Usage Took Hit in 2013," *Wall Street Journal*, January 17, 2014, available at http://blogs.wsj.com/chinarealtime/2014/01/17/report -china-microblog-usage-took-hit-in-2013/.
14. Shannon Tiezzi, "Xi Jinping's Vision for China's Courts," *The Diplomat*, January 9, 2014, available at http://thediplomat.com/2014/01/xi-jinpings-vision-for -chinas-courts/.
15. "Quashing Expectations for Rule of Law in China," *Wall Street Journal*, January 17, 2014, available at http://blogs.wsj.com/chinarealtime/2014/01/17/quashing -expectations-for-rule-of-law-in-china/.
16. "Chinese Economy Lost $3.79 Trillion in Illicit Financial Outflows since 2000, Reveals New GFI Report," *Global Financial Integrity*, October 25, 2012, available at http://www.gfintegrity.org/content/view/581/70/.
17. "Asia 2050: Realizing the Asian Century," Asian Development Bank, August 2011, available at http://www.adb.org/publications/asia-2050-realizing-asian-century.

18. Robert A. Manning and Banning Garrett, "Does Beijing Have a Strategy? China's Alternative Futures," Atlantic Council, March 19, 2013, http://www.atlantic-council.org/publications/issue-briefs/does-beijing-have-a-strategy-chinas-alternative-futures.

19. Richard Wike, "Americans and Chinese Grow More Wary of Each Other," Pew Research Center, June 5, 2013, available at http://www.pewresearch.org/fact-tank/2013/06/05/americans-and-chinese-grow-more-wary-of-each-other/.

## CHAPTER 6: WILL TECHNOLOGY BE A BOON OR A CURSE?

1. "Vision 2016: Towards Prosperity for All," available at http://paris21.org/sites/default/files/3144.pdf.

2. "Transformational Technologies, Implications for Change in Africa," conference held in Gabarone, Botswana, under the auspices of the Global Futures Forum, July 11–13, 2012.

3. Meetings with IBM in Brazil during visit, April 19–25, 2012.

4. It's also being called the Second Machine Age; see Erik Brynjolfsson and Andrew McAfee, *The Second Machine Age: Work, Progress and Prosperity in a Time of Brilliant Technologies* (New York: W. W. Norton & Co., 2014).

5. My colleague Banning Garrett's work has been my guide in thinking through the consequences of 3D printing. Banning Garrett, "Will 3D Printing Change the World?," Atlantic Council blog, October 17, 2011, available at http://www.atlanticcouncil.org/blogs/new-atlanticist/will-3d-printing-change-the-world; "Envisioning 2030: US Strategy for the Coming Technology Revolution," Atlantic Council, December 9, 2013, pp. 16–19, available at http://www.atlanticcouncil.org/publications/reports/envisioning-2030-us-strategy-for-the-coming-technology-revolution.

6. National Intelligence Council, *Global Trends 2030: Alternative Worlds*, p. 93.

7. "Robots Don't Complain," *Economist*, August 6, 2011, available at http://www.economist.com/node/21525432. "Suicide-Stricken Chinese iPhone-Maker Replacing 1 Million Workers," *Foreign Policy*, August 1, 2011, available at blog.foreignpolicy.com/posts/2011/...company_replacing_1...with_robots.

8. In December 2013, the Atlantic Council's Strategic Foresight Initiative (which I now direct) published a report, "Envisioning 2030: US Strategy for the Coming Technology Revolution," available at http://www.atlanticcouncil.org/publications/reports/envisioning-2030-us-strategy-for-the-coming-technology-revolution. I am indebted to my co-authors of that report, Banning Garrett, Robert Manning, and Peter Engelke, for many insights in this section on the political, social, and economic impacts of the new technologies.

9. US Department of Transportation, "National Motor Vehicle Crash Causation Survey," Report to Congress, Washington, DC, July 2008, available at http://www-nrd.nhtsa.dot.gov/Pubs/811059.PDF.

10. "Envisioning 2030," p. 20.

11. Ibid., p. 20.

12. "A World Run on Algorithms?," Atlantic Council, July 24, 2013, available at http://www.atlanticcouncil.org/publications/issue-briefs/a-world-run-on-algorithms.

13. Edward P. Thompson's classic history is one of the best guides in understanding the link between the elimination of craft industries resulting from rapid technological change and the development of more rigid class structures in the

nineteenth century. *The Making of the English Working Class* (London: Vintage, 1966).

14. Brian Fung, "The House Is Really Worried about 3D Printed Guns," *Washington Post*, December 3, 2013, available at http://www.washingtonpost.com/blogs/the-switch/wp/2013/12/03/the-house-is-really-worried-about-3d-printed-guns-so-its-voted-to-ban-them/.

15. J. Craig Venter, *Life at the Speed of Light: From the Double Helix to the Dawn of Digital Life* (New York: Viking, 2013).

16. "Envisioning 2030," p. 18.

17. *Positioning Synthetic Biology to Meet the Challenges of the 21st Century* (Washington, DC: National Academies Press, 2014), p. 10, available at http://www.nap.edu/openbook.php?record_id=13316&page=10.

18. "Envisioning 2030," p. 18.

19. Ibid., pp. 18–19.

20. Ibid., p. 18.

21. Laurie Garrett, "Biology's Brave New World," *Foreign Affairs*, November/December 2013, available at http://www.foreignaffairs.com/articles/140156/laurie-garrett/biologys-brave-new-world.

22. Ibid.

23. "Envisioning 2030," p. 7.

24. Ibid., p. 7.

25. Mariana Mazzucato, *The Entrepreneurial State: Debunking Public vs. Private Sector Myths* (London: Anthem Press, 2013).

26. Mariana Mazzucato, "Startup Myths and Obsessions," *Economist*, February 3, 2014, available at http://www.economist.com/blogs/schumpeter/2014/02/invitation-mariana-mazzucato.

27. Ibid.

## CHAPTER 7: A RETURN TO WORLD AT WAR?

1. Margaret MacMillan, "The Rhyme of History: Lessons of the Great War," *The Brookings Essay*, December 14, 2013, available at http://www.brookings.edu/research/essays/2013/rhyme-of-history-print.

2. P. Collier, A. Hoeffler, and M. Söderbom, "2008 Post-Conflict Risks," *Journal of Peace Research* 45, no. 4 (July 2008): 461–78, doi: http://dx.doi.org/10.1177/0022343308091356.

3. Benedetta Berti and Jonathan Paris, "Beyond Sectarianism: Geopolitics, Fragmentation, and the Syrian Civil War," Strategic Assessment, vol. 16, no. 4, January 2014. p. 30, available at http://d26e8pvoto2x3r.cloudfront.net/upload-Images/systemFiles/Beyond%20Sectarianism.pdf.

4. Sara Assaf, "I Am Not a Terrorist… Yet," *NOW*, November 9, 2013, available at https://now.mmedia.me/lb/en/commentaryanalysis/519760-i-am-not-a-terrorist-yet.

5. Benedetta Berti and Jonathan Paris, "Beyond Sectarianism: Geopolitics, Fragmentation, and the Syrian Civil War," *Strategic Assessment* 16, no. 4 (January 2014): 30, available at http://d26e8pvoto2x3r.cloudfront.net/uploadImages/sys-temFiles/Beyond%20Sectarianism.pdf.

6. Erica Chenoweth and Maria J. Stephan, "Why Civil Resistance Still Works," *Foreign Affairs* (forthcoming).

7.  Ibid.
8.  "Government Budgets Are Increasingly Vulnerable to a Decline in Oil Prices," in "Middle East and North Africa Regional Economic Outlook," International Monetary Fund, November 12, 2013, available at https://www.imf.org/external /pubs/ft/reo/2013/mcd/eng/pdf/mreo1113p.pdf.
9.  "Non-Farm Jobs to Slump by 25 Percent in FY 13–19 Period: Crisil," *Economic Times*, January 8, 2014, available at http://articles.economictimes.indiatimes .com/2014-01-08/news/45991274_1_crisil-research-ratings-agency-crisil-gdp.
10. Dan Twining, "Pakistan and the Nuclear Nightmare," *Foreign Policy*, September 4, 2013, available at thttp://nuclear-news.net/2013/09/05/usas-intense-worry -about-nuclear-pakistan/.
11. "Indians View the World," Pew Research Center, March 31, 2014, available at http://www.pewglobal.org/2014/03/31/chapter-2-indians-view-the-world/.
12. Dr. Daniel Twining, Senior Fellow for Asia at German Marshall Fund researched and forged the groundwork for the scenarios used in *Global Trends 2030*. He has later published himself on the possible scenarios for South and East Asia, "Global Trends 2030: Scenarios for Asia's Strategic Future," *Foreign Policy*, December 11, 2012, available at http://www.gmfus.org/archives/global-trends-2030-scenarios -for-asias-strategic-future/.
13. Aaron L. Friedberg coined the term in his well-known article "Ripe for Rivalry: Prospects for Peace in a Multipolar Asia," *International Security* 18, no. 3 (Winter 1993–94): pp. 5–33. Available at http://links.jstor.org/sici?sici=0162 -2889%28199324%2F199424%2918%3A3%3C5%3ARFRPFP%3E2.0.CO%3B2-X. International Security is currently published by the MIT Press.
14. Erica Chenoweth and Maria J. Stephan, *Why Civil Resistance Works: The Strategic Logic of Nonviolent Conflict* (New York: Columbia University Press, 2011).
15. Erica Chenoweth, "The Dissident's Toolkit," *Foreign Policy*, October 25, 2013, available at http://www.foreignpolicy.com/articles/2013/10/24/the_dissidents _toolkit.
16. "The U.S. Won't Match Russia's Gas Exports to Europe for Years," *MIT Technology Review*, March 20, 2014, available at http://www.technologyreview .com/news/525601/the-us-cant-really-undermine-russia-by-exporting-gas/.
17. Zachary Keck, "Why Did BRICS Back Russia on Crimea?," *The Diplomat*, March 31, 2014, available at http://thediplomat.com/2014/03/why-did-brics-back-russia -on-crimea/.
18. Jason Healey, *A Fierce Domain: Conflict in Cyberspace, 1986 to 2012* (Vienna, VA: CCSA Publications, 2013), pp. 20–25.
19. Ibid., p. 231.

## CHAPTER 8: THE LAST DAYS OF PAX AMERICANA?

1.  Robert Kagan, "The Myth of American Decline," *New Republic*, January 11, 2012, http://www.newrepublic.com/article/politics/magazine/99521/america-world -power-declinism.
2.  "The American-Western European Values Gap: American Exceptionalism Subsides," Pew Research Global Attitudes Project, February 29, 2012, http:// www.pewglobal.org/2011/11/17/the-american-western-european-values-gap/. The original poll was in 2011, but then Pew Research Center updated results in early 2012.

3. US leaders' criticism spiked during the Second Gulf War with former Defense Secretary Donald Rumsfeld's attack on "old Europe." In its quadrennial polling of Council on Foreign Relations members, Pew Research Center's results showed in the last poll in 2009 a shift in the elite's attitudes toward seeing more US interests in rising Asia: "There is a growing belief among CFR members that China, along with India, will be more important U.S. allies in the future." See "U.S. Seen as Less Important, China as More Powerful," Pew Research Center, December 3, 2009, available at http://www.people-press.org/2009/12/03/us-seen-as-less -important-china-as-more-powerful/. The German Marshall Fund, which annually surveys US, Canadian, and European publics, shows in their latest 2013 polling a shift in US views of Asia—defined as "countries…such as China, Japan, and South Korea." They are now seen as more important to US national interests than countries of the European Union, a reversal of last year's result and a return to attitudes first expressed in the 2011 survey. Forty-five percent described Asia as more important, up 11 percentage points from last year, while 44 percent, down 11 percentage points from last year, described Europe as more important. "Transatlantic Trends: Key Findings 2013," German Marshall Fund, available at http://trends.gmfus.org/files/2013/09/TT-Key-Findings-Report.pdf.

4. "EU Poll: Faith in European Union Plummets," Reuters report, *Voice of America*, July 24, 2013, available at http://www.voanews.com/content/reu-eu-poll-shows -faith-in-european-union-plummets/1709503.html.

5. Bruce Stokes is director of global economic attitudes in the Pew Research Center's Global Attitudes Project, where he assesses public and expert views about economic conditions, values, and policies. He is the former international economics correspondent for the *National Journal*, a former senior transatlantic fellow at the German Marshall Fund, and a former senior fellow at the Council on Foreign Relations.

6. Bruce Stokes, "The Transatlantic Trade and Investment Partnership: Completing the Strategic Vision; The Next Step in a Beautiful Friendship," (private paper).

7. For more on the necessity of the United States' new trade negotiations for not isolating China, see Arvind Subramanian, "Preserving the Open Global Economic System: A Strategic Blueprint for China and the United States," Peterson Institute, June 2013, available at http://www.piie.com/publications/pb/pb13–16.pdf.

8. Tyler Cowen, "Crimea through a Game-Theory Lens," *New York Times*, March 15, 2014, available at http://www.nytimes.com/2014/03/16/business/crimea -through-a-game-theory-lens.html?ref=todayspaper&_r=0; Jay Ulfelder, "Is the World Boiling Over or Just Getting Back to Normal?," *Dart-Throwing Chimp*, February 23, 2014, available at http://dartthrowingchimp.wordpress .com/2014/02/23/is-the-world-boiling-over-or-just-getting-back-to-normal/.

9. Barry Eichengreen, "The Irresistible Rise of the Renminbi," *Project Syndicate*, November 23, 2009, available at http://www.project-syndicate.org/commentary /the-irresistible-rise-of-the-renminbi.

10. Ibid. More recently, Professor Eichengreen has speculated about whether the weaker renminbi we've seen in early 2014 are "paradoxically, part of the Chinese government's strategy for encouraging its wider international use.…So long as investors believe that the renminbi can only appreciate, opening the country's markets will cause it to be flooded by foreign money, with unpleasant financial consequences, not the least of which is inflation." Barry Eichengreen, "Yuan Dive?," *Project Syndicate*, March 12, 2014, available at http://www.project-syndicate .org/commentary/barry-eichengreen-offers-two-explanations-for-the-renminbi

-s-depreciation-in-recent-weeks#AHcWJj03IZ7D4srO.99. For more on the needed steps by Chinese authorities to turn the renmimbi into a reserve currency, see Barry Eichengreen, "The Renminbi Challenge," *Project Syndicate*, October 9, 2012, available at http://www.project-syndicate.org/commentary/can-china -have-an-international-reserve-currency-by-barry-eichengreen.

11.  Marie Charrel, "How the Chinese Yuan Is Threatening the Dollar's Hegemony," *Le Monde*, October 21, 2013, available at http://www.worldcrunch.com/world -affairs/how-the-chinese-yuan-is-threatening-the-dollar-039-s-hegemony /currency-market-bond-shanghai-shenzhen/c1s13723/#.UmaN3I3D-Un.

12.  Eichengreen, "The Irresistible Rise of the Renminbi."

13.  "The 2013 Long-Term Budget Outlook," Congressional Budget Office, September 17, 2013, available at http://www.cbo.gov/publication/44521.

14.  Deng Xiaoping's "24-Character Strategy" first emerged in 1990 in response both to the global backlash from the 1989 Tiananmen Square crackdown and to the CCP's sense of alarm following the collapse of the communist states of Eastern Europe. The strategy provided basic principles on how China should protect its national interests while increasing its interactions with the world. The "24-Character Strategy" has been roughly translated as: "Observe calmly; secure our position; cope with affairs calmly; hide our capacities and bide our time; be good at maintaining a low profile; and never claim leadership." For more on the origins and meaning of Deng's strategy, see "Deng Xiaoping's '24-Character Strategy,'" *Global Security*, available at http://www.globalsecurity.org/military /world/china/24-character.htm.

15.  Jane Perlez, "Chinese President to Seek New Relationship with U.S. in Talks," *New York Times*, May 28, 2013, available at http://www.nytimes.com/2013/05/29 /world/asia/china-to-seek-more-equal-footing-with-us-in-talks.html.

16.  Paul Kennedy, "The Great Powers, Then and Now," *New York Times*, August 13, 2013, available at http://www.nytimes.com/2013/08/14/opinion/global/the -great-powers-then-and-now.html?pagewanted%3Dall&_r=0&pagewanted=pri nt&pagewanted=print.

17.  Atlantic Council, "Envisioning 2030: US Strategy for a Post-Western World," Atlantic Council, December 10, 2012, available at http://www.atlanticcouncil .org/publications/reports/envisioning-2030-us-strategy-for-a-postwestern-world.

18.  *Foreign Policy in the New Millennium, Results of the 2012 Chicago Council Survey of American Public Opinion and U.S. Foreign Policy*, Chicago Council on Global Affairs, 2012, available at http://www.thechicagocouncil.org/UserFiles/File /Task%20Force%20Reports/2012_CCS_Report.pdf.

## CHAPTER 9: THE ENEMY OF MY ENEMY IS MY FRIEND

1.  "Military Strikes on Iran Would Trigger Humanitarian Catastrophe," Omid for Iran and Hinckley Institute of University of Utah, 2012, available at http:// nucleargamble.org/.

## CHAPTER 12: MAKING THE SYSTEM WORK

1.  "The Coming Tech-Lash," *Economist*, November 18, 2013, http://www .economist.com/news/21588893-tech-elite-will-join-bankers-and-oilmen-public -demonology-predicts-adrian-wooldridge-coming.

2. "Apple may not make the smartphones with the biggest screens, but the company sure has the biggest cash stockpile. With $146.6 billion in the bank, the tech behemoth had 10 percent of all the cash held by Corporate America in 2013 (not counting financial firms), according to an analysis by ratings agency Moody's. Apple's Silicon Valley siblings also have enormous piles of dollars. Seventeen tech companies held one-third of all the money in corporate America last year, according to the analysis. Microsoft had the second highest cash holdings with $77 billion, followed by Google and Cisco Systems with $54.4 billion and $50.6 billion." Dino Grandoni, "Look: Apple Holds a HUGE Amount of Corporate America's Cash," *Huffington Post*, January 23, 2014, available at http://www.huffingtonpost.com/2014/01/23/silicon-valley-money_n_4652326.html.

3. The actual quotation is: "Only a crisis—actual or perceived—produces real change. When that crisis occurs, the actions that are taken depend on the ideas that are lying around. That, I believe, is our basic function: to develop alternatives to existing policies, to keep them alive and available until the politically impossible becomes the politically inevitable." Milton Friedman, *Capitalism and Freedom, Fortieth Anniversary Edition* (Chicago: University of Chicago Press, 2002), ix.

## CONCLUSION: ARE WE PREPARED FOR THE FUTURE?

1. Connie Cass, "Americans Forecast Downhill Slide to 2050," *Huffington Post*, January 3, 2014, available at http://www.huffingtonpost.com/2014/01/03/americans-2050_n_4535892.html.

2. Ibid.

3. Richard Stone, "Scientists Campaign against Killer Robots," *Science* 342 (December 20, 2013): pp. 1428–29, available at http://www.sciencemag.org/content/342/6165/1428.full.

4. Michael Specter, "Letter from Shenzhen, the Gene Factory," *New Yorker*, January 6, 2014, available at http://archives.newyorker.com/global/print.asp?that=/djvu/Conde Nast/New Yorker/2014_O.

5. Leon Fuerth with Evan M. H. Faber, "Anticipatory Governance Practical Upgrades: Equipping the Executive Branch to Cope with Increasing Speed and Complexity of Major Challenges," October 2012. Available on George Washington University and Wilson Center websites: http://www.gwu.edu/~igis/assets/docs/working_papers/Anticipatory_Governance_Practical_Upgrades.pdf; http://wilsoncenter.org/sites/default/files/Anticipatory_Governance_Practical_Upgrades.pdf.

# Index